The Fundamentals of Trade Finance

WILEY PROFESSIONAL BANKING AND FINANCE SERIES
EDWARD I. ALTMAN, Editor

THE STOCK MARKET, 4TH EDITION
Richard J. Teweles and Edward S. Bradley
TAX SHELTERED FINANCING THROUGH THE R & D LIMITED
PARTNERSHIP
James K. La Fleur
CORPORATE FINANCIAL DISTRESS: A COMPLETE GUIDE TO
PREDICTING, AVOIDING, AND DEALING WITH BANKRUPTCY
Edward I. Altman
CREDIT ANALYSIS: A COMPLETE GUIDE
Roger H. Hale
CURRENT ASSET MANAGEMENT: CASH, CREDIT, AND
INVENTORY
Jarl G. Kallberg and Kenneth Parkinson
HANDBOOK FOR BANKING STRATEGY
Richard C. Aspinwall and Robert A. Eisenbeis
THE BANKING JUNGLE: HOW TO SURVIVE AND PROSPER IN A
BUSINESS TURNED TOPSY TURVY
Paul S. Nadler and Richard B. Miller
ELECTRONIC BANKING
Allen H. Lipis, Thomas R. Marschall, and Jan H. Linker
BUSINESS OPPORTUNITIES FROM CORPORATE BANKRUPTCIES
Rees Morrison
DEREGULATING WALL STREET: COMMERCIAL BANK
PENETRATION OF THE CORPORATE SECURITIES MARKET
Ingo Walter
CONTROLLING INTEREST RATE RISK
Robert B. Platt
EXPORT-IMPORT FINANCING, 2ND EDITION
Harry M. Venedikian and Gerald Warfield
THE FUNDAMENTALS OF TRADE FINANCE: THE INS AND OUTS
OF IMPORT-EXPORT FINANCING
Jane Kingman-Brundage and Susan A. Schulz

The Fundamentals of Trade Finance

THE INS AND OUTS OF IMPORT-EXPORT FINANCING

JANE KINGMAN-BRUNDAGE

SUSAN A. SCHULZ

A WILEY-INTERSCIENCE PUBLICATION
JOHN WILEY & SONS,
New York • Chichester • Brisbane • Toronto • Singapore

Library of Congress Cataloging in Publication Data:

Kingman-Brundage, Jane.
    The fundamentals of trade finance.

    (Wiley professional banking and finance series,
ISSN 0733-8945)
    "A Wiley-Interscience publication."
    Bibliography: p.
    1. International finance. 2. Financial institutions,
International. 3. Commerce. I. Schulz, Susan A.
II. Title. III. Series.

HG3881.K5326   1986   332.1′5   86-954
ISBN 0-471-81488-1

Printed in the United States of America

10 9 8 7 6 5 4 3 2 1

SERIES PREFACE

The worlds of banking and finance have changed dramatically during the past few years, and no doubt this turbulence will continue through the 1980s. We have established the Wiley Professional Banking and Finance Series to aid in characterizing this dynamic environment and to further the understanding of the emerging structures, issues, and content for the professional financial community.

We envision three types of book in this series. First, we are commissioning distinguished experts in a broad range of fields to assemble a number of authorities to write specific primers on related topics. For example, some of the early handbook-type volumes in the series concentrate on the Stock Market, Investment Banking, and Financial Depository Institutions. A second type of book attempts to combine text material with appropriate empirical and case studies written by practitioners in relevant fields. An early example is a forthcoming volume on The Management of Cash and Other Short-Term Assets. Finally, we are encouraging definitive, authoritative works on specialized subjects for practitioners and theorists.

It is a distinct pleasure and honor for me to assist John Wiley & Sons, Inc. in this important endeavor. In addition to banking and financial practitioners, we think business students and faculty will benefit from this series. Most of all, though, we hope this series will become a primary source in the 1980s for the members of the professional financial community to refer to theories and data and to integrate important aspects of the central changes in our financial world.

EDWARD I. ALTMAN

Professor of Finance
New York University,
Schools of Business

PREFACE

In recent years, international trade practices have assumed increased importance in both the business and banking communities. Trade practices, never static, are in flux now more than ever before, and there is intense competitive demand on the banks to provide appropriate, even innovative, trade payment and financing services. Moreover, every trade transaction is made up of a unique configuration or mix of possibilities and constraints. As a seasoned trade banker observed, "In international trade, *constraints* drive innovation. Innovative trade practices are a direct response to constraints in the environment—regulatory, funding, risk, interest rates, or whatever. Environmental constraints make trade challenging. A day seldom passes that I don't learn something *new*—how to do something *differently*."

As Americans we have long been recognized for our ingenuity. It is our hope that this book will contribute to the development of innovative trade practices by identifying the structural elements that underlie invention. Or, as the eminent letter of credit expert Henry Harfield wrote, "Hope combines with commercial history to create the expectation that bankers will accept the challenge [to balance security and risk] and that the result will be new techniques of foreign and domestic commerce."*

In 1978 Stephen I. Davis asked 30 senior corporate financial officers to identify the criteria they use in selecting a new bank relationship. Roughly 40 percent of the respondents named "the offering . . . of a new or imaginative solution to a specific problem."† In the same survey, Davis asked for a critique of the business development approach used by bankers representing the major international banks. Almost one-half of the respondents named "lack of prep-

---

*Henry Harfield, *Bank Credits and Acceptances* (5th ed.), Wiley, New York, 1974, p. 194.
†Stephen I. Davis, *The Management Function in International Banking*, Wiley, New York, 1979, p. 75.

aration and understanding of [our] business and requirements." Or, as a U.S. corporate treasurer phrased it, "I am somewhat indignant when [bankers] start off with the desire and expectation of doing business with this office without doing a nominal amount of homework from readily available sources." Finally, Davis characterized the next comment as typical of the view held by many financial officers critical of bankers "who clearly intend to sell the bank and really have no interest in our group."

Faced with the incontrovertibly fungible character of their basic product, how then do bankers develop a "new or imaginative solution" in what is essentially an undifferentiated product line? Davis suggests that *expertise* differentiates a bank's offering in the absence of an otherwise clearcut product or service distinction. This expertise may consist in regional knowledge or in specialty functional sectors such as oil or shipping. It may develop as an ability to execute certain kinds of transactions (such as foreign exchange or funds movement) exceptionally well. Historically, technical expertise has resided in a bank's operating areas quite separate from the credit function. Widespread changes in the structure of banking, however, are mirrored in changes in the traditional bank-customer relationship. Where credit officers once asked, "How much can I lend?" the more forward-looking among them now ask, "What service can I perform to enable this customer to transact this business faster, cheaper, more easily or with less risk?" Developing answers to this question has led generalist bankers to explore their bank's technical capability as a natural complement to the credit function. More often than not, the end result has been development of the "innovative solution to a specific problem" sought by Davis' respondents.

Trade does not exist in a vacuum. Trade is conducted in specific commercial, economic, and political contexts which alternately or simultaneously nurture or threaten it. Consequently, it is our intention to present an orderly way of thinking about trade problems. Four dynamics—customer, technical, environmental and marketing—taken together convey the "big picture" surrounding a given transaction. We assume that the business manager engaged in international trade and the generalist banker who services the transaction share a common need: to refine their ability to view a trade transaction *as a whole*.

There is a related problem. Those relatively inexperienced in international trade who attempt to discuss even "routine" trade issues are often unprepared to respond to the information they receive from a more experienced counterpart, whether banker or corporate manager. We propose that the remedy to this situation lies in mastery of the basics of trade payment and financing structures. Thus we have developed this book as a primer in the area of the classical trade services. Information is presented on two levels: In Part I we introduce a working knowledge of the technical logic underlying a bank's trade services because we believe that such knowledge is a prerequisite for understanding sophisticated trade issues. In Part II we introduce the Transaction Profile as a systematic way of thinking about trade problems because we believe that systematic thought is the root of the ability to structure innovative payment and financing arrangements tailored to unique transaction requirements. By advocating a working knowledge of the trade services, we are not suggesting that the reader master technicalities at an inappropriate level of detail. Rather by showing readers systematically exactly what they *should* know, we hope to increase their ability to identify accurately information they are *not* expected to know and hence their confidence in calling in an appropriate technical expert.

Our goal is to present a solution-oriented approach to the marketing of trade banking services. It is a relatively new approach, one which challenges credit officers and technical specialists to find new ways to work together to produce innovative payment and financing arrangements. We have observed a consistent "trickle-down" effect associated with their collaboration: over time generalist bankers are able to integrate technical expertise with their traditional credit skills. In the area of trade the result has been the emergence of the specialist trade banker. Dedicated to developing trade business within the bank's customer base, the trade banker becomes a resource for other generalist bankers and their corporate customers.

Someone once observed that no book is solely the creation of its authors. Every book is, in an important sense, the collective product of a professional community. Because this volume attempts to synthesize perspectives and skills which bankers have historically kept apart, the observation is appropriate to this book. We wish to acknowledge the role of our clients in challenging us to think systematically about trade issues. More specifically, we wish to acknowledge the contribution of Carl R. Meyer, Vice President with the Letter of Credit Division at Bankers Trust Company and former head of the Letter of Credit Department at Marine Midland Bank, who provided invaluable technical assistance throughout the book, but whose influence is most keenly felt in Part I.

In addition we wish to acknowledge the contribution of the following people who read various parts of the manuscript and made valuable suggestions: Louise I. Borke, Vice President, State Street Bank, Boston; Thomas E. LaMonica, Vice President, The Hibernia Bank, San Francisco; M. Elizabeth Moffett, Vice President, Morgan Guaranty Trust Co., New York; Mark F. Sullivan, Vice President, Midland International Trade Services, New York; and Stellan P. Wollmar, Vice President, Bankers Trust Company, New York.

Finally, we wish to acknowledge the contribution of John E. Foster, V.P., senior letter of credit technician now retired from The Chase Manhattan Bank, who was our first letter of credit mentor and who had both the patience and the imagination to repeat basic principles in different forms until we understood.

It is commonly recognized that banking practice is not standard from one part of the world to another, or even from bank to bank within the same geographic area. In the pages that follow, we describe what we believe to be generic procedures; we encourage the taking of notes which will enable the reader to tailor the material to the practices of specific banking or market environments.

JANE KINGMAN-BRUNDAGE
SUSAN A. SCHULZ

North Salem, New York
New York, New York
April 1986

CONTENTS

PART I

LIST OF TABLES

LIST OF FIGURES

The Fundamentals
of Trade Finance

Part **1**

INTRODUCTION

International trade is grounded in the desire of a buyer and seller to exchange goods for payment across national borders, and international trade practices are techniques developed to facilitate the exchange in specific commercial, economic, and political contexts. Employed when buyer or seller request the assistance of a bank to complete an international transaction, the trade services—letter of credit, documentary collection, and bankers acceptance—are the classic examples of these techniques. Banks have traditionally been reactive and limited in their response to the needs of their customers engaged in international trade. Thus, for example, an exporter's need to receive payment at shipment rather than when the buyer actually received the goods has been met by a bank when it agrees to provide on request a letter of credit payment service.

Today, however, many banks are taking a more aggressive role. Innovative bankers are looking beyond the limited needs arising out of an immediate transaction. Innovators are looking for opportunities to improve the customer's current payment/financing practices in such a way that they contribute significantly to achievement of the customer's overall business goals—the desire, for example, not only to obtain financing but to improve a company's liquidity position or return on cash.

THE ORGANIZATION OF TRADE BANKING

At one time the corporate finance officer's role vis-à-vis a company's banking relationships was presumed to be the ability to obtain working capital loans at a rate favorable to the company. Conversely, a bank's calling officer was rewarded on the basis of the ability to negotiate large working capital loans at a rate of return profitable to the bank. Times have changed. Many companies now go directly into the money market to obtain the capital they need, and bankers are looking beyond their customers' working capital needs for financial opportunities emerging in other areas. A company's buying and selling activities are one such area of focus. The transaction-based financing opportunities arising out of the company's trading activities make up what is known as trade finance.

The successful practice of trade finance has always relied on the ability of trade experts to devise payment/financing arrangements to satisfy the needs of both the trading parties. Such expertise has historically resided in trade specialists attached to the operating areas responsible for processing a bank's trade services. In recent years many of the larger money center banks have established trade banking sales groups dedicated to developing this specialized business and have staffed them with technical specialists transferred from the processing areas and with "trade bankers," that is, loan officers who have developed special trade expertise as a result of working with a bank's technical specialists. Because trade bankers combine technical expertise with credit skills, they are often exceptionally qualified to design payment/financing structures tailored to either specific transaction requirements or to the customer's business goals. In the smaller banks, a single trade officer may perform this function. Where such a capability is lacking in-house, a smaller bank can usually refer its customer to a trade specialist available in a correspondent bank.

THE ROLE OF INNOVATION

Although innovation is a tradition in the international trade arena, the banker's conscious cultivation of innovative techniques to satisfy a company's broader business goals is relatively new. Bankers have discovered their customers are willing to pay top prices for innovative arrangements that provide tangible, often measurable, business results. Because of the distinct, often competitive, advantages they offer to the customer, innovative techniques command top prices when initially introduced. The passage of time, however, erodes the market value of the invention. As the technique becomes familiar and is employed widely, what originated as an innovative practice becomes state-of-the art, and profit margins shrink significantly.

Real profit rests with the innovators; therefore the most creative trade bankers are found at the cutting edge of current trade practice developing the innovative structures destined to become tomorrow's customary trade practice. The pattern is an old one. For example, variations on the classic letter of credit structure can be traced to innovations on the traditional letter of credit instrument, which in itself evolved as an innovative response to the commercial needs of a bank's trading customers in colonial times.*

This condition raises an interesting side issue. Under the laws of the United States all banks offer the same financial services, and competitive distinctions derive precisely from the banker's ingenuity in assembling certain basic financial "building blocks" into an arrangement tailored either to a customer's

---

*Henry Harfield, *Bank Credits and Acceptances* (5th ed.), Wiley, New York, 1974, p. 17.

special goals, or into a practice that uniquely capitalizes on a little known regulatory niche, to the distinct advantage of the bank's customer. It may be argued that such an innovative arrangement, packaged as a bank proposal, is essentially proprietary in nature.

These circumstances have altered the ground rules governing the marketing relationship existing between banker and company representative. The fungible character of money in a traditional lending sense is widely recognized. Money is money no matter how or where obtained. When "rate" governed the negotiation of credit arrangements, the underlying dynamic was competitive, sometimes even adversarial, and a corporate finance officer felt justified in handing over one bank's proposal to another bank saying, "Here. Can you give me a better rate on this?" However, such an action violates the contemporary marketing relationship in two ways. First, it negates the intrinsic value of the innovative arrangement by reducing a buy decision to one based solely on rate. Second, and more seriously, it violates the integrity of the buyer–seller relationship by delivering to a competitive bank the innovative technique itself. Such conduct may occasionally earn a company a short-term gain, but it short-circuits the company's access to future innovations. These misunderstandings seem most marked during periods of transition such as the one characterizing current marketing practices in the trade banking context.

The international trade arena operates from a set of premises quite different from those governing a strictly credit-oriented banking relationship. Success in trade requires the cooperation and collaboration within established commercial boundaries of all parties to a transaction. Theodore Levitt has characterized this practice as a "system of reciprocal dependencies" in which both buyer and seller need to realize a "profit" or the relationship cannot last.* In attempting to discuss the inherent give-and-take nature of international trade relationships, trade bankers observe, "On the other side of every export is an import." They invoke this statement to dramatize the system of reciprocal commercial dependencies which typically characterize the practice of international trade.

PROFILING A COMPANY'S TRADE FLOWS

The pattern of a company's international purchases and sales constitutes its *trade flows*. The individual transactions that make up a trade flow are usually repetitive in nature, involving the same countries and often the same trading

*Theodore Levitt, *The Marketing Imagination*, Free Press, New York, 1984, p. 121.

partners. Each transaction is made up of a special combination of possibilities and constraints derived from the "demographics" of the underlying commercial transaction—the agreed-upon exchange of goods for payment.

In Chapter 8 we introduce the Transaction Profile, a detailed method for analyzing the characteristics of a given trade transaction or trade flow. This detailed analysis precedes the design of arrangements tailored to a specific situation. However, before committing bank resources to this time-consuming and hence expensive design process, a banker must assess the business potential that is represented by a customer's international business. Answers to the following questions provide the trade banker with a profile of a company's trade flows.

- *What* is being bought/sold across national borders?
- *Who* are the trading partners? What is their relative negotiating strength? What is their relative market dominance?
- *Where* are the purchases/sales being made? What are the ports of origin and destination?
- *How Much* is being traded? What are the volumes?
- *How Often* are the shipments? What is the frequency?
- *On What Trade Terms?* (Delineates the allocation of risk, responsibility, and control in the transaction.)

Additionally a trade banker needs to know what the company is trying to do and *why*. Two companies with identical trade flows but different sets of business resources and goals may call for two very different payment/financing arrangements.

THE COLLABORATIVE NATURE OF TRADE BANK MARKETING

The trade banker is a solution-oriented salesperson keenly aware that the design of optimal payment/financing structures depends on the informed cooperation of the bank's customer. The trade banker bases the design of innovative arrangements on elements occurring in three basic areas: the *company's current processing methods and practices* (discussed in Chapters 3 and 7); *technical components* of the trade services themselves (described in detail in Chapters 4–6); and *government laws and regulations* applicable to a specific transaction. Being familiar with the technical possibilities inherent in the trade services and with the relevant trade regulations, the trade banker must elicit the company's cooperation to understand its current methods, practices, and fundamental goals.

Ultimately the adequacy of a payment/financing structure depends as much on the company's ability to describe its current situation as on the skill of the trade banker in tailoring a structure to satisfy those requirements. Successful trade bankers are proficient at assisting company representatives to articulate clearly their business goals and current practices.

The research and analytic process required to devise innovative trade finance arrangements often surprises both generalist bankers and the corporate finance officer who is their normal company contact. The generalist banker may be surprised by the additional company contacts the trade banker needs to make, and corporate treasurers are sometimes taken aback by the range of the trade banker's questions. Both may be unsettled to discover the trade banker has questions that can only be answered by others in the company— by a purchasing agent, for example, or a production manager, or the export credit manager or manager of export sales. At such times it is helpful to remember the trade banker's basic goal: to find a way to enable the customer to do a piece of business faster, cheaper, more easily, or with less risk.

Such collaboration may be a new experience for the generalist banker and the corporate finance officer accustomed to operating under an older set of marketing premises. Sometimes termed "need-satisfaction" selling, the underlying rules derive from this simple paradigm: A *customer need*, satisfied by a *product feature*, produces a *customer benefit*. Under this scenario the marketer's task is to sell customer *benefits* rather than product *features*, thus answering the customer's implicit question, "What's in it for me?" This model is often formalized in a product profile format (customer "needs" are matched by corresponding product "features" that yield customer "benefits"). When applied to a bank's trade services this selling model has three severe limitations:

- First, the product profile format conveys the mistaken impression that the trade services are static in nature, whereas in fact trade is a *process* driven by dynamics in the environment that either constrain or foster it.
- Second, the product profile format provides an incomplete framework for guiding the marketing process because it tends to focus attention on the "banking needs" of the bank's customer—either exporter or importer—*in isolation from the needs of other parties to the transac-*

tion. The fact is that successful completion of a trade transaction requires the collaborative efforts of all parties to the transaction, and the value of individual actions is found in assessing their impact on the transaction as a whole and by judging their effect on the other trading parties.

- Third, to the extent that the product profile format neglects the technical logic governing trade transactions, it encourages a simplistic view of the mechanical aspects of the trade services. In fact very specific rules and regulations govern trade transactions. These rules derive from at least two separate sources: the regulations and customary practices associated with the individual trade services and governmental laws and regulations applicable to a given transaction.

By contrast, commitment to problem solving characterizes the modern relationship-based trade marketing process in which products are viewed as problem-solving tools. Although identification of business problems worthy of marketing focus commonly begins with analysis of a company's current methods, practices, and company goals, it probably will not stop there. A bank's need, for example, to achieve operational efficiency may provide the impetus for finding new ways to structure a customer's international business to the mutual advantage of bank and company. The generalist banker and corporate finance officer play a potentially important role in the initial fact-finding phase. The generalist banker may be needed to explain to the corporate finance officer the kind of information the trade banker is seeking and the advantage to the company in providing it. In turn the corporate finance officer is in a position to introduce the trade banker to others in the organization, many of whom have never met before with a banker and may need some explanation of the trade banker's purpose and method before they will volunteer needed information.

In the broadest sense, then, a trade banker seeks information about the company that makes it possible to tailor payment/financing structures to satisfy the requirements of specific transactions in a way that enables the company to achieve other business goals. Therefore optimal arrangements can be structured only when the trade banker has a firm grasp on the total commercial context within which a company transacts a piece of business. Conversely, the more informed the company representatives are about trade banking capability in general, the more efficiently and completely they will be able to identify and provide needed information.

Information sought in the initial data-gathering process may be classified under the following four dynamics:

1. The *customer* dynamic describes the business strategy developed by
    a banking customer to capitalize on opportunities and/or to overcome
    constraints in the environment (see item 4 below). Answers to the
    following questions provide the trade banker with insight into the
    business dynamics underlying a trading customer's motivations:

    -   What is the bank's customer trying to do, and why?
    -   What business goals is the company trying to achieve?
    -   What problems is it trying to solve?
    -   What is the role of imports and exports in the company strategy as
        a whole? What might it be?

2. The *product* dynamic describes the technical logic of given transac-
    tions. Answers to the following questions provide banker and cus-
    tomer alike with the tools they need to manipulate the constituent
    elements of the trade services to obtain payment/financing structures
    tailored to the practical requirements of specific transactions.

    -   What government laws or regulations govern the transaction?
    -   What are the technical requirements or operating constraints asso-
        ciated with the trade term currently employed for this trade flow?
    -   What is the bank's service capability ("product line")?

3. The *environmental* dynamic describes the contexts in which trade is
    conducted and a trade service offered. Answers to the following ques-
    tions help reveal the motivations and business strategies of customer
    and bank and suggest areas for collaboration.

    -   What obstacles/opportunities does the *bank's customer* see in the
        relevant commercial, economic, and political environments?
    -   What obstacles/opportunities does the *bank* perceive in the com-
        mercial, economic, or political environments?

4. The *marketing* dynamic describes a bank's strategic response to ob-
    stacles and opportunities occurring in the environment. At a bank-
    wide level, the answer to the following question characterizes a
    bank's marketing program. At the individual account level, the an-
    swer to this question describes (or should describe) a banker's mar-

keting program tailored to the needs of individual importing and/or exporting customers.

- What activities (tactics) must a bank's marketing officer perform in order to establish vital connections between customer realities ("needs") and product/service capabilities ("features"), thus producing customer satisfaction ("benefits")?

The marketing dynamic may also describe the tactics of a corporate finance officer intent on obtaining improved trade service from the company's current banks. A generalist banker can be asked to locate the bank's trade specialist, and the trade expert can be invited to assess the company's current methods and practices to see where significant improvements might be made.

This is the basic framework guiding discussion of the classical trade services. By asking, "What is the customer problem for which a given trade service capability is the appropriate solution?" we focus attention on the essential problem-solving character of the trade services. The trade map presented in Figure 0.1 schematizes these issues. Subsequent chapters treat individual topics in detail.

One purpose of this book is to assist bankers to identify the necessary activities to make the vital connection between customer need, broadly conceived, and bank capability; an equally important goal is to assist companies engaged in international trade to gain perspective on the transaction as a whole and insight into the technical and processing requirements associated with delivery of each of the trade services. Improved business results await bank and customer willing to put forth the needed collaborative effort.

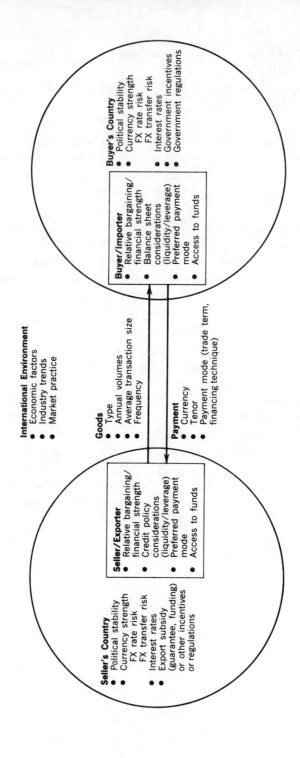

International Environment
• Economic factors
• Industry trends
• Market practice

Goods
• Type
• Annual volumes
• Average transaction size
• Frequency

Payment
• Currency
• Tenor
• Payment mode (trade term, financing technique)

Buyer's Country
• Political stability
• Currency strength
  FX rate risk
  FX transfer risk
• Interest rates
• Government incentives
• Government regulations

Buyer/Importer
• Relative bargaining/financial strength
• Balance sheet considerations (liquidity/leverage)
• Preferred payment mode
• Access to funds

Seller's Country
• Political stability
• Currency strength
  FX rate risk
  FX transfer risk
• Interest rates
• Export subsidy (guarantee, funding) or other incentives or regulations

Seller/Exporter
• Relative bargaining/financial strength
• Credit policy considerations (liquidity/leverage)
• Preferred payment mode
• Access to funds

Figure 0.1 Trade map.

1 The Commercial Context

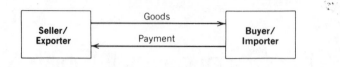

Figure 1.1   Trade.

The buying and selling that occurs between businesses is the heart of trade, which may be described simply as the exchange of goods for payment (see Fig. 1.1).

Certain dynamics act to complicate this apparently simple exchange. First, corporate customers conduct business in specific national, industrial, and competitive environments that generate pressures that either aid or impede successful completion of a trade transaction (see Fig. 1.2).

Second, sellers also buy and buyers also sell. The seller in the preceding figures must purchase raw materials and supplies from sources outside the company and process them, or "add value," before selling the finished product to the buyer. The buyer usually adds value in some way and resells the product to customers outside the company. These suppliers and customers also operate in particular national, industrial, and competitive markets and are also engaged in trading and value-added activities. Figure 1.3 illustrates the structural network implicit in these relationships.

The cash-to-cash or cash conversion cycle depicted in Figure 1.4 is a conventional method used to plot a company's flow of cash through purchase of raw materials or supplies into finished goods and back into cash through conversion of receivables.

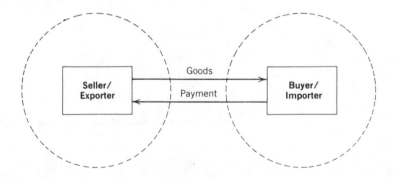

Figure 1.2   Trade environment.

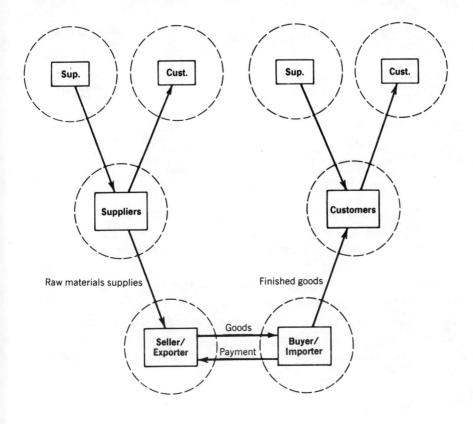

Figure 1.3 Network of trade relationships.

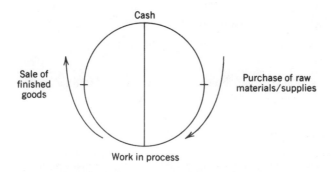

Figure 1.4 Simple cash–to–cash cycle.

13

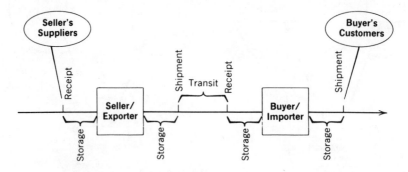

Figure 1.5 Movement of goods from seller to buyer.

In an ideal world the cash-to-cash cycle would be in equilibrium: Available cash would equal that needed both to fund purchases and to extend credit to the company's own buyers when necessary. In reality the cycle is seldom balanced and gaps frequently occur. These gaps represent the difference between the credit terms a company receives from its suppliers and the credit terms it extends to its own buyers.

Trade Financing

Figure 1.5, derived from the asset or cash conversion cycle, charts the normal movement of goods from seller to buyer. Buyers and/or sellers may require financing at any point along this path. For example:

- The seller may need financing to purchase the goods and prepare them for shipment, or for the period between shipping goods to and receiving payment from the buyer.
- The buyer may need financing to meet his payment obligations to the seller.

Transaction-based techniques commonly used to finance these gaps are introduced in later chapters.

Risk, Responsibility, and Control

Within the context of any sales transaction it seems obvious that the goal of the seller is to get paid, and the goal of the buyer is to receive goods as ordered. Their respective risks, then, are that the seller will not receive payment and the buyer will be unable to take timely delivery of goods as ordered.

In a domestic sale the relative geographic proximity of the trading companies and the common legal and cultural environment in which they operate enable the trading partners to transact their business in a way that takes many things for granted. The bank normally plays a minimal role in domestic transactions, specifically processing the buyer's check and effecting payment to the seller, thus settling the account by debiting the buyer and crediting the seller.

But businesses buying and selling across national borders face special problems. In addition to the complications presented by the often significant geographic distances, differences in language, culture, and legal systems may impede the successful completion of the transaction. Table 1.1 lists the risks of international trade from both the exporter's and importer's points of view and describes the potential impact on each. (Note that the "sellers" and "buyers" in domestic trade transactions become "exporters" and "importers" in cross-border transactions.)

Documents are the principal means available to reduce or eliminate the risks inherent in international trade. The International Chamber of Commerce (I.C C.) classifies four major categories of trade documents:*

- The *commercial* documents, principally the invoice, are the seller's description of the goods shipped and the principal means by which the buyer gains assurance that the goods shipped are those ordered.
- The *transport* documents are "documents indicating loading on board or dispatch or taking in charge" (I.C.C. Publication 400, Section D1). The bill of lading (the principal transport document) is the carrier's acknowledgment of receipt of the goods and, when issued in negotiable form, controls title to them.
- *Insurance* documents, normally an insurance certificate, represent that the goods are duly insured, hence mitigating the risk if they are lost in transit.
- Other documents may include *official* documents required by governments in order to regulate and control the passage of goods across their borders; they typically include consular documents, import or export licenses, and certificates of origin. Other documents may also include certificates of weight, quality, or analysis named by the buyer.

The buyer and the seller employ specific documents as the means by which they allocate risk, responsibility, and control in the transaction.

* Uniform Customs and Practice for Documentary Credits (rev. ed.) 1983, International Chamber of Commerce (I.C.C.), Publication 400, is included in the appendices of this book.

Table 1.1 Risks of International Trade

Risk	Impact on Seller/Exporter	Impact on Buyer/Importer
Performance: The seller will fail to deliver the goods as specified in the sales contract.	Potential damage to business reputation; potential financial loss.	May adversely affect ability to perform under sales contracts with *own* customers; potential financial loss and/or damage to reputation.
Transaction: The goods will fail to arrive at their destination and/or to clear customs in the importer's country.	Financial loss for value of goods.	Same.
Payment: The seller will fail to receive payment for goods shipped due to one or more of the following:		
• *Nonacceptance:* The buyer will fail to accept the goods shipped.	Stuck with goods in a foreign port, seller must either find another foreign buyer (risking a loss on the forced sale) or bear the cost of shipping the goods for domestic sale.	Potential damage to reputation; same.
• *Commercial credit:* The buyer will be unwilling or unable to pay as agreed when payment is due.	Financial loss for value of goods.	Potential damage to reputation, which could adversely affect ability to draw from international sources of supply in the future.
• *Political:* The government of the importing country will take sovereign action to renege on public and private international commitments; or wars, strikes, revolutions, or other civil disturbances in the	Financial loss for value of goods.	Same.

Table 1.1 (Continued)

Risk	Impact on Seller/Exporter	Impact on Buyer/Importer
importing country will prevent or delay payment.		
• *Foreign exchange transfer:* If payment is due in foreign currency, the required foreign exchange will not be available or allocated in the importer's country to permit the buyer to remit payment to the seller in the agreed-upon currency.	Payment will be delayed, requiring additional financing.	Same.
• *Foreign exchange rate fluctuation:* At payment time, the foreign exchange rate will be unacceptable.	Financial loss if payment is to be *received* in foreign currency.	Financial loss if payment is to be *made* in foreign currency.

SALES CONTRACT

The sales contract* is the document in which the trading partners confirm their respective rights and responsibilities in the transaction. Ideally, sales contracts would always be structured to avoid ambiguity and the possibility of future conflicts; however, sales agreements are often concluded on nothing more than a handshake. Usually in this case the mutual goal of buyer and seller is to move the goods and effect payment, and each will do whatever is required to achieve that goal. In other words, regardless of the terms of sale a transaction will be successful when the buyer wants to buy and the seller

*For a more detailed discussion, see Chapter 6 in Gerhard W. Schneider, *Export–Import Financing: A Practical Guide,* Wiley, New York, 1974.

wants to sell. The difficulty arises when one of the trading partners wants out of the transaction or when the approval of a third party (such as a government entity) is required. In those instances protection in the event of dispute is the reward of those who have taken care to make underlying assumptions explicit in the sales contract.

It is our goal in this section to describe the major elements of a sales agreement and to spell out several of the most common underlying assumptions.

Description of the Goods

Universal definitions for weight, measurement, and quality (including grades) do not exist and may differ from country to country. In order to prevent misunderstanding or conflict, the trading partners may need to define these terms precisely as they will be used in a given transaction. Once weight, quantity, and quality have been defined the goods may be described accurately.

Inspections, Warranties, Guarantees

Inspection certificates, usually issued by the buyer's agent, may be required in order to ensure that the goods are as specified in the sales contract. The seller may be required to issue a warranty against product defects, the extent of which should be explicitly stated in the sales contract. The buyer may require the seller to back up either the product or delivery with a guarantee in the form of a standby letter of credit from a bank.

Packaging and Marking

The nature of the goods, how they are to be shipped (i.e., by air or steamship, truck, and/or rail), and customs regulations in the country of destination usually determine the mode of packaging. In addition, customs regulations in the importing country usually govern the marking of both inner and outer cartons.

Insurance

Theoretically the buyer assumes the cost of insuring the goods in transit. As a practical matter in some markets, however, payment of the insurance premium may become a matter of negotiation, and the seller may agree to pay the premium as a way of reducing overall transaction costs. Moreover, either buyer or seller may agree to accept responsibility for arranging insurance coverage. The terms of sale (see below) identify who is responsible for arranging the coverage and for paying the premium.

The bank takes an active role in insurance coverage when it takes a security interest in the transaction, as in a letter of credit transaction. In that case the bank will make sure that the goods are insured, that the coverage is in proper form, and that the amount is appropriate to the value of the goods.

Price Specifications

The unit price must specify the currency in which the price is expressed and should name who will accept the foreign exchange risk. The following adjustments to price must be specified:

- Discounts for quantity, early payment, and so forth.
- Additions to compensate for finance charges (in case of deferred payment) or transportation charges, insurance fees, or other surcharges.

Terms of Sale

In the process of exchanging goods for payment, the terms of sale (sometimes referred to as "selling terms" or "shipping terms") name the precise moment when responsibility for the goods passes from seller to buyer. Familiar as FOB, C&F, CIF, and so on, the *Revised American Foreign Trade Definitions (1941)* constitute the customary basis in the United States for defining who is responsible for the goods at each moment they are in transit. In an attempt to standardize international trade practices, the International Chamber of Commerce has developed the *IncoTerms* now widely accepted outside the United States.*

Payment Terms

Finally the trading partners will agree in the sales contract to a specific payment term. The term selected depends on a number of factors, principally:

- Relative negotiating (including financial) strength of buyer and seller.
- Industry practices or customs.
- Competitive practices.

Revised American Foreign Trade Definitions (1941) and a "Summary of Incoterms" are included in the appendices.

The classical payment terms are:

- Open account.
- Documentary collections:
  Documents against payment.
  Documents against acceptance.
- Letter of credit (unconfirmed):
  Sight
  Time
- Confirmed letter of credit:
  Sight
  Time
- Cash in advance.

In an *open account* transaction the seller ships the goods and sends the required documents directly to the buyer who pays after accepting the goods. In that case the seller assumes all the risk in the transaction. Open account terms are common in markets characterized by long-standing commercial relationships, for example, domestic trade and trade conducted between Europe and the United States.

At the other end of the spectrum, when the selling terms are *cash in advance*, the seller does not ship until he has received the buyer's payment. Again, however, the seller sends the documents directly to the buyer. In this instance the seller retains total control over the transaction, and the buyer assumes all the risk, that is, that the goods ordered and paid for may not be received by the desired date.

In both open account and cash in advance, the buyer pays the seller directly via check or money transfer, and the bank's role is limited to moving the funds from buyer to seller.

Sometimes, however, the trading parties require more than the bank's impartial money transfer services. In such instances buyer and seller may employ the bank's services to allocate elements of risk and control between them in a given transaction. The key elements of the bank's role at this level are *regulation of timing* and *risk taking;* the bill of lading and draft are the primary control documents in such transactions. (We describe these two key documents in more detail in the next section.)

The documentary collection and the letter of credit, described in detail in Chapters 4 and 5, may be regarded as practical alternatives to cash in advance and open account terms. In a *documentary collection* transaction, the bank acts as *agent* for the seller/exporter in seeking payment from the overseas buyer/importer. Each party retains important elements of control: The importer is not required to pay the exporter before the merchandise ordered is shipped, and the exporter is able to retain title to the goods until the importer either pays the draft (documents against payment) or accepts it (documents against acceptance). In both cases the bank acts solely as agent for the exporter, regulating the *timing* of the transaction—specifically by holding the documents, including the bill of lading, until the buyer/importer either pays or accepts the draft.

The bank is a legal party in a *letter of credit* transaction and for a fee assumes most of the risk. The importer's bank obligates itself to pay the exporter against his presentation of documents that conform to (i.e., match) the terms and conditions of the letter of credit. In effect the importer's bank says to the seller/exporter, "I know your buyer, and I judge him to be creditworthy. Therefore for a fee I will assume his credit risk, and I undertake to pay you directly for the goods, provided that you submit documents which conform to the terms and conditions of the letter of credit." If the letter of credit is *confirmed,* a bank in the exporter's country also obligates itself to pay the exporter against conforming documents, thus substituting *its* credit for that of the importer's bank. In such a case, the exporter has the obligation to pay of two banks—one of which is located in his own country and is presumably known to him.

THE PRINCIPAL CONTROL DOCUMENTS

Payment of a sight draft or acceptance of a time draft must precede release of the documents to the buyer, thus allowing the seller and/or his bank to retain control of the goods until the buyer either pays or acknowledges the obligation to pay. In this section we will describe certain characteristics of the two documents that make this control possible.

Draft or Bill of Exchange

The seller's unconditional written demand for payment, the *draft* or *bill of exchange* supplements the commercial invoice as the means by which the seller charges the buyer for the goods. Figure 1.6 shows a typical draft format. The draft is written by the *drawer* (seller) to the *drawee,* and it requires

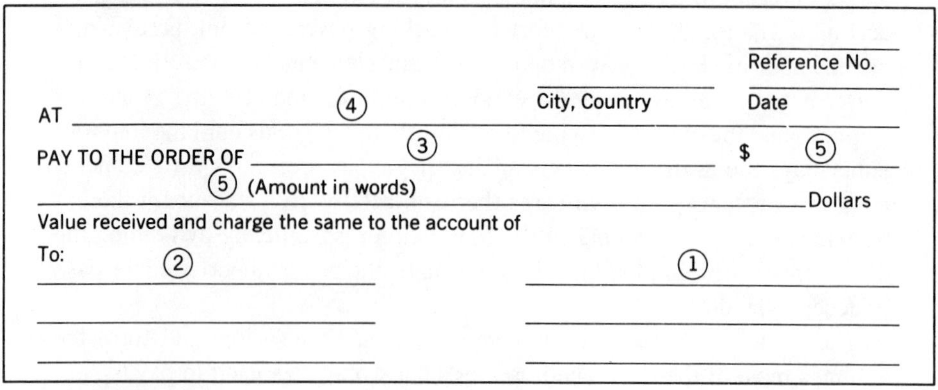

1. Drawer/seller
2. Drawee/buyer or bank
3. Payee
4. Tenor
5. Amount

Figure 1.6 Typical draft format.

payment of a fixed amount at a specific time to a named *payee*. In a documentary collection the drawee is usually the buyer; in a letter of credit transaction it is a bank. The drawer and payee will normally be the same party (the seller), and in this case the named payee is often simply "ourselves."

The *tenor* of a draft indicates when payment is to be made by making it possible to determine when the draft matures. A draft payable upon presentation is called a *sight draft* and the tenor is stated simply "at sight." A draft payable on a specified or determinable date in the future is a *time* (or *usance**) *draft*. The maturity date or tenor of a time draft may be expressed in various ways, the most common being:

- As a *fixed date;* for example, June 30, 1985.
- As a specified number of days after presentation of the draft to the drawee, called *days sight;* for example, 60 days sight.
- As a specified number of days from the date of the draft (based on a particular document, usually the bill of lading) called *days date;* for example, 30 days date.

---

*F. E. Perry explains the term "usance bill" as follows. "Bills [of exchange] drawn for a term usually specify three months but may also, of course, be for other periods, according to the

An *acceptance* is created when the drawee writes "Accepted," the date, and his signature on the face of a time draft. A draft accepted by the buyer becomes a *trade acceptance;* one accepted by a bank becomes a *bankers acceptance*.

Drafts are *negotiable instruments* as defined by the Uniform Commercial Code (U.C.C.). Article 3-104 of U.C.C. says that to be negotiable an instrument must:

- Be signed by the maker or drawer.
- Contain an unconditional promise or order to pay a certain sum in money.
- Be payable on demand or at a definite time.
- Be payable to order or to bearer.

Because they are negotiable, drafts may be sold and ownership transferred by endorsement to another party termed the *holder in due course*. There is no limit to the number of times ownership may be transferred. Whoever owns the draft at maturity presents it to the drawee (buyer or bank) for payment. In other words, the drawee is the *primary obligor*, who is the party unconditionally obligated to make payment at maturity to whoever presents the draft at that time. If the primary obligor fails to meet the payment obligation, the holder in due course has recourse through all previous endorsers in turn back to the drawer (seller) of the draft who is the *secondary obligor*. Under negotiable instruments law the secondary obligor has the unconditional obligation to pay the draft if the primary obligor and subsequent endorsers dishonor it. This characteristic makes the accepted draft *two-name paper*.

Examples of specific drafts are included in the relevant chapters: a sight draft, and a time draft accepted by the buyer in a documentary collection (a trade acceptance) in Chapter 4; a sight draft under a letter of credit in Chapter 5; and a time draft accepted by a bank (bankers acceptance) in Chapter 6.

Bill of Lading

The bill of lading is a far more complex document than the discussion here suggests. Our goal is to introduce the document and show how it may be used

time estimated to be necessary for the goods to reach their destination, be resold, and for the proceeds to become available to meet the due dates of the bills. These periods of time became customary for certain places; thus a usance bill was one drawn at a term governed by the custom in the trade, for example, three months' date for bills on Paris, ninety days' date for bills on Lisbon, thirty days' sight for bills on Bombay." F. E. Perry, *The Elements of Banking* (3rd ed.), Methuen, London, 1981, pp. 110–111.

to control the exchange of goods for payment. Additional information may be obtained from trade specialists located in the trade banking departments of the major banks, or in the finance areas of businesses engaged in international trade.

A *bill of lading* is the receipt given by the freight company (called the carrier) to the exporter/shipper and is evidence of the shipping contract between them. It may be issued in either negotiable form (called an order bill of lading) or in nonnegotiable form (a straight bill of lading). In its negotiable form it is also the title document for the goods being shipped; as such it permits ownership of the goods to be independent of actual possession of them. In other words, whether the bill of lading is negotiable or nonnegotiable determines whether the exporter or the importer controls title to the goods.

In an *order bill of lading*, the shipper consigns the shipment "to the order of" a named party, usually themselves. Because the order bill of lading is negotiable, the exporter can transfer title to another party (usually a bank in the importer's country) by endorsing it and delivering it to the bank. *Under an order bill of lading, the consignee (exporter or bank) retains title to the goods until the importer pays or acknowledges the obligation to pay.* However, carriers usually issue bills of lading in sets of three or more originals. To keep title the consignee must have a "full set," because whoever presents a properly endorsed original to the carrier may receive the goods.

The order bill of lading is the preferred form in a documentary collection or a letter of credit transaction if the goods are to be used as collateral in a financing arrangement.

A shipment sent under a *straight bill of lading* is consigned to a specific party, usually the importer. It is nonnegotiable. The consignee named on the straight bill of lading can receive the shipment by presenting adequate identification instead of the actual bill of lading. *Under a straight bill of lading, both the exporter and the bank lose control of the shipment before the importer pays or accepts the obligation to pay.*

Straight bills of lading might be used in situations in which the exporter trusts the importer to pay (open account), or if the exporter has already received payment (cash in advance), or in consignment shipments where no financing is involved. They are also used if the importing country prohibits order bills of lading.

Cross-border shipments can be made by air as well as by sea, but there is an important difference between the two. Goods shipped by sea usually spend several days, even weeks, in transit. Hence there is adequate time before the goods arrive at their destination for the exporter to assemble the documents and present them to his bank (a process that may take two–three days), for the bank to process and send them (another one–three days), and for them to arrive at the importer's bank (another two–five days, depending on the transit mode). By contrast, goods sent by air often arrive several days before the documents. Because warehouse space at airports is limited, the importer must be able to take possession of the goods without waiting for the title documents.

The *air waybill* is a bill of lading issued by an air freight company.* As with the ocean bill of lading, it is the carrier's receipt for the goods and evidence of the contract between the carrier and the exporter/shipper. Because of the timing problem described above, air waybills are usually issued in nonnegotiable form and consigned to the importer who can take possession of the goods upon presentation of adequate identification to the carrier. As with the straight bill of lading, the exporter loses control of the goods before the importer pays for them.

SUMMARY

Buyer/importers and seller/exporters employ the documents described in the preceding sections to reduce or eliminate the risks commonly associated with the cross-border exchange of goods for payment. Table 1.2 summarizes the banking services associated with open account, documentary collection, and letter of credit payment terms from the respective points of view of buyer and seller.

In Chapter 2 we investigate the procedures established by banks to make and receive payments associated with international transactions.

---

*The U.C.C. paragraph 1-201(6) provides: "'Bill of lading' means a document evidencing the receipt of goods for shipment issued by a person engaged in the business of transporting or forwarding goods, and includes an airbill. 'Airbill' means a document serving for air transportation as a bill of lading does for marine or rail transportation, and includes an air consignment note or air waybill."

Table 1.2 Risks and Bank Products

Risk		Payment Term	Bank Function	Bank Service
Seller/Exporter	Buyer/Importer			
"I have confidence in this buyer. His country is stable, and I know he will accept and pay for the goods."	"I want to hold transaction costs to a minimum."	Open account	Settlement	Funds transfer • Cable • Mail payment order Bank draft • Foreign currency draft • U.S. dollar check payable overseas Regular business check
"I want to control the goods until the buyer pays, but his country is stable, and I'm confident he will accept the goods."	"I want to minimize transaction costs."	Documentary collection	Settlement plus Timing	Documents against payment (D/P)
"I'm willing to give terms, but I need legal evidence of the buyer's debt in his own country."	"I want to hold financing costs down."	Documentary collection	Settlement plus Timing	Documents against acceptance (D/A)

Customer situation	Method	Functions	Instruments
"The buyer's country is stable, and I know his bank is a good one, but "I need some control over the seller's performance, for example, over • Quality of the goods. • That goods were modified as per the sales contract. • Compliance with the latest shipping date."	Letter of credit (unconfirmed)	Settlement plus Timing plus Risk taking	Unconfirmed irrevocable letter of credit
• I don't know the buyer. • I've modified the goods and/or • his country requires a letter of credit." "I'm not willing to take the risk of the buyer's bank and/or country." If exporter pays fees: "I'll incur the fees to mitigate the risk and conclude the sale." "I need to obtain these goods and will do whatever is required to expedite the process, including paying the bank fees" (if importer pays fees).	Confirmed letter of credit	Settlement plus Timing plus Risk taking	Confirmed irrevocable letter of credit
"I am confident I will receive the goods as ordered and paid for be-cause the seller is a major supplier with a solid international repu-tation and frankly, I am in a weak bargaining po-sition." "I'll ship when I have the buyer's payment in hand."	Cash in advance	Settlement	Funds transfer • Cable • Mail payment or-der Bank draft • Foreign currency draft • U.S. dollar check payable overseas

2 The Banking Context: Settlement and Foreign Exchange

The demand deposit account (DDA) lies at the core of a customer's banking relationship. Bank and customer—whether retail, commercial, or institutional—communicate with each other principally by means of debits and credits to the DDA. In its simplest form, *settlement* may be described as the simultaneous debit and credit to the respective demand deposit accounts of a buyer and seller engaged in a trade transaction. A simultaneous debit and credit on the books of a commercial bank is termed a *book transfer;* it is the basic settlement mechanism for payments made on either a funds transfer or a negotiable instrument basis. A book transfer occurs when both parties to a transaction maintain business checking accounts at the same bank, thus enabling that bank to debit and credit the respective parties simultaneously on its own books, as schematized in Figure 2.1. The parties in a book transfer transaction for the settlement of a negotiable instrument, as say, a regular business check, are:

- *Payor* is the party from whose account the funds will be debited (the buyer).
- *Payee* is the party to whose account the funds will be credited (the seller).
- *Depository bank* is defined by U.C.C., Section 4-105, to be the first bank to which an item is transferred for collection even though it is also the payor bank,* in which case the depository bank maintains accounts for both payor (buyer) and payee (seller).

In the following flows a word of clarification is in order regarding the direction of arrows used to indicate debits and credits to the accounts of the various parties to the transaction. The arrows indicate the *flow of funds* rather than the direction of the accounting entry, that is, a debit represents a flow of funds out of an account and a credit represents a flow of funds into an account. The debit and credit entries made by any one bank are indicated by a single number and a letter (for example, the accounting entry performed by a single bank is represented by 2a debit and 2b credit). In the strictest sense a bank debits the payor before it credits a payee. The book transfer procedure outlined in Figure 2.1 follows this format.

---

*Uniform Commercial Code, Section 4-105.

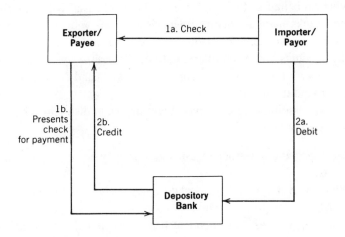

Figure 2.1   Book transfer settlement of check.

TRANSACTION FLOW

Transaction Steps	Notes
1. Payor (buyer) writes a check and sends it to the payee (seller).	In this way the buyer instructs the bank to debit his account to pay the seller.
2. Depository bank *debits* payor's account and *credits* payee's account on its books.	Settlement is final.

Because the bank is able to debit the buyer or payor's account directly (resulting in a collected debit), the funds are obviously immediately "good," that is, they are *available* for the seller either to withdraw or transfer to another account.

Correspondent Bank Relationships

Unfortunately, customers rarely maintain accounts at the same bank. Thus it has been necessary for the banking system to devise a way to send payments to each other on behalf of their customers. The mechanism is a deceptively simple one: Banks maintain demand deposit accounts with each other and remit cross-border payments by debits or credits to these accounts. Banks maintaining accounts with each other are termed *correspondent banks*. The accounting network formed by these correspondent demand deposit accounts links banks around the world.

Bankers have traditionally employed Latin names to distinguish between correspondent accounts:

- A *nostro* account is *our* account in your currency on your books; therefore it is:

    What a U.S. bank calls its local currency account on the books of an overseas correspondent bank.

    What an overseas correspondent bank calls its U.S. dollar account on the books of its U.S. correspondent bank.

- A *vostro* account is *your* account in our currency on our books; therefore it is:

    What a U.S. bank calls the U.S. dollar account it maintains on its books for an overseas correspondent.

    What an overseas correspondent bank calls the local currency account it maintains on its books for a U.S. correspondent.

In other words, one bank's *nostro* is its correspondent bank's *vostro*. Bankers employ these accounts to effect international payments. However, in order to locate the account relationships for making the requisite debit and credit entries, it is often necessary to route a payment through several correspondent banks before it reaches the payor bank and final settlement is possible.

THE COLLECTION PROCESS

The collection process associated with effecting an international payment by means of a negotiable instrument involves two major procedures:

- *Clearance* of an item is the path it takes physically through banking channels to return to the payor bank for final collection of the debit.
- *Settlement* of the item occurs by a chronological sequence of debit and credit entries to the accounts of correspondent banks acting on behalf of buyer and seller and culminating in a direct debit to the buyer's own account.

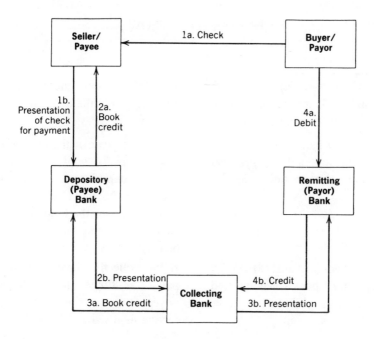

Figure 2.2 Clearance and settlement of a check by collection.

Figure 2.2 describes the basic collection process involved in effecting a cross-border payment by means of a negotiable instrument.* The sequence is chronological, that is, each step in the process depends upon successful completion of all preceding steps. The parties† to this collection process are:

- *Collecting bank* receives items from the depository bank, *credits* the depository bank's account on a book credit basis, and presents the items for payment to the proper remitting bank.
- *Remitting (payor) bank* is the payor's (buyer's) bank. As such it is the bank on which the item is drawn, and it *debits* the payor's demand deposit account on its books. A collecting bank may or may not also be the remitting bank, depending on whether or not it is also the payor's bank and hence on whether or not it is the bank on which the item is drawn.

*For the sake of simplicity we have chosen the regular business check to illustrate a "bare bones" or generic collection process. Bank drafts, which clear and settle in a similar manner, are discussed later in the chapter.
†Uniform Commercial Code, Section 4-105.

TRANSACTION FLOW

Transaction Steps	Notes
1. Payor (seller) (a) writes the check and sends it to the seller who (b) presents it for payment.	The seller presents the item by depositing it into the demand deposit account.
2. Depository bank (a) *credits* the payee's account and (b) *presents* the item to a collecting bank for payment.	The credit given at the time of deposit is termed *book credit;* however, the depository bank does not usually make the funds available until it receives the funds from the payor or remitting bank (see Step 4 below).
3. The collecting bank (a) *credits* the depository bank's account and (b) *presents* the item to the remitting bank for payment.	If the collecting bank is also the payor (remitting) bank, it debits the buyer's account directly, thus effecting final settlement.
4. The remitting bank verifies that there are sufficient funds in the payor's account and then (a) *debits* that account and (b) *credits* the collecting bank's account.	Settlement is now final.
	If the remitting bank determines that the item cannot be paid from the payor's account (e.g., because of insufficient funds), the remitting bank notifies the collecting bank and returns the item. To "unwind" the string of book credits, each intermediary bank debits the account of the bank that preceded it in the collection process. Ultimately funds are recovered from the payee (seller's) account, and the check item is returned to that party.

In actual practice, the settlement issue is a complicated one as the following passage from the Uniform Commercial Code indicates:

> The term "settle" is used as a convenient term to characterize a broad variety of conditional, provisional, tentative and also final payments of items. Such a

comprehensive term is needed because it is frequently difficult or unnecessary to determine whether a particular action is tentative or final or when a particular credit shifts from the tentative class to the final class. Therefore its use throughout the Article indicates that in that particular context it is unnecessary or unwise to determine whether the debit or the credit of the payment is tentative or final. However, when qualified by the adjective "provisional" its tentative nature is intended, and when qualified by the adjective "final" its permanent nature is intended.

Examples of the various types of settlement contemplated by the term include payments in cash; the efficient but somewhat complicated process of payment through the adjustment and offsetting of balances through clearing houses; *debit or credit entries in accounts between banks;* the forwarding of various types of remittance instruments, sometimes to cover a particular item but more frequently to cover an entire group of items received on a particular day.* (Emphasis added)

For our purposes, we shall adopt a strict definition of settlement to mean *final* settlement and restrict our discussion to consideration of settlement via debit or credit entries to accounts between banks. In everyday usage, however, the term *settlement* will be heard in the broader scope described in the passage cited.

FOREIGN EXCHANGE

A trade transaction may be denominated in the currency of the importer or the exporter, or in a third currency. Transactions denominated in U.S. dollars typically pass over the books of a bank in the United States. Many companies outside the United States who regularly engage in cross-border buying and selling find it convenient to maintain a U.S. dollar account, provided that such accounts are permitted under local exchange controls. Such an account gives them the capability to make U.S. dollar deposits and to write U.S. dollar checks. However, many trade payments are also made in currencies other than dollars. Fortunately, the basic exchange and transfer mechanism is the same whether applied to U.S. dollar or nondollar payments. Although the procedure may seem at first glance like accounting sleight of hand, this not-so-simple mechanism lies at the heart of the international payments system; the surest way to understand it is to trace at a basic level the typical sequence

*Uniform Commercial Code, Section 4-104, Official Comment.

of bookkeeping entries that constitute international settlement of a trade payment.

In this section we examine the pivotal role of the nostro account in the conversion of one currency to another and in the transfer of funds from one country to another. Using this international settlement mechanism, banks remit payments to their customers' foreign suppliers on either an open account ("Send me the goods and bill me") or cash in advance ("Pay me first, and I'll ship the goods") basis. It is important to remember that for every credit there must be a corresponding debit, and vice versa. It is also important to identify the currency in which the sale price is stated because it determines the structure of the payment, as shown in Table 2.1. The table suggests two variations of the basic foreign exchange and settlement procedure. These variations depend on which trading partner agrees to assume the foreign exchange rate risk in the transaction. In the following discussion, we examine first the case in which the importer agrees to remit payment in foreign currency, thus assuming the risk.

Remitting a Foreign Currency Payment.   Using the current rate of exchange (i.e., the spot rate), the importer's bank calculates the local currency equivalent of a foreign currency payment. Depending on fluctuations in the current rate of exchange, the importer may either gain (pay less in his own currency) or lose (pay more) to obtain the necessary foreign currency amount. In either case the importer is exposed to the rate risk until the bank debits the importer's account for the *local currency equivalent* of the foreign currency

**Table 2.1 Relationship of the Currency of
the Sale and Structure of the Foreign Exchange**

If	Then	And
Importer remits payment in	Foreign exchange rate risk is assumed by	Foreign exchange conversion is performed by
Own currency	Exporter	Exporter's bank
Exporter's currency	Importer	Importer's bank
Third currency	Importer and exporter	Importer's bank[a]

[a]The importer assumes the foreign exchange rate risk until his account is debited and the bank delivers the invoice amount in the stated currency, thus fulfilling the importer's payment obligation. At that point the exporter assumes a foreign exchange rate risk and his bank performs any additional exchange conversions.

amount. Generally speaking, a U.S. bank remits a foreign currency payment for its customer in three basic bookkeeping steps.

- First, it *converts* the foreign currency amount to dollars, using the current rate of exchange.
- Second, it *debits* the customer's (dollar) account for the dollar equivalent of the payment expressed in foreign currency.
- Third, it *credits* the foreign currency amount to its (nostro) account that it maintains with its correspondent located in the country of the currency.

The bank mechanically posts the credit in an account book or ledger that it maintains in that currency.* At the same time, the bank advises its correspondent and authorizes the correspondent to *debit* the (local currency) account for *credit* (payment) to the account of the designated beneficiary (exporter or supplier).

A bank's foreign exchange traders manage their bank's foreign exchange position, working closely with the Foreign Exchange Operations Department. The bank maintains sufficient balances in the major currencies to cover most payments in those currencies on behalf of the bank's customers. In the event of an expected deficit (i.e., an anticipated payment in an amount that exceeds the account's current balance), the foreign exchange trader transfers funds to cover the anticipated payment. In a trade context, a second source of funds for a local currency account derives from the deposits received in payment for goods purchased from U.S. merchants by importers located in the country of the currency. The issue of whether all this activity results in a net surplus or a deficit at the end of the day approaches balance of payments theory and practice, which lies outside the scope of our discussion.†

In a similar manner overseas banks remit U.S. dollar payments ("foreign currency" payments from their point of view) by employing the same accounting mechanism as described in the following transaction flow.

---

*Foreign currency nostro accounts are generally maintained like any other demand deposit account. The correspondent sends a regular statement of account describing activity (debits and credits) in the account, and the Foreign Exchange Department reconciles the correspondent's statement to its own account record or ledger.

† See Brian Kettell, Chapter 2, "International Financial Flows," in *The Finance of International Business,* Quorum Books, Westport, CT, 1981.

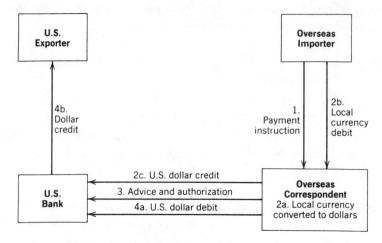

Figure 2.3   Overseas importer paying U.S. exporter in dollars.

TRANSACTION FLOW (Fig. 2.3)

Transaction Steps	Notes
1. The overseas importer instructs own bank to pay the U.S. exporter in dollars.	The importer assumes the foreign exchange rate risk.
2. The importer's bank (a) converts the local currency to dollars; (b) debits the importer's account for the local currency equivalent of the U.S. dollar payment; and (c) credits the U.S. dollar amount to its own U.S. dollar (nostro) account with a U.S. correspondent.	Using the current rate of exchange, the bank calculates the local currency equivalent of the U.S. dollar payment. The net result of the foreign exchange conversion is an increase in the U.S. dollar (nostro) account of the importer's bank with its U.S. correspondent.
3. The importer's bank notifies its U.S. correspondent and authorizes the U.S. correspondent to debit that nostro for payment to the account of the U.S. exporter.	

TRANSACTION FLOW (Continued)

Transaction Steps	Notes
4. The U.S. correspondent (a) debits the overseas (importer's) bank's account and (b) credits in dollars the account of the U.S. exporter.	In the event the exporter does not have an account with the U.S. correspondent, that bank will either issue a check or transfer the funds via U.S. domestic wire transfer procedures.

Receiving a Foreign Currency Payment. By contrast, an exporter who agrees to receive payment in foreign currency assumes the foreign exchange rate risk in the transaction. As a practical matter, exporters invoicing in foreign currency usually instruct the importer to place the currency with a specific local bank for the account of the exporter's own bank. Technically the importer has fulfilled his or her payment obligation at this point. To convert the funds the exporter's bank debits its own local currency (nostro) account for the stated invoice amount, performs the necessary conversion, and credits the exporter's account with an equivalent amount of the desired currency at the current rate of exchange.

These procedures are summarized in Table 2.2. The outcome is the same (i.e., the importer remits and the exporter receives payment), but the mechanics differ according to which trading partner assumes the foreign exchange rate risk in a given transaction.*

The authorization a bank gives to its correspondent to act on its behalf to remit payment to the designated beneficiary is a primary component of the international funds transfer mechanism. Authorization is transmitted in one of two principal ways: either telegraphically via telex or cable, or the bank may deliver to the buyer/importer an instrument that upon presentation entitles the bearer to receive payment. Thus the mode of authorization may be used to distinguish between the two classes of international payment mechanisms, that is, telegraphic funds transfer and negotiable instruments. These mechanisms are examined in more detail in the next chapter.

---

*For a discussion of techniques employed by companies to control foreign exchange exposure, see Chapters 8 and 9 in Brian Kettell, *The Finance of International Business*, Quorum Books, Westport, CT, 1981.

Table 2.2 Summary of Funds Transfer Settlement Procedures

U.S. Importer Instructs Own U.S. Bank to Pay Overseas Supplier in		Overseas Importer Instructs Own Bank to Pay U.S. Supplier In	
U.S. Dollars	Foreign Currency	U.S. Dollars	Local Currency
U.S. bank debits importer's account in dollars and credits dollars to U.S. dollar account of overseas correspondent located in supplier's country. Importer has fulfilled his payment obligation. To obtain local currency exporter authorizes own bank to convert dollars to local currency equivalent. Overseas bank debits own U.S. dollar nostro and credits exporter with local currency proceeds of exchange conversion.	U.S. bank calculates U.S. dollar equivalent for the invoice amount stated in foreign currency, debits importer's account in U.S. dollars, and credits the foreign currency amount to its own foreign currency (nostro) account with correspondent in country of the currency. U.S. bank notifies[a] overseas correspondent of credit for account of exporter and authorizes correspondent to debit U.S. bank's local currency (nostro) account and credit the funds to the designated beneficiary, the exporter.	Overseas bank calculates the local currency equivalent of the invoice amount stated in U.S. dollars, debits importer's account in local currency, and credits the U.S. dollar amount to its own U.S. dollar (nostro) account with U.S. correspondent. Overseas bank notifies[a] correspondent of credit for account of exporter and authorizes U.S. correspondent to debit overseas bank's dollar account and credit the funds to the designated beneficiary, the exporter.	Overseas bank debits importer's account for the invoice amount stated in local currency and credits the funds to (local currency) account of its U.S. correspondent for the account of the U.S. supplier. Importer has fulfilled his payment obligation. To obtain U.S. dollars, exporter authorizes own bank to convert local currency to U.S. dollar equivalent. U.S. bank debits own local currency nostro and credits U.S. exporter with U.S. dollar proceeds of exchange conversion.

[a]The initiating bank may notify its correspondent by either telegraphic means or by mail payment order. (See Chapter 3.)

3 Payment Methods Under Open Account Terms

The banking system offers four principal methods for effecting cross-border payments under open account terms: (1) telegraphic transfer, (2) mail transfer (mail payment order), (3) bank draft, and, where permitted by exchange controls, (4) regular business check.* Ultimately each of these methods requires a bank to debit the account of the buyer and arrange credit to the account of the seller for the stated amount represented by the sale price.

Although these methods are neither identical nor interchangeable, nonetheless they all have this trait in common: They all depend upon the buyer to initiate the payment process. Additionally bankers classify them according to the specific settlement procedures they employ to debit the buyer's account and arrange credit to the seller's account. The funds transfer mechanisms (telegraphic transfer and mail payment order) are primarily bank-to-bank procedures that utilize the formal account relationships maintained between banks. These procedures make it possible for banks to deliver payment to the seller in *cleared funds* (funds that are immediately usable, i.e., available for withdrawal or transfer to another account). By contrast, the various kinds of bank drafts and the regular business check are payment instruments that require the funds to be *collected* following presentation of the item. In these cases the seller's bank does not make the funds available to the seller until it receives them. Depending on the location of the banks involved, the collection process—based on traditional clearing and settlement procedures described later in this chapter—may take days or even weeks.

All payment methods are composed of two primary elements—financial messages and accounting entries. Depending on the specific instrument chosen, the buyer authorizes, orders, or instructs his bank to pay the seller by debiting the buyer's account, and banks advise their customers (buyer and seller) when they have completed the requisite accounting entries that constitute settlement. Innovations to the payment process have generally revolved around finding faster, cheaper, or easier ways to transmit financial messages; or developing ways to expedite the settlement or accounting process in order to "move" funds faster, that is, to make them available sooner.

In this chapter we investigate the payment methods available under open account terms.

---

*Brian Kettell, *The Finance of International Business*, Quorum Books, Westport, CT, 1981, pp. 120–121.

**Table 3.1 Summary of International Payment Methods
on Open Account Terms**

Funds Transfer

Importer instructs own bank to pay the exporter (the *beneficiary* of the payment).
The bank makes the payment in *cleared funds*, thus providing the exporter with
immediately available funds.

Cable transfer: The financial message is sent by telegraphic means, and payment
is effected via a debit to the initiating bank's nostro account with a correspondent in
the exporter's country and is completed with a credit to the exporter's account at the
exporter's bank.

Mail payment order: The financial message is sent through the mail, and payment
is made via a debit to the initiating bank's nostro account with a correspondent in the
exporter's country and a credit to the exporter's account via book or electronic transfer, check or bank draft (see below). Mail payment orders are especially useful in
countries where telegraphic capabilities are unreliable.

Negotiable Instruments

Bank draft: A bank draft is like a cashier's check, except that it is used to remit
international payments. The importer purchases the draft and sends it through the
mail to the exporter, who deposits it like any other check. Payment is normally on a
collection basis; that is, the item is sent out for collection, and the bank makes the
funds available to the exporter when it receives them. The principal forms of bank
draft are the *foreign currency draft* drawn either by a U.S. bank on its overseas
correspondent or by an overseas bank on itself; a *U.S. dollar draft payable overseas*
drawn by a U.S. bank on either its own overseas branch or on its designated overseas
correspondent; and a *U.S. dollar draft payable in the U.S.* drawn by an overseas
bank on its own U.S. branch or on its designated U.S. correspondent.

A U.S. business check: A regular business check may be used when it is acceptable
to the exporter and when it is permitted under exchange control regulations in the
exporter's country.

FUNDS TRANSFER

The basic mechanics of the international payment procedure are identical for
all four payment methods. Moreover, contrary to uninformed expectation,
currency does not actually leave a country in the international equivalent of
armored cars. Rather *international payments are made via bookkeeping entries to the demand deposit accounts that banking correspondents maintain
with each other,* as discussed in Chapter 2.

Table 3.1 summarizes the methods available for remitting international payment under open account terms. To simplify the discussion, we assume that importer and exporter maintain accounts with banking correspondents in their respective countries; thus final settlement can occur via a book transfer. In real life, of course, the funds transfer process is complicated by the fact that importer and exporter normally do not maintain accounts with banks who are correspondents. When that is the case, a check is issued or a transfer routed domestically through appropriate banking channels, that is, through banking intermediaries who maintain the needed account relationships.

Telegraphic Funds Transfer

Financial messages exchanged telegraphically between banks both authorize and advise of activity in the demand deposit accounts of the various parties to an international payment transaction. Thus the international funds transfer system is made up of two primary elements:

- *Financial messages* communicated between correspondent banks authorizing or advising debits or credits to their nostro accounts.
- *Accounting entries* (debits and credits to demand deposit accounts) by which settlement actually occurs.

Message Systems.   Payment instructions and advices may be sent either by cable (telegraphic transfer) or by mail (mail payment order). Today, however, these financial messages are most often sent electronically via SWIFT (The Society for Worldwide Interbank Financial Telecommunications), the wire services (telex or cable), or proprietary communication systems offered by the commercial banks to their business customers (see the Introduction to Part II). Obviously security is a key issue in the exchange of these financial messages, and the banks have devised a system of authenticating messages to make sure that the person giving a payment instruction is in fact authorized to do so. Each cable or telex containing instructions to pay out money must have a special code called the *test key*. The test key serves the same function as does the bank's signature on a cashier's check.

The impact of SWIFT on the processing of interbank payments deserves special mention. SWIFT is a Belgian nonprofit corporation founded in 1973 to provide a telecommunication system for exchanging financial messages among member banks. Designed as an alternative to the slower, more paper-intensive and error-prone wire systems, SWIFT has gained wide acceptance in the banking community with over 40 SWIFT member nations. SWIFT messages are transmitted in English and are highly structured to conform to standards agreed upon by SWIFT members. This structuring eliminates language and interpretation problems common in most other, less structured communication modes. The rigid structure also facilitates automatic processing and enables automated account reconciliation.

Security and control procedures make SWIFT a safe and workable system, and SWIFT takes responsibility from acceptance of the message to receipt by the member bank. It also sends an acknowledgment to the sending member that the message has been transmitted. Responsibility for accurately structuring (formating) the message rests, however, with the sending bank, a responsibility many of the major banks are assisting their business customers to share.

Settlement Systems.   Message systems are sometimes mistaken for settlement systems. We have seen, however, that settlement is an accounting function and can only occur where a ledger is present to enable the appropriate accounting (debit and credit) entries. In the United States, settlement occurs only on the books of a commercial bank or on the books of a District Federal Reserve Bank via debits and credits to member banks' reserve accounts.

NEGOTIABLE INSTRUMENTS

Negotiable instruments, including various types of bank drafts and regular business checks, are employed to effect cross-border payments. To be negotiable a writing must:

- Be signed by the maker or drawer.
- Contain an unconditional promise or order to pay a certain sum in money.
- Be payable on demand or at a definite time.
- Be payable to order or bearer.*

The settlement of a negotiable instrument thus requires physical presentation of the item to the payor bank, a requirement that delays the availability of the funds under such payments.

*Uniform Commercial Code, Section 3-104.

Bank Draft

A bank draft is like a cashier's check except that it is denominated in a foreign currency. The concept of "foreign" currency is, of course, relative in this context. The basic mechanics of the various types of bank draft (described below) are the same whether employed by U.S. or non-U.S. buyers and sellers. A buyer purchasing a bank draft sends it through the mail to the seller who deposits it like any other check.

Negotiable instruments settle on a *collection* basis; that is, the seller's bank sends the item out for collection and normally does not make the funds available to the seller until it receives credit for them. When an item must clear, availability of funds frequently becomes a paramount issue to customers. *Availability* refers to the moment when funds are usable, that is, when the payee/seller may withdraw or transfer them to another account. As we shall see, a bank grants availability when it knows that final settlement has occurred (i.e., when the sequence of debits and credits is complete) or when it is willing to extend credit to its customer because it is confident it will receive payment for the item.

Foreign Currency Draft.   To pay an overseas supplier in local currency a U.S. buyer may choose to purchase a draft denominated in the designated foreign currency. Such a draft is commonly drawn by a U.S. bank on its overseas correspondent, in which case the draft is paid by a debit to the U.S. bank's local currency nostro account on the correspondent's books. From the overseas supplier's point of view the collection time is thus comparable to that associated with any other domestic check.

Conversely, an overseas importer may choose to pay a U.S. supplier in local currency by purchasing from his local bank a draft denominated in local currency. When a U.S. supplier receives the foreign currency draft, the supplier presents the draft to his bank, obtaining book credit for the dollar equivalent of the foreign currency amount. The U.S. bank obtains funds by sending the draft out for collection; that is, it asks the overseas bank to credit the proceeds of the draft to the U.S. bank's local currency (nostro) account, and it considers the item settled when it is advised of the credit to its account.

U.S. Dollar Draft Payable Overseas.   A U.S. importer may purchase a U.S. dollar draft to pay an overseas supplier in dollars. Such a draft is typically drawn by a U.S. bank either on its own overseas branch or on an overseas correspondent. To effect payment the U.S. bank debits its customer's account in dollars, and credits the invoice amount to the U.S. dollar account (on its books) of a correspondent in the exporter's country. At the same time it advises the correspondent ". . . of a credit in [the stated amount of] dollars to cover our draft number xxx."

The U.S. bank gives the draft to the U.S. importer who sends it to the overseas supplier. Upon receiving the draft, the overseas supplier presents it to his or her bank. The overseas correspondent purchases the draft at the current rate of exchange by debiting its U.S. dollar (nostro) account and crediting the local currency proceeds of the conversion to the account of the supplier. From the point of view of the overseas supplier, such a collection is comparable to that for collection of a domestic check. It should be noted, however, that the exporter assumes the foreign exchange rate risk in the transaction.

U.S. Dollar Draft Payable in the U.S. Drawn by an Overseas Bank. An overseas buyer may purchase a U.S. dollar draft to pay a U.S. supplier in dollars. Such a draft is drawn on the U.S. branch of the overseas bank or on the U.S. correspondent of the overseas bank. Notice that from the point of view of the overseas bank, this "U.S. dollar draft" is actually a foreign currency draft.

Summary

The settlement mechanism is identical for each of the payment methods analyzed here: Banks make and receive foreign currency payments by means of authorized debits and credits to the nostro accounts that they maintain with each other.

United States Domestic Check

Where the exchange controls of the exporter's country permit, a U.S. importer may choose to pay an overseas U.S. dollar invoice with a check drawn on his regular business checking account. If the overseas exporter maintains a U.S. dollar account, he will deposit the check item in that account, and the item will clear according to procedures described in Step 3 below. If he does not have a U.S. dollar account, his bank will accept the item for deposit on a collection basis, that is, it will make the funds available to the exporter only after it has received them.

The domestic clearing process described in this section is fundamental to a working knowledge of the mechanics of banking. Outside the United States central banks usually perform the clearing function, that is, they sort items and distribute them to the appropriate commercial banks. Within the United States the Federal Reserve plays the major clearing and settlement role. The United States is divided into 12 Federal Reserve districts. Individual banks within a district may choose to maintain a reserve account on the books of their regional Federal Reserve Bank, that is, at "the Fed." Final settlement occurs either *directly* via entries to the demand deposit accounts on the books of banks that maintain correspondent relationships with each other, or *indirectly* via entries to member banks' reserve accounts at their local Federal Reserve Bank. A District Federal Reserve Bank may also act as a clearing mechanism for the banks within its district by distributing presorted packages of checks to member banks.

The length of time required for an item to clear varies by geographic location of the banks involved. In London, for example, a clearing house (similar to the New York Clearing House described below) has been established to process U.S. dollar checks. In other parts of the world the clearing process may take several weeks.

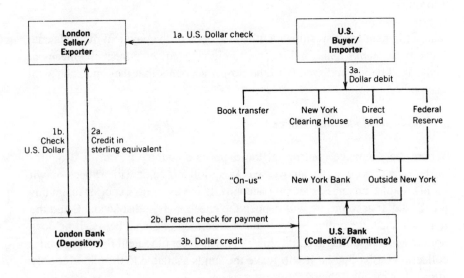

Figure 3.1   United States domestic check clearance and settlement.

TRANSACTION FLOW (Fig. 3.1)

Transaction Steps	Notes
1. The U.S. importer (a) writes a U.S. dollar check and sends it to the London exporter who (b) presents it to a London bank.	
2. The London bank (a) calculates the sterling equivalent of the U.S. dollar amount, credits the exporter's account, and (b) presents the item for payment to its U.S. correspondent.	The London bank accepts the item on a collection basis; that is, it agrees to make the funds available (for withdrawal or transfer to another account) only after it receives them from the importer's (payor) bank.
3. The New York bank receives the U.S. domestic check. *If the item is drawn on itself ("on us")*, settlement occurs by a book transfer on its own books.	The New York bank verifies that the importer's account has sufficient funds; then it (a) *debits* the importer's account and simultaneously (b) *credits* the London bank's dollar nostro account.
If the item is drawn on another New York Clearing House bank, settlement occurs through the New York Clearing House (NYCH).	Settlement at the NYCH occurs as follows: • The collecting bank presents the item to the remitting bank at the New York Clearing House. • The remitting bank verifies that there are sufficient funds in the payor's (importer's) account; then (a) debits that account for the amount of the item and (b) credits dollar nostro of the London bank. *Note: Net settlement* (total of debits and credits rather than of individual items) between the two banks occurs at the end of the day on the books of the New York Federal Reserve Bank.

TRANSACTION FLOW (Fig. 3.1) (Continued)

Transaction Steps	Notes
If the item is drawn on a bank outside New York City, settlement may occur in one of two ways. The New York bank may present the check item to the remitting bank either by "direct send" or through the Federal Reserve system.	Under *direct send,* the New York bank delivers the checks directly to its domestic correspondent, the remitting bank, usually by courier. The remitting bank (a) *debits* the payor's account, and (b) *credits* the collecting bank's account on its books.

Note: A collecting bank might choose direct send when the checks are high-value items and/or if it has a particularly efficient correspondent relationship with either the remitting bank or with a correspondent located near the remitting (drawee) bank.

Under the *Federal Reserve system,* a collecting bank delivers presorted check packages for credit to its New York Federal Reserve account. The New York Federal Reserve delivers them either to the appropriate District Federal Reserve or to the Regional Check Processing Center (RCPC) for presentation. The District Federal Reserve or the RCPC *debits* the remitting (drawee) bank's reserve account and *credits* the collecting bank's reserve account. (These debits and credits to reserve accounts are effected electronically through the Federal Reserve.) After verify-

TRANSACTION FLOW (Fig. 3.1) (Continued)

Transaction Steps	Notes
	ing that sufficient funds exist in the payor's account, the remitting (drawee) bank *debits* the buyer's account on its books. This final debit to the payor's account constitutes final settlement.

SUMMARY

As we have already seen, a foreign depository bank avoids the risk that a check will not be paid by accepting the item for deposit on a collection basis; that is, it makes the funds available to the seller only after it collects them from the remitting (payor) bank. Depending on the location of the banks, this process may take days or even weeks. Banks recognize the operational efficiency of telegraphic transfers by employing the telegraphic transfer (TT) rate as the basic rate at which they buy and sell foreign exchange. Because of the longer time required to collect bank drafts, the exchange rates that banks apply to the purchase of drafts and other negotiable instruments are generally slightly less favorable than the telegraphic transfer (TT) rate. For these reasons banks and their customers have preferred timelier and more direct methods such as telegraphic transfers for effecting international payments.

It is also important to remember that the domestic clearing procedures described here (and which have a telegraphic counterpart) are common in the overseas countries to which payment is directed or from which it is received. By making it necessary to route a payment through several intermediary banks, such domestic clearing and settlement arrangements quickly complicate the international transfer of funds.

4 Documentary Collection

In Chapter 1 we defined trade as the exchange of goods for payment. Domestically, open account payment terms dominate. Typically, a buyer orders goods. The seller ships them and sends along a packing slip. A few days later the seller sends a commercial invoice, the bill. The buyer then pays the invoice more or less promptly. Some international transactions are conducted the same way. However, the added risks of international trade often demand different trade practices and greater control over a transaction. To maintain this control the trading partners may elect to exchange the draft and the bill of lading through banking channels via a documentary collection.

The documentary collection is a payment mechanism that allows exporters to retain ownership of the goods until they receive payment or are reasonably certain that they will receive it. In a documentary collection the bank, acting as the exporter's agent, regulates the timing and sequence of the exchange of goods for value by holding the title documents until the importer either pays the draft—termed *documents against payment* (D/P)—or accepts the obligation to do so—termed *documents against acceptance* (D/A).*

The exporter will agree to a documentary collection if he or she is willing to assume the risks inherent in international trade, namely:

- The acceptance risk that the importer will refuse to accept the goods shipped.
- The credit risk of the importer.
- The political risk of the importer's country.
- The exchange transfer risk that foreign exchange will not be available in the importer's country.
- The documentary risk that the shipment may fail to clear customs.

If the exporter is reluctant to assume any of these risks he or she will seek to negotiate an alternative payment term, probably a letter of credit.

THE PRINCIPAL CONTROL DOCUMENTS

In Chapter 1 we said that the draft or bill of exchange is the seller's unconditional written demand for payment. In a documentary collection the draft is written by the drawer (seller/exporter) to the drawee (usually the buyer/im-

---

*"The Uniform Rules for Collections," International Chamber of Commerce Publication 322, is a compilation of accepted international practice in documentary collections. This publication is included in the appendices. United States regulations governing collections are gathered in the Uniform Commercial Code, Article 4.

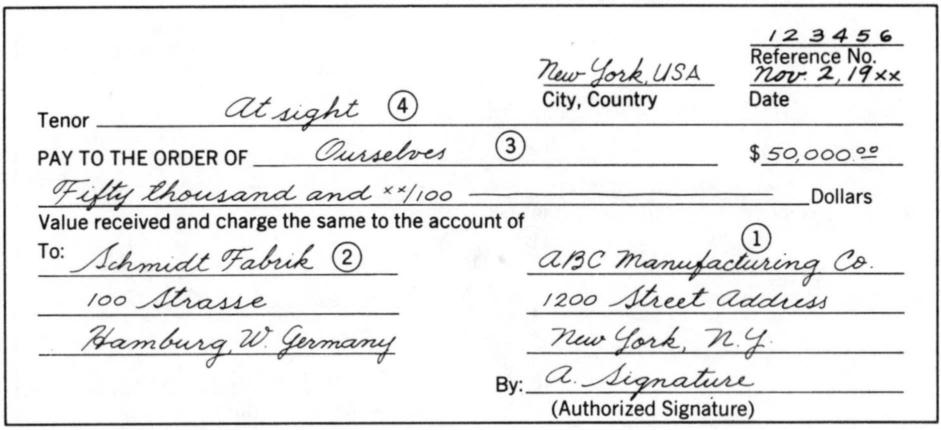

Figure 4.1 Typical sight draft (documents against payment).

porter) and requires payment of a fixed amount at a specific or determinable date to the payee—usually the exporter himself. A draft is a negotiable instrument that normally requires physical presentation as a condition for payment. A draft may be either a sight or a time draft.

Figure 4.1 is a typical sight draft in a documentary collection, that is, one that is payable upon presentation. The exporter would use such a draft in a documents-against-payment transaction to enable himself to retain ownership of the goods until the importer actually pays the draft. In Figure 4.1, ABC Manufacturing Company demands payment to themselves of $50,000 from Schmidt Fabrik upon presentation (at sight) of this draft to Schmidt.

Figure 4.2 is a typical trade acceptance, that is, a time draft accepted by the importer and payable at a determinable date in the future. Exporters would use this kind of draft in a documents-against-acceptance transaction when they are willing to relinquish the title documents at the time the importer accepts the obligation to pay but before he actually does so. In Figure 4.2, Johann Schmidt accepts Schmidt Fabrik's obligation to pay the ABC Manufacturing Company the sum of $50,000 on or before the 60th day after the draft is presented to and accepted by Schmidt on November 10, 19xx.

As you recall from Chapter 1, the bill of lading is the carrier's receipt for the goods being shipped and in its negotiable form is the title document for

		1 2 3 4 5 6
	New York, USA	Reference No.
	City, Country	*Nov. 2, 19xx*
Tenor __*At 60 days sight*__ ④		Date
PAY TO THE ORDER OF __*Ourselves*__ ③		*50,000.⁰⁰*

*Fifty thousand and **/100* ———————————————————— Dollars

Value received and charge the same to the account of

To:
Schmidt Fabrik ②   ⑤   *ABC Manufacturing Co.* ①
100 Strasse   *1200 Street Address*
Hamburg, W. Germany   *New York, N.Y.*

Accepted Schmidt Fabrik by Johann Schmidt Nov. 10, 19xx

By: *a. Signature*
(Authorized Signature)

1. Drawer/seller (secondary obligor)
2. Drawee/buyer (primary obligor)
3. Payee
4. Tenor
5. Drawee's acceptance

Figure 4.2 Typical trade acceptance (documents against acceptance).

the shipment. In a documentary collection the negotiable ocean order bill of lading is the preferred form. If goods must be shipped by air, or if the importing country does not permit order bills of lading, then a documentary collection may not be the ideal payment term for the transaction. The exporter must decide: "Do I trust the importer enough to go with open account terms? If not, can I get the importer to accept the costlier letter of credit terms in order to lessen my risk of nonpayment?"

THE MAJOR PARTICIPANTS

The parties to a documentary collection are:

- *Seller/exporter* (drawer) who initiates the collection; also called the principal.
- *Remitting bank*—the local bank to which the seller submits the collection.
- *Collecting bank*—any bank other than the remitting bank that is involved in processing the collection. Usually, the collecting bank is a correspondent or branch of the remitting bank in the importer's country.

- *Presenting bank*—if the collecting bank is not located near the importer, it would send the documents to a presenting bank in the importer's city.
- *Buyer/importer* (drawee).

Operationally banks classify collection items as either outward collections or inward collections. For the remitting bank in the exporter's country, the item is called an *outward collection* or *payable overseas*. For the collecting bank in the importer's country, the item is called an *inward collection* or *payable domestic*.

In the following pages we will present a step-by-step flow of a documents-against-payment transaction using a sight draft, followed by a documents-against-acceptance transaction using a trade acceptance.

DOCUMENTS AGAINST PAYMENT

Figure 4.3 illustrates the documents–against–payment (D/P) transaction flow. Notice that the collection procedure is chronological: The banks in a documentary collection transaction do not act until the preceding steps have been completed. This means that the exporter does not receive payment until his or her bank has received the funds from its correspondent, the overseas collecting bank.

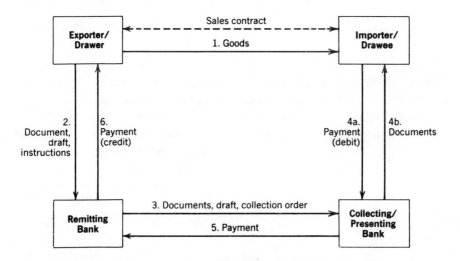

Figure 4.3 Documents against payment.

TRANSACTION FLOW

Transaction Steps	Notes
1. The exporter ships the goods to the importer as agreed in the sales contract.	
2. The exporter submits to his bank—the remitting bank—documents, a sight draft drawn on the importer, and written instructions governing the collection.	The documents include a title document, usually the bill of lading, plus any other documents required by the importer or by customs in the importer's country. The remitting bank is under no obligation to examine the documents except to verify that they appear to be those stipulated by the exporter. According to General Provision C of I.C.C. Publication 322, every documentary collection must be accompanied by a collection order that gives the exporter's instructions precisely and completely. Most U.S. banks have their own collection forms that are accompanied by clear instructions for completion.
3. The remitting bank sends documents, draft, and collection order to the collecting/presenting bank in the importer's country which notifies the importer.	The exporter may specify the collecting bank, usually the bank requested by the importer. If the exporter does not name a bank, the remitting bank will use a branch or correspondent in the importer's country. The collecting bank is responsible only for verifying that the documents named in the instructions are present and for presenting the draft to the importer "without delay" (I.C.C. 322, Article 9).

TRANSACTION FLOW (Continued)

Transaction Steps	Notes
4(a) The importer pays the face amount of the draft plus any charges the importer is responsible for, as stated in the collection order.	If the importer maintains an account with the collecting bank, the bank will collect payment by simply debiting that account. The exporter's instructions must specify which charges are for the account of the importer (e.g., bank fees, cable, telex, exchange commission). In the absence of specific instructions, all fees and charges are for the account of the exporter. If the importer refuses to pay any charges, the usual practice is for the exporter to waive them. Waived charges are for the account of the exporter. If the importer refuses to honor the draft, the collecting bank is responsible for protesting or not, according to the exporter's instructions on the collection order (I.C.C. 322, Article 17).
(b) The collecting/presenting bank releases the documents to the importer, who can then claim the goods.	In countries that require a stamp tax on drafts, the sight draft may be eliminated altogether in order to avoid the tax. In this case, the presenting bank releases documents upon receipt of payment in cash from the importer.
5. The collecting bank deducts its fee and sends the importer's payment to the bank from which the collection order was received, either an intermediate collecting bank or the remitting bank.	If the two banks have a correspondent relationship, the collecting bank will simply credit the account of the remitting bank and advise it of the credit.

TRANSACTION FLOW (Continued)

Transaction Steps	Notes
6. The remitting bank credits the exporter's account for the face val⹂e of the draft minus any fees and charges for which the exporter is responsible.	

DOCUMENTS AGAINST ACCEPTANCE

Figure 4.4 illustrates a documents–against–acceptance (D/A) transaction flow.

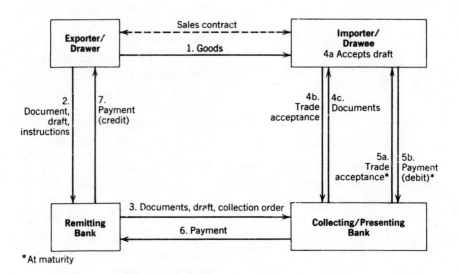

Figure 4.4   Documents against acceptance.

TRANSACTION FLOW

Transaction Steps	Notes
1. The exporter ships the goods to the importer as agreed in the sales contract.	
2. The exporter submits to the remitting bank documents including a time draft drawn on the importer and a written collection order giving complete, precise instructions governing the collection.	
3. The remitting bank sends documents, time draft, and collection order to the collecting/presenting bank in the importer's country, which notifies the importer.	
4(a) The importer writes "Accepted" and the date and signs across the face of the draft, thereby creating a trade acceptance.	By accepting the draft, the importer acknowledges an unconditional obligation to pay the face amount at maturity to whoever presents the draft at that time.
	Usually the bank holds the acceptance in safekeeping until maturity. Technically the exporter could hold it in portfolio and present it directly to the importer, but this option is seldom exercised.
(b) The collecting/presenting bank releases the documents to the importer who can then take possession of the goods.	The exporter relinquishes title to the goods before receiving payment. If necessary, the exporter may make financing arrangements with the bank for the period until payment is received. United States financing mechanisms include conventional loans, discounting, bankers acceptance financing, and factoring.

TRANSACTION FLOW (Continued)

Transaction Steps	Notes
5(a) At maturity the collecting/presenting bank presents the acceptance to the importer.	
(b) The importer pays the face amount of the acceptance plus any fees or other transaction costs that are the buyer's responsibility.	Normally at maturity the bank will simply debit the importer's account and advise the importer.
6. The collecting/presenting bank deducts its fee and either sends the payment to the remitting bank or credits the remitting bank's account if they have a correspondent relationship.	
7. The remitting bank credits the exporter's account for the face value of the draft less whatever fees and charges the exporter is responsible for.	

SUMMARY

Rights, Responsibilities, Obligations

Banks.   According to Article 1 of the Uniform Rules for Collections, all banks involved in a documentary collection have the responsibility to "act in good faith and exercise reasonable care."

Each bank is also responsible for verifying that the documents received appear to be as listed in the collection order, and for immediately advising the party from whom they received the order of any missing documents. They have no further obligation to examine the documents (Article 2).

The collecting bank is responsible for presenting the draft to the importer for payment or acceptance "without delay," which is usually interpreted to mean within three days.

Each bank has a right to a fee for its services. These fees are usually collected at each step of the collection process.

Exporter/Principal.   The exporter is responsible for giving the remitting bank complete, precise instructions regarding the collection.

The exporter is responsible for paying all collection fees and other charges not specifically allocated to the importer in the collection order, and all fees and charges refused by the importer or waived.

The exporter has a right to receive the collection proceeds from the bank "without delay."

The exporter retains title to the goods in the event the draft is not paid or accepted.

Importer/Drawee.   The importer has an obligation to pay the exporter's draft either at presentation (documents against payment) or maturity (documents against acceptance), as stated in the collection instructions.

Risks and Liability

The exporter assumes most of the risks including:

- Acceptance risk (i.e., that the importer will not accept the goods shipped).
- Credit risk of the importer.
- Political risk of the importer's country.
- Foreign exchange transfer risk (i.e., that the foreign exchange will not be available).
- Documentary risk that the shipment may fail to clear customs.

The importer has the risk that the goods shipped may not be as ordered.

Banks assume no risks in a documentary collection. They have no liability for loss to the exporter unless the loss was caused by negligence on the bank's part.

Cost Considerations.   Normally U.S. banks charge a flat fee for their services at each step in a documentary collection. Banks outside the United States usually express these charges as a percentage of the face value of the draft.

Summary of Relative Advantages

A documentary collection represents a trade-off of relative advantages for elements of control in the transaction. The attractiveness of the documentary collection for the buyer or seller depends on whether it is considered to be an alternative to open account (which favors the buyer) or to a letter of credit (which favors the seller).

5 Letter of Credit

A letter of credit is a complex, practical instrument whose governing principles have developed over time as a result of customary banking practice. These principles (collectively called "The Uniform Customs and Practice" or "UCP")* interpret current practice and create a basic framework for conducting documentary credit transactions. Practically everything written about letters of credit begins with a definition like this:

> A letter of credit is a written undertaking issued by a bank at the request of its customer (the buyer) in which the bank obligates itself to pay the seller up to a stated amount, within a prescribed time frame, upon presentation of documents that conform to all the terms and conditions of the Credit.

A letter of credit may also be defined as a conditional payment mechanism, that is, one in which the bank's obligation to pay the seller for the goods is conditional only upon the seller's presentation of documents that are in strict accordance with the terms and conditions of the Credit.

What does it mean? This chapter is intended to clarify that definition. But first it might help to clarify the language. Banking operations personnel refer to a letter of credit as an L/C, an LOC, or simply a Credit—not to be confused with credit used in an accounting sense. In this book, Credit (capital C) refers to the letter of credit instrument; and credit (lower case c) refers to the bookkeeping entry, or to the credit extended in a borrowing sense.

We have already pointed out that open account terms favor the buyer and that the documentary collection may be viewed as a compromise payment term between open account at one end and letter of credit at the other. (Table 1.2 summarizes the relative advantages of each of these payment terms.)

Although the letter of credit generally favors the seller, to the extent that documents can verify performance it may also offer the buyer important elements of control over the transaction prior to taking possession of the goods. For example, a buyer may exert some control over the condition of the shipment upon arrival by having the Credit require a *clean bill of lading,* that is, one on which the carrier's representative has made no notations as to apparent defective condition of goods or packaging. Or the Credit may specify what notation is acceptable on the bill of lading, such as "5% damaged bags acceptable." Or a buyer may arrange to have the goods inspected by his or her agent prior to shipment, in which case the Credit will specify presentation of an inspection certificate.

Buyers might also exert control over when they actually receive the goods by specifying an earliest and/or latest shipping date in the Credit. The carrier's

---

*"Uniform Customs and Practice for Documentary Credits" (rev. ed.) 1983, International Chamber of Commerce (I.C.C.), Publication 400, is included in the appendices of this book.

representative will issue an *on-board bill of lading* when the goods are loaded on board the vessel for shipment. If the carrier has received the goods but is not able to load them on board for whatever reason, the representative will issue a *received-for-shipment bill of lading*. Goods received for shipment might sit in a warehouse for weeks before being loaded on board. In other words, the on-board date of an on-board bill of lading is documentary evidence of the shipping date; the issuance date of a received-for-shipment bill of lading is not.

To give a feeling for the logic of the letter of credit in the following pages, we first provide a bare-bones description of the two major stages of a basic sight Credit transaction—issuance and payment. Then we introduce the intermediary functions (advising, paying as agent, confirming, and negotiating). We show the procedural flow of each of these functions and describe the role of each party to the transaction. Summaries or discussion sections put these operational descriptions in perspective.

THE BARE BONES

The Draft

As you will recall from the previous sections, the draft is the financial spine of international trade. As the seller's demand for payment, it supplements the commercial invoice. Figure 5.1 is an example of a sight draft in a letter of

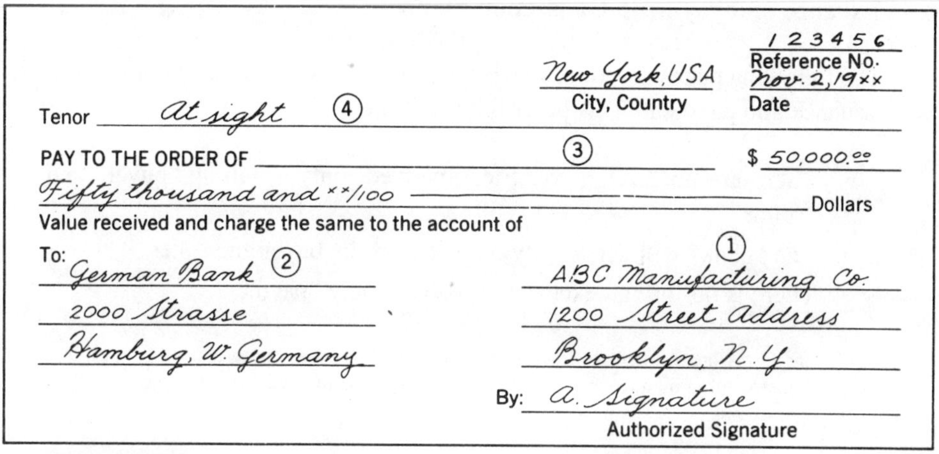
123456
Reference No.
New York, USA
City, Country
Nov. 2, 19xx
Date
Tenor At sight (4)
PAY TO THE ORDER OF (3) $ 50,000.00
Fifty thousand and xx/100 Dollars
Value received and charge the same to the account of
To: (1)
German Bank (2)
2000 Strasse
Hamburg, W. Germany
ABC Manufacturing Co.
1200 Street Address
Brooklyn, N.Y.
By: A. Signature
Authorized Signature

1. Drawer/seller
2. Drawee Bank
3. Payee
4. Tenor

Figure 5.1 Typical sight draft in a letter of credit.

credit transaction (i.e., a draft payable upon presentation). The exporter would draw a sight draft if the trading parties had agreed during their negotiations that the exporter would not extend credit to the importer by deferring the payment date. Notice that the drawee on this draft is a bank, not the importer as was the case in a documentary collection. Notice also that the importer is not named on the draft.

If the exporter had agreed to help the importer finance the transaction by allowing the importer to make payment at a later date, say 60 days after presentation, the tenor of the draft would read "At 60 days sight." (Time letters of credit are covered in detail in Chapter 6, *Bankers Acceptance.*)

The Major Participants

The three major parties* to a letter of credit are:

- The *buyer/importer/account party* who is the applicant for the Credit.
- The *seller/exporter/beneficiary* who is the recipient of the Credit.
- The *issuing bank* who issues the letter of credit and acts between buyer and seller.

Issuance and Payment Transaction Flows

The following pages describe, step by step, the two stages of a letter of credit: issuance and payment. This description assumes:

- There are no foreign countries involved, only a willing "buyer" and "seller."
- The "bank" will act equally on behalf of the buyer and seller.
- There is no foreign exchange involved, only "payment."

*Different terms are applied to describe the different roles that buyer and seller play in a transaction structured on a letter of credit basis. These terms include the following:

Seller	Buyer
Exporter	Importer
Beneficiary	Applicant
Shipper	Account party
Consignor	Consignee

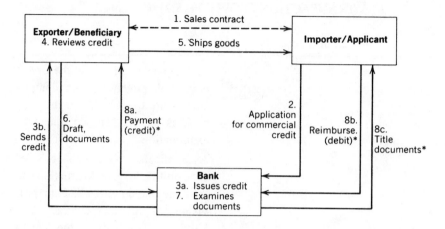

*Step 8 assumes that documents conform. If they do not conform, the bank will notify the exporter.

Figure 5.2   Issuance and payment.

TRANSACTION FLOW (Fig. 5.2)

Transaction Steps	Notes
1. Buyer and seller agree on certain terms and conditions regarding the sale of the goods and spell them out in the sales contract.	As we discussed in Chapter 1, the sales contract sets forth the payment terms and sales terms and specifies required documentation—commercial, transport, insurance, and official. Thus the sales contract defines the terms and conditions under which the sale will be completed.
2. If they agree that the payment mechanism will be a letter of credit, the buyer applies for the Credit at his or her bank.	The credit application, or related security agreement, is a contract between the issuing bank and the buyer/applicant in which the applicant agrees to reimburse the bank for any payments made under the letter of credit. Conversely the

TRANSACTION FLOW (Fig. 5.2) (Continued)

Transaction Steps	Notes
	bank agrees to pay under the Credit only if documents are in compliance with the Credit terms. The bank is at risk for "documentary examination."
	As applicant, it is the buyer's responsibility to give instructions to the bank that do not violate the provisions of the sales contract. The buyer must also indicate the date on which the Credit will expire.
	At the bank the account officer for the buyer/applicant decides whether or not to approve the application based on the buyer's credit-worthiness. In general, the officer applies the same criteria as would pertain to any other borrowing request on an unsecured basis for a time frame represented by the expiry date of the Credit.
3. The bank (a) issues a letter of credit in favor of the seller/beneficiary in which it agrees to pay against the terms and conditions of the Credit and (b) sends the Credit to the seller/beneficiary.	The letter of credit is an arrangement between bank and seller/beneficiary in which the bank undertakes to pay the beneficiary upon presentation of documents that conform to all the terms and conditions of the Credit.
	In the Application for the Credit the bank also obligates itself to the buyer/applicant *not* to pay if the seller/beneficiary fails to meet all the terms and conditions of the Credit, that is, if there is a documentary discrepancy.

TRANSACTION FLOW (Fig. 5.2) (Continued)

Transaction Steps	Notes
	What then is a discrepancy? The Application for the Credit contains a complete description of documents the seller/beneficiary is required to present, and it describes the information that must appear on them. At issuance, the bank translates that description into the terms and conditions of the Credit itself.

When the letter of credit operations area examines the documents, it is looking for any difference between the documents named and described in the application and those actually presented by the seller/beneficiary. Such a difference is a documentary discrepancy, and constitutes legitimate grounds for the bank to refuse payment.

The bank's obligation under a letter of credit is irrevocable. What does that mean?

Generally it means that the letter of credit may be amended or canceled only with the agreement of the seller/beneficiary and bank (I.C.C. Publication 400, Article 10D). More specifically it means that the bank's promise to pay the seller/beneficiary (on condition that the documents conform) cannot be unilaterally broken.

Note: Credits can also be issued in *revocable* form. The buyer/applicant can ask the issuing bank to

TRANSACTION FLOW (Fig. 5.2) (Continued)

Transaction Steps	Notes
	change or withdraw a revocable Credit without prior notice to the seller/beneficiary. Therefore they are commonly used only between branches or subsidiaries of a company or to satisfy an external requirement, such as a governmental (foreign) exchange control regulation, rather than as a means for the trading partners to control the transaction.
4. Upon receiving the letter of credit, the seller/beneficiary reviews it.	The beneficiary is the party obligated to assemble documentation that conforms to the terms and conditions of the Credit; therefore it is in his own best interest to review the Credit to ensure that it conforms to the provisions of the sales contract and that it is deliverable, that is, that the beneficiary can ship the goods and present the documents specified within the time allowed for an amount not to exceed that stipulated in the Credit.
	If he cannot perform as specified but wishes to ship under the Credit, the seller must ask the buyer to have the Credit amended.
	(A common source of discrepancies is for buyer and seller to agree to change the terms but neglect to ask the bank to amend the Credit.)

TRANSACTION FLOW (Fig. 5.2) (Continued)

Transaction Steps	Notes
5. The seller ships the goods to the buyer.	The seller/beneficiary has no obligation *under the Credit* to ship the goods. In this sense, a letter of credit is a one-way contract: The bank is obligated to pay against conforming documents, but the seller is not obligated to ship.
6. The seller/beneficiary presents documents and a draft to the bank.	Presentation of documents and draft begins the payment process that culminates in settlement of the transaction.
	The draft may be drawn on the issuing bank or on any other party named in the Credit.
7. The bank examines the documents.	The bank conducts a thorough documentary review to ensure that it does not pay against a discrepancy. A letter of credit operations specialist examines the documents the seller has presented against the terms and conditions of the Credit itself in the light of I.C.C. Publication 400, that is, by the "rules" as they are contained in the 55 articles of I.C.C. Publication 400. The clerk notes any differences (discrepancies) between the terms and conditions of the Credit and the documents as presented. (Discrepancies are discussed in more detail later in this chapter.) Documents that match the terms and conditions of the Credit are said to *conform*.

TRANSACTION FLOW (Fig. 5.2) (Continued)

Transaction Steps	Notes
8. *If documents conform,* the bank pays the Credit by (a) arranging to credit the seller/beneficiary's account and (b) debiting the buyer/applicant's account.	Normally a bank debits the payor (buyer) before it credits the payee (seller). In a letter of credit transaction, however, the bank is obligated to pay without reference to the solvency of the buyer and *without recourse* to the seller/beneficiary. In other words, the bank cannot recover funds from the seller/beneficiary if the buyer/applicant cannot reimburse the bank for financial reasons, or will not reimburse it for any other reason.
	At this point, the seller/beneficiary is out of the transaction. Any disputes that arise now must be settled between the bank and the buyer/applicant.
If documents do not conform, the bank notifies the seller/beneficiary who has two immediate options:	
• Correct the documents and present them again.	A beneficiary can correct documents that are still under his control.
• Ask the buyer/applicant to waive the discrepancy.	An applicant is likely to waive a discrepancy when obtaining the goods is the primary concern, because the bank may not release the documents until and unless the buyer/applicant pays the draft.
(c) The bank transfers title and releases the documents to the buyer, thus concluding the letter of credit transaction.	After receiving the title documents the buyer can pick up the goods at the dock. A cautionary note is needed, however. Should a buyer/

TRANSACTION FLOW (Fig. 5.2) (Continued)

Transaction Steps	Notes
	applicant find even a minute discrepancy he can refuse to accept the documents and to reimburse the bank.
	A buyer/applicant might try to refuse to pay, for example:
	• When the price of the goods has moved against him since the sales contract was concluded.
	• Or when he suspects fraud on the part of the seller/beneficiary.
	• Or simply because he does not want to.

Risks.   Strictly from a credit point of view, the bank has the commercial credit risk of the buyer/applicant. Unless the bank takes a security interest in the underlying goods, this risk is generally regarded to be in the same class as any other unsecured borrowing.

If the issuing bank has a security interest in the goods, it will normally have the bill of lading consigned to the order of itself. It mitigates the risk that the goods will be lost or damaged by making sure that the shipment is insured, that the coverage is in the proper form, and that the amount is appropriate to the value of the goods. However, the bank incurs an additional risk in having the bill of lading consigned to its order, that is, that it will actually become owner of the merchandise. Such goods are called "distressed goods" and typically command extremely low prices in the marketplace. Ultimately the bank mitigates these risks by determining to issue letters of credit only on behalf of applicants who can and will pay under their letters of credit. In addition, a bank considers the expiry date of the Credit. A Credit with an expiry date 30 days from issuance differs in a credit sense from a Credit with an expiry date 180 days from issuance. The duration of exposure is normally reflected in the rate that the account officer quotes for the Credit.

Operationally a bank has both issuance and documentary review risks; that is, if a bank issues a letter of credit incorrectly or pays the seller/beneficiary against a discrepancy, the buyer/applicant may legitimately refuse to reimburse the issuing bank. Two sets of dynamics are at work with documentary discrepancies. The first dynamic comes from the bank's need to protect its right to reimbursement from the buyer/applicant for *legitimate* payments it makes under the credit by paying only against documents that conform 100% to the terms and conditions of the credit. The second set derives from the pragmatic concern of the seller/beneficiary to obtain prompt payment under the Credit, technical nonconformity of the documents notwithstanding. The problem of discrepancies is discussed once more following consideration of the intermediary functions.

The seller risks shipping without being able to comply with the terms of the Credit, thus losing its protection against payment and acceptance risks.

The buyer risks fraud on the part of the seller (i.e., that the goods shipped may not be as ordered and described on the documents and that the documents are thus fraudulent).

Rights, Responsibilities, Obligations

The Bank:

- Has a responsibility to structure the Credit to ensure that the terms are explicit, workable, and in compliance with I.C.C. Publication 400.
- Has a responsibility to examine the documents submitted by the seller/ beneficiary to make sure they conform to the terms and conditions of the Credit and to the articles of I.C.C. Publication 400.
- Is obligated to pay the beneficiary's draft if documents conform to all the terms and conditions of the Credit, and not to pay if documents do not conform.
- Has a right to receive reimbursement from the buyer/applicant if documents conform.

The Buyer/Applicant:

- Has a responsibility when applying for the Credit to give precise instructions to the bank that agree with the provisions of the sales contract.
- Is obligated to reimburse the bank if the documents conform to the terms and conditions of the Credit.

- Has a right to refuse to reimburse the bank if the documents do not conform.

The Seller/Beneficiary:

- Has a responsibility to examine the letter of credit upon receipt to ensure that he can ship goods and present documents specified within the time allowed for an amount not to exceed that stipulated in the Credit.
- Has a responsibility to request the buyer/applicant to have the Credit amended if he cannot perform as stipulated.
- Has a responsibility to submit conforming documents to the bank.
- Has a right to receive payment from the bank against conforming documents.

The Bank's Exposure. The bank's role in a letter of credit, then, is a risk-taking one. In fact, the bank assumes significant exposure at both the issuance and payment stages. At issuance it risks *financial exposure*. Because the bank is substituting its credit for that of the buyer/applicant, the bank *must* pay against presentation of conforming documents, even if the applicant lacks the funds to reimburse the bank.

When a bank approves issuance of the Credit, it must take into consideration the tenor of the draft in addition to the proposed expiry date of the Credit itself. For example, a Credit due to expire in 30 days calling for time drafts at 60 days is not the same credit risk to the same customer as a Credit due to expire in 90 days and calling for time drafts at 60 days. In the first case, the total potential time span is only 90 days (expiry date of the Credit *plus* tenor of the draft) as contrasted to 150 days in the second.

To help protect itself against the financial exposure, the bank may take a security interest in the goods being shipped. It does so by stipulating that the bill of lading be consigned to the order of the bank. Some banks eliminate financial exposure by debiting the account party at issuance, but in the majority of cases issuance of a letter of credit is based on a credit judgment and not on cash collateral.

At both issuance and payment the bank risks *operational exposure*. Should a bank make an error at issuance or pay against discrepant documents, it cannot recover payment from the beneficiary (seller) because payment under the Credit is without recourse; nor does it have recourse to the account party (buyer) because the account party is obligated to reimburse the bank only against conforming documents. The bank seeks to protect itself against the operational exposure by maintaining a letter of credit technical staff competent in both the issuance and payment functions and thoroughly familiar with the rules of I.C.C. Publication 400.

Liability.   A bank's liability at issuance is *contingent;* that is, it depends upon the seller/beneficiary's presentation of conforming documents. The contingent liability becomes *actual* when the beneficiary presents and the bank pays against conforming documents. In the case of a sight Credit the liability is of a "now you see it, now you don't" nature, because the debit to the applicant's account extinguishes the *actual* liability as soon as it is incurred. We will return to the issue of liability in the discussion of time (usance) credits. (See Chapter 6, *Bankers Acceptance*).

A letter of credit does *not* protect the buyer/applicant against fraud on the part of the seller/beneficiary. The bank is responsible for reviewing the documents with reasonable care to ascertain that they are, on their face, in compliance with the terms and conditions of the Credit. The bank is not liable or responsible for the effect of fraudulent documents (I.C.C. Publication 400, Article 17).

THE INTERMEDIARY FUNCTIONS

The preceding description assumed a single bank acting equally on behalf of buyer and seller. This assumption is usually not practical. International borders and long distances are involved. Language, cultural, and political differences can complicate transactions and result in the risks normal to international trade. Moreover, timing is vital because every letter of credit has an expiration date, and the goods may be perishable. In reality buyer and seller each usually require banking services in their respective countries in order to conclude a letter of credit transaction successfully. Why?

In the preceding section we described a "bank"—in reality the issuing bank—which received a letter of credit application from its customer, the buyer/applicant (importer). This bank issued and paid a letter of credit to a seller/beneficiary (exporter) located in another country. Because, from the seller's perspective, he is the beneficiary of a letter of credit opened by a "foreign bank," he typically has three sets of practical concerns:

- "Has the Credit been *opened?*"
- "Is it a *valid* Credit?"
- "What are the *risks* that I will fail to obtain payment against presentation of documents that conform to the terms and conditions of the Credit?"

Letter of credit functions have developed as the "customary practice" to mitigate these common risks:

- The process of issuance includes selection of a bank in the exporter's country to *advise* the Credit, that is, to test the issuing bank's cable or verify its signature, and then to inform the exporter/beneficiary that a valid letter of credit has been issued in his or her favor. When the terms of sale were negotiated, the exporter/beneficiary would have accepted an advised letter of credit provided he was comfortable with:
  The commercial credit risk of the issuing bank.
  The foreign exchange transfer risk.
  The political risk of the importer's country.
- An exporter/beneficiary who was not willing to take these risks could have asked that the Credit be *confirmed,* that is, that it also carry the irrevocable payment obligation of a bank in his or her own country. When issuing a confirmed letter of credit, the bank must use the services of another bank to obtain confirmation of its Credit. In this instance the exporter/beneficiary has the irrevocable obligation of *two* banks to pay, provided that he submits conforming documents.

The issuing bank is obligated to settle a letter of credit that it has issued, provided that the exporter/beneficiary presents conforming documents. It settles via one of three basic settlement procedures:

- By *payment,** either on its own books or on the books of a correspondent bank in the exporter's country. This payment is independent of the

---

*Article 10 of I.C.C. Publication 400 also states that "if the credit provides for deferred payment [the issuing bank is obligated] to pay, or [ensure] that payment will be made, on the date(s) determinable in accordance with the stipulations of the credit. . . ." For our purposes, deferred payment is a variation of the basic payment procedure, and we do not treat it separately here.

actions of any other party to the Credit. In other words, it is final and *without recourse*. This is true whether payment is made directly by the issuing bank or indirectly by a bank acting as its agent. This type of Credit is issued in *straight* form and is identified on the letter of credit by a statement to the effect that "We hereby engage with *you* [beneficiary] that all drafts drawn under and in compliance with the terms of this Credit will be duly honored."

- By *negotiation,* whereby an intermediary bank purchases the draft and documents from the beneficiary, transmits them to the issuing bank, and waits to be reimbursed by that bank. Negotiation is normally undertaken *with recourse,* that is, if the issuing bank fails to reimburse the negotiating bank for any reason, the negotiating bank can recover the funds from the beneficiary. This type of Credit is issued in *negotiable* form and is identified by a statement to the effect that "We hereby engage with *drawers, endorsers, and bona fide holders* that drafts drawn under, and in compliance with the terms of said Credit, and accompanied by the documents specified above, will be duly honored if drawn and negotiated on or before (date)."

- By *acceptance,* discussed in detail in Chapter 6, *Bankers Acceptance.*

As part of negotiation of the sales contract, importer and exporter decide how a Credit is to be structured. Exporters negotiating overseas sales often include their trade bankers at early stages to ensure that payment and financing arrangements are structured to their best advantage. The optimal letter of credit structure is then specified in the sales contract, and the buyer/applicant subsequently instructs the issuing bank via the Application for a Commercial Credit regarding the preferred structure. However, in the absence of explicit instructions, an issuing bank will advise the buyer/applicant on the best structure, taking into account the denomination of the Credit, the country in which it (issuing bank) is located, and the country in which the beneficiary is located.

The denomination of a Credit may be described as follows: "A credit which stipulates that drafts are to be drawn in the currency of the domicile of the beneficiary is a 'local currency' credit, while a credit which stipulates that drafts are to be drawn in a foreign currency, whether that of the accredited buyer or not, is a 'foreign currency' credit."* Generally speaking a local cur-

---

*Henry Harfield, *Bank Credits and Acceptances* (5th ed.), Wiley, New York, 1974, p. 49.

rency Credit (i.e., one denominated in the currency of the beneficiary's country) is structured in *straight* form (i.e., for payment); conversely a foreign currency Credit (whether or not denominated in the currency of the buyer's own country) is structured in *negotiable* form. This common practice enables classification of geographic "markets" for letters of credit based on the prevailing settlement mechanism. The United States, for example, is judged to be a payment market for dollar-denominated Credits, whereas the rest of the world is a negotiation market for them. Similarly, London is the payment market for sterling-denominated Credits, whereas the rest of the world is a negotiation market for them. As a practical matter, then, dollar-denominated Credits issued by banks in the United States are issued in negotiable form, whereas dollar-denominated Credits issued by banks outside the United States are issued in straight form. Table 5.1 summarizes letter of credit forms and settlement mechanisms associated with various currency denominations and geographic locations. Notice in the table that Credits issued in negotiable form ultimately settle by means of payment at the counters* of the issuing bank.

One final point is necessary before continuing: The bank processing a letter of credit classifies it as either an import or export Credit. A single Credit thus carries two names: to the importer/applicant's bank (issuing bank) it is an import Credit, and to the exporter/beneficiary's bank it is an export Credit. In other words, these terms represent the bank's point of view and not classification in a technical sense.

In the following sections, we will look at the functions commonly associated with these typical forms—advising, paying, negotiating, and confirming. Assume throughout that the letter of credit is a *sight Credit* (i.e., payable upon presentation of a sight draft and conforming documents). Note, however, that under certain circumstances the sight draft may be omitted entirely. This practice is possible because the Credit is payable upon presentation of conforming documents and hence the draft is not essential.

---

*The term "at own counters" is an operations expression that derives from historic banking practice. The exporter (or more typically, his messenger) would deliver documents to a window or counter (much like the teller's window at a bank branch), and the bank would make payment to the exporter at this same window or counter; hence the expression "payable at our counters." Even though most payments under letters of credit are now made via a credit to the beneficiary on the bank's books, the term is still used.

Table 5.1 Typical Letter of Credit Structures

Issuing Bank and Denomination of Credit	Beneficiary	Type of Credit	Settlement Mechanism
U.S. Import Credit: U.S. bank issues			
U.S. dollar credit	Non-U.S. exporter	Negotiation	*Negotiable* by bank in exporter's country. *Payable* at own counters in the U.S. or at foreign bank's counters via cable reimbursement.
Non-U.S. dollar credit	Non-U.S. exporter	Straight	Payable at counters of: Named bank in exporter's country. Named bank in third country. At their own counters in the United States.
U.S. Export Credit: Non-U.S. bank issues			
U.S. dollar credit	U.S. exporter	Straight	*Payable* at counters of U.S. correspondent of issuing bank
Non-U.S. dollar credit	U.S. exporter	Negotiation	*Negotiable* by U.S. bank. *Payable* at counters of U.S. bank via cable reimbursement or at counters of issuing bank.
Reimbursement Credit: Non-U.S. bank issues			
U.S. dollar credit	Non-U.S. exporter	Straight or Negotiation	*Reimbursable* at counters of issuing bank's U.S. correspondent (bank–to–bank reimbursement).

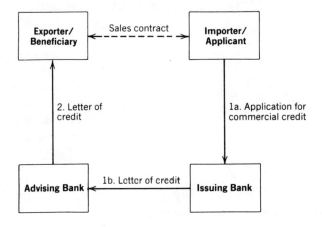

Figure 5.3   Advising.

Advising

TRANSACTION FLOW (Figure 5.3)

Transaction Steps	Notes
1. In accordance with the terms of the sales contract, the importer applies to the bank for a letter of credit. As part of issuance, the issuing bank selects another bank to advise the Credit to the exporter/beneficiary.	The exporter may tell the importer to have the Credit advised through the exporter's own bank. In the absence of such an instruction, the issuing bank selects a correspondent, usually according to a predetermined routing schedule.
2. The advising bank advises the exporter that a Credit has been opened in his favor.	In advising, the bank undertakes only the transmission of the Credit to the exporter "without engagement" (I.C.C. Publication 400, Article 8). The advising function is technically over at this point. Normally an advising bank will assume one or more additional functions: confirming, negotiating, or paying

TRANSACTION FLOW (Continued)

Transaction Steps	Notes
	as agent. However, it is not obligated to do so. (The risks and obligations attending assumption of these other functions are discussed in the next three sections.)

Risks.   A bank acts as merely a conduit or "mail box" for Credits that it advises; therefore its risk is minimal.

Rights, Responsibilities, Obligations.   Under Article 8 of I.C.C. Publication 400, an advising bank "shall take reasonable care to check the apparent authenticity of the credit which it advises." Operationally that means cable testing, verifying the signature, and transmitting the credit to the exporter/ beneficiary in a timely fashion. The advising bank receives a fee for its service.

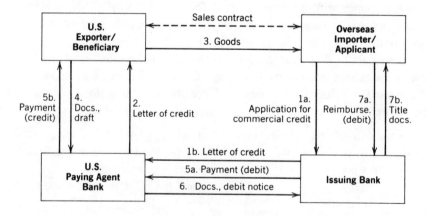

Figure 5.4   Paying.

Paying

TRANSACTION FLOW (Fig. 5.4)

Transaction Steps	Notes
1. According to the terms agreed upon in the sales contract (a) the overseas importer applies for a letter of credit; (b) the issuing bank issues the Credit calling for U.S. dollar drafts drawn on a named U.S. correspondent and sends it to that bank.	From the point of view of the U.S. bank, this is an export credit structured by an overseas issuing bank as a straight credit payable in the United States. (Such a credit is commonly termed an "advised credit.") In this way, the overseas issuing bank can arrange funding of the payment by directing that it be made from a specific U.S. dollar account maintained at its named correspondent bank in the United States.
2. Acting as the advising bank, the U.S. correspondent transmits the Credit to the exporter/beneficiary.	
3. The beneficiary examines the Credit, prepares the goods, and ships them.	
4. The beneficiary presents the draft and documents to the advising bank, now in its role as paying agent.	
5. After reviewing the documents, the paying agent bank (a) receives payment by debiting the U.S. dollar account of the issuing bank and (b) arranges payment to the exporter/beneficiary by credit to his	The paying agent has no credit risk, because it pays with funds provided by the issuing bank. However, it does have a documentary review risk and must examine the documents carefully, because if it pays

TRANSACTION FLOW (Fig. 5.4)

Transaction Steps	Notes
account, by a check, or by electronic funds transfer.	against a discrepancy the issuing bank may request a reversal of the debit.
	Payment to the exporter is *without recourse*, that is, the bank has no right to reclaim the funds from the beneficiary if the issuing bank refuses discrepant documents.
	Occasionally an overseas issuing bank will neglect to provide sufficient funds in its U.S. dollar account. When this happens the paying agent bank has three options:
	• It may tell the beneficiary to wait for payment until the opening bank funds the account.
	• At the beneficiary's request, it may cable the issuing bank for funds.
	• The account officer for the issuing bank may approve an overdraft.
6. The paying agent bank sends the documents and debit notice to the issuing bank.	
7. After reviewing the documents, the issuing bank (a) debits the buyer/applicant's account and (b) transfers title and releases the documents to the applicant.	If the issuing bank finds a discrepancy, it may recover the funds from the paying agent bank by requesting reversal of the debit.

Risks.   A bank that pays as agent has a documentary review risk. If it pays the beneficiary against a discrepancy, the issuing bank may request a reversal of the debit.

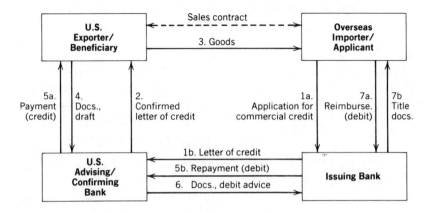

Figure 5.5 Confirming.

Rights, Responsibilities, and Obligations. A bank paying as agent:

- Has a right to refuse to pay the beneficiary if the issuing bank's account has insufficient funds to cover the draft.
- Has a responsibility to review the documents carefully for discrepancies, and to transmit conforming documents to the issuing bank.
- Has a right to a commission (a percentage of the face value of the draft) from the issuing bank.

Confirming

TRANSACTION FLOW (Figure 5.5)

Transaction Steps	Notes
1. In accordance with the terms of the sales contract (a) the overseas importer applies to the bank for a letter of credit to be confirmed by a U.S. bank; and	An exporter will request confirmation of a letter of credit when he or she is uncomfortable with the credit risk of the issuing bank and/or the political and foreign exchange transfer risk of the importer/applicant's country.

TRANSACTION FLOW (Fig. 5.5) (Continued)

Transaction Steps	Notes
(b) as part of issuance, the issuing bank selects a bank, usually a correspondent in the beneficiary's country, to confirm the Credit.	The contractual obligations between the issuing and confirming banks rest in the issuing bank's request for confirmation and in I.C.C. Publication 400.
2. The confirming bank adds its obligation and advises the confirmed Credit to the beneficiary.	From the point of view of the beneficiary's bank, the decision to confirm is primarily a credit decision that is based on an assessment of the commercial credit risk of the issuing bank as well as the political and foreign exchange transfer risk of the importer's country.
	The notation is similar to "This Credit bears our confirmation, and we engage that documents presented in conformance with the terms of this Credit will be duly honored on presentation." By adding this notation, the confirming bank *irrevocably* obligates itself to pay the beneficiary upon presentation of a draft and documents that conform to the terms and conditions of the Credit—even if the issuing bank is unable to provide reimbursement.
	A fourth "contract," the confirming bank's undertaking to pay, has now been added to the three already in effect (i.e., the sales contract between importer and exporter, the Application for Commercial Credit

TRANSACTION FLOW (Fig. 5.5) (Continued)

Transaction Steps	Notes
	between importer and issuing bank, and the letter of credit between issuing bank and exporter/beneficiary).
3. The exporter/beneficiary reviews the letter of credit, prepares the shipment, and ships the goods.	
4. After shipment, the beneficiary presents a draft and documents to the confirming bank.	The payment process begins with presentation of the documents.
5. The confirming bank reviews the documents for discrepancies. If they conform, the confirming bank (a) *pays* the beneficiary and (b) *debits* the issuing bank's U.S. dollar account on its books.	Payment to the beneficiary is *without recourse* (i.e., if the issuing bank refuses to reimburse the confirming bank for any reason, the confirming bank cannot recover the funds from the beneficiary). In other words, the confirming bank becomes the paying bank.
6. The confirming/paying bank transmits the documents and debit advice to the issuing bank.	
7. The issuing bank reviews the documents. If they conform, it (a) *debits* the account of the importer/applicant; (b) *transfers* title and *releases* the documents to the importer; and responds to the confirming bank's debit by crediting that bank's local currency account on their books.	If the issuing bank determines that the confirming bank has paid against a discrepancy, it can recover the funds from the confirming bank by requesting reversal of the debit. In such cases the issuing bank promptly notifies the confirming bank that it is holding the documents at the disposal of the confirming bank pending further instructions.

Risks.   A confirming bank assumes these risks:

- The commercial credit risk of the issuing bank.
- The political risk of the issuing bank's country.
- The documentary review risk that it may fail to identify a discrepancy.

Rights, Responsibilities, Obligations.   A confirming bank:

- Has a right to a payment commission, usually a percentage of the face value of the Credit for the duration of the confirmation; this is in addition to commissions for any other services.
- Has a responsibility to review documents carefully for discrepancies.
- Is obligated to pay the seller/beneficiary's draft upon presentation of documents that conform to the terms and conditions of the Credit.
- Is obligated to transmit documents to the issuing bank (or as otherwise instructed by the issuing bank).
- Has a right to receive reimbursement from the issuing bank if documents conform.
- Is obligated not to pay if documents do not conform.

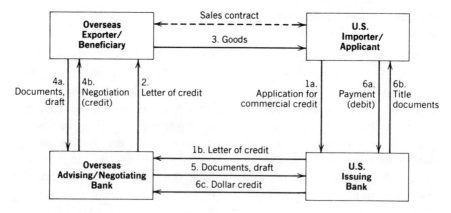

Figure 5.6   Negotiating.

Negotiating

TRANSACTION FLOW (Fig. 5.6)

Transaction Steps	Notes
1. In accordance with the terms of the sales contract (a) the U.S. importer applies for a letter of credit; (b) the issuing bank issues a U.S. dollar Credit and sends it to a correspondent in the exporter/beneficiary's country which it has named as the advising bank.	The U.S. issuing bank classifies this as an import credit. Dollar-denominated Credits in favor of beneficiaries located outside the United States are normally structured as negotiation Credits.
2. The advising bank transmits the Credit to the exporter/beneficiary.	
3. The beneficiary reviews the Credit, prepares the goods, and ships them.	
4. After shipping, the beneficiary (a) presents draft and documents to the advising bank (or to any other bank) and asks it to negotiate the Credit (i.e., to purchase the draft).	A bank's decision to negotiate or not is primarily a credit decision based on these factors: • The credit standing of the seller (beneficiary). • The credit standing of the issuing bank. • The duration of exposure, if applicable. Non-U.S. banks are usually willing to negotiate drafts drawn on the major U.S. money center banks.
(b) The negotiating bank reviews the documents and buys the draft from the exporter at a discount from the face value, usually with	Unlike a bank paying as agent (which pays with funds received from the issuing bank), a bank electing to negotiate buys the draft

TRANSACTION FLOW (Fig. 5.6) (Continued)

Transaction Steps	Notes
recourse. The net amount is paid to the beneficiary's account.	and documents from the seller/beneficiary and advances its own funds to him, normally *with recourse*. Consequently, if the issuing bank refuses or is unable to reimburse the negotiating bank for any reason, the negotiating bank has the right to reclaim the advance from the seller/beneficiary.
5. The negotiating bank sends the documents to the issuing bank for reimbursement.	The negotiating bank is without the monies advanced until it is reimbursed by the issuing bank. Therefore it charges the seller/beneficiary interest for the estimated number of days until reimbursement. This "transit" or "mail" interest is generally incorporated as part of the foreign exchange rate and subtracted from the face value of the draft.
6. The issuing bank reviews the documents and if they conform, it (a) *debits* the importer/applicant and (b) *releases* the documents to the importer; it then	
(c) *credits* the negotiating bank's U.S. dollar account on its books.	At this point, the transaction looks like any other international payment described in Chapter 2.

Risks. A bank electing to negotiate the seller/beneficiary's draft drawn under a letter of credit incurs the following risks:

- Political risk of the issuing bank's country.
- Credit risk of the issuing bank.
- Documentary review risk.
- Beneficiary credit risk.

Ideally a negotiating bank will pass on all these risks to the beneficiary via a full recourse agreement. In that case, the negotiating bank retains full recourse to the beneficiary should the issuing bank fail to repay it. Sometimes, however, these agreements become the subject of negotiation between beneficiary and negotiating bank. In those instances the beneficiary will argue for limited recourse and may be able to persuade the bank to accept the documentary review risk, saying in effect, "If you miss a discrepancy, it's your problem."

Rights, Responsibilities and Obligations.   A negotiating bank:

- Has the right to decide whether or not to negotiate the seller/beneficiary's draft and documents.
- Has a right to charge the beneficiary interest for the period of time it has advanced funds, for negotiation fees, and for a foreign exchange spread.
- Has a responsibility to review documents carefully for discrepancies.
- Has a responsibility to transmit the documents to the issuing bank.
- Has a right to be reimbursed by the issuing/paying bank if documents conform.
- Has a right to reclaim funds advanced to the beneficiary if the issuing bank does not pay e.g., because of legal intervention, failure of issuing bank, foreign exchange clampdown, etc., provided said right is secured by a full recourse agreement with the beneficiary.

Cable Reimbursement.   Transit interest charges can be reduced by having the buyer/applicant structure the Credit for cable reimbursement. In this case the beneficiary presents the documents to a bank in his or her country. After reviewing the documents, the bank cables the issuing bank to credit its account. The issuing bank debits the buyer/applicant and cables back the credit. The issuing bank retains recourse to the foreign bank if the documents are not in order.

Restricted Negotiation.   In a restricted negotiation the issuing bank names a specific negotiating bank in the letter of credit. The purpose is primarily to keep revenues derived from negotiation in-house, that is, within the issuing bank's branch network. To ensure that the issuing bank does earn the commission, the notation on the letter of credit would read, "This Credit is negotiable only at the counters of (name of bank and local branch)." When negotiation is restricted to a bank other than a branch of the issuing bank, the purpose is to assist the importer to track the arrival of documents at the bank.

Seller/Beneficiary Alternatives to Advising Bank's Refusal to Negotiate. Should an advising bank decide not to negotiate, the seller/beneficiary has two alternatives: Ask another bank to negotiate, or ask the advising bank to send the documents to the issuing bank for collection. In the latter case the advising bank becomes a collecting bank, and the funds remain uncollected until the issuing bank has reviewed the documents and credited the collecting bank, at which time the collecting bank will pay the beneficiary. Note that the seller/beneficiary retains protection under the Credit provided that the documents reach the issuing bank before the Credit expires.

Exporter/Beneficiary Options in the Event of Documentary Discrepancies.   The distances normally involved in a letter of credit transaction complicate the handling of discrepancies. As a practical matter an exporter/beneficiary faced with discrepant documents has four options:

- *Correct a discrepancy in documents that he prepared and resubmit the documents*. This is not always possible after shipment, because many of the documents relate directly to the shipment.
- *Ask the bank to telex the issuing bank for the applicant's authorization to pay.*
- *Ask the bank to submit the documents and draft to the buyer/applicant via the issuing bank as a collection item*. The item becomes a documentary collection (see Chapter 4) and the exporter/beneficiary loses the advantages and protection of the letter of credit. The exporter must wait for payment until the issuing bank collects the funds from the

importer/applicant, and the intermediary bank collects from the issuing bank.

- *Ask the intermediary bank to pay against reserve* (indemnity). Under an indemnity, the exporter/beneficiary agrees to hold the bank harmless in the event the importer/applicant refuses the documents, in which case the bank will seek repayment from the beneficiary. In effect the beneficiary says to his bank, "I acknowledge that there are discrepancies. Pay me anyway, and I guarantee to refund the amount of the Credit plus charges plus interest plus any other costs if the issuing bank fails to pay." The exporter's bank's decision to pay against reserves is based on three considerations: (1) whether or not the Credit disallows reserves; (2) whether or not the account officer for the issuing bank will allow the arrangement; and (3) whether or not the account officer for the beneficiary makes a favorable credit decision.

SUMMARY

The procedural differences between paying, negotiating, and confirming letters of credit are demonstrated in close analysis of their respective settlement mechanisms. The mechanism underlying settlement of a negotiation credit, for example, is based essentially on the collection procedure. By contrast, the funds transfer settlement mechanism forms the accounting basis for a Credit structured in straight form. Moreover, the accounting entries also show clearly the credit risk a confirming bank takes in paying a Credit it has confirmed.

Banks customarily charge either a flat processing fee or a negotiated commission for each step involved in a letter of credit transaction. In the United States flat fees are usually charged for issuing and amending letters of credit. A commission (normally a percentage of the drawing under a Credit) is charged for the assumption of risk, that is, for paying or accepting drafts drawn under letters of credit and for confirming letters of credit opened by non-U.S. banks. Banks outside the United States charge a commission for issuance based on a percentage of the face value of the Credit and for a specific availability period (e.g., for the 90 days from issuance to expiry). In the United States, a payment commission is charged when documents are honored; this commission represents a percentage of the face value of the drawing under the Credit. All charges levied under a letter of credit are for the account of the importer/applicant, unless the letter of credit explicitly states that charges are for the account of the exporter/beneficiary.

The remarkable flexibility of the letter of credit instrument is beginning to show itself. Generally speaking a letter of credit is a seller's payment term. In its simplest form it makes it possible for the seller/beneficiary to eliminate the risks of nonpayment and nonacceptance from an international sale. Moreover, when confirmed it eliminates political risk (including foreign exchange transfer risk) and the commercial credit risk of the issuing bank as well.

Historically the basic letter of structure has been adapted to meet the specific needs of buyers and sellers engaged in cross-border trade. These classic letter of credit variations are found in Appendix II. In Chapters 9 and 10 we shall show how the structure of customary practice that has evolved around this remarkable instrument forms a reliable model for the design and evaluation of financing arrangements tailored to the practical requirements of very unusual transactions.

6 Bankers Acceptance

One of the principal advantages of the classic sight letter of credit instrument is that it provides a mechanism by which the importer can finance the transit time in the transaction, thus enabling the exporter to obtain payment shortly after shipment. The basic variation on the standard sight letter of credit format is the time (usance) credit, which enables the exporter to finance the importer by agreeing to receive payment at a specified future date. In this chapter we introduce bankers acceptances (BAs), focusing specifically on the dual nature of the instrument as both financing tool and investment vehicle.

As you will recall from Chapter 1, bankers acceptances are time drafts drawn on and accepted by banks. Their purpose is to stimulate international trade by providing relatively low cost financing to the buyer or seller for certain eligible trade transactions as defined by the Federal Reserve. Eligibility criteria are summarized later in this chapter. United States dollar acceptance financing is used primarily for:

- United States imports and exports.
- Shipment between foreign countries (creating what are known as "third-country bills").

Other uses include:

- United States domestic shipments.
- Pre-export financing.
- Domestic and foreign storage.
- Extension of dollar exchange credits to foreign countries ("dollar-exchange bills").

THE INSTRUMENT

The bankers acceptance (BA) is a two-armed instrument with one branch in financing and the other in investment. To understand the instrument, we must first understand this dual nature. It may help to think of the BA as being shaped like a boomerang, with one arm labeled "Financing" and the other "Investment." Bank officers and their corporate customers are completely in

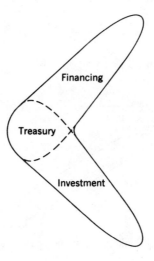

Figure 6.1 Dual nature of bankers acceptances.

the financing arm. Funding for the BA is usually in the investment arm. The bank's treasury department sits at the head of the boomerang where these arms meet (see Fig. 6.1).

- The customer requests BA financing from his or her account officer at the bank.
- The account officer prices the BA, quoting a rate within guidelines set by the bank's treasury department.
- Treasury decides on the funding mechanism; normally it sells the BA in the acceptance market.

Interaction of the Participants

Now let's add these major participants at each point of the diagram and introduce the primary functions:

- Creation
- Discount
- Sale (rediscount)
- Settlement (payment and repayment)

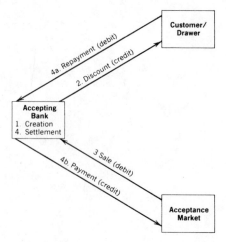

Figure 6.2   Bankers acceptance parties and functions.

TRANSACTION FLOW (Fig. 6.2)

Transaction Steps	Notes
1. The bank *creates* the BA by stamping "Accepted" on the face of a draft presented by its customer, the drawer.	The bank will have established an acceptance facility and line of credit for this customer before it accepts a draft.
2. The bank *discounts* the BA, that is, it pays the drawer a sum less than the face value of the draft.	
3. The bank *sells* (*rediscounts*) the BA to an investor in the acceptance market.	Normally the bank receives a sum less than the face value of the draft but more than it paid the drawer.
4. At maturity the bank *settles* the BA, that is, it debits the drawer for the full amount of the BA and pays the full value to the investor who presents it.	

KEY TERMS DEFINED

Before we flesh out the preceding description it will be useful to introduce or review several key terms and concepts important for understanding bankers acceptances.

Bankers acceptances originate either as the time draft required under a time (usance) letter of credit or independently of letters of credit. Although terminology differs from bank to bank, most operations areas distinguish between these two types. In this chapter we will refer to letter of credit-related BAs as *documentary* and to independent BAs as *clean*.

In Chapter 1 we pointed out that drafts are negotiable instruments, which means that they can be sold and ownership transferred by endorsement to another party, termed the *holder in due course*. There is no limit on the number of times ownership can be transferred. Whoever owns the draft at maturity presents it to the drawee for payment. By accepting a draft and creating a BA, a bank substitutes its credit for its customer's and assumes the irrevocable obligation to pay the face amount of the acceptance at maturity to whoever presents it at that time. Normally an accepting bank pays with funds received by debiting the account of its obligor—the party whose credit risk the bank assumes. It is important not to confuse the bank's obligor in the trade transaction with the primary and secondary obligors of the bankers acceptance itself. Under negotiable instruments law, an accepting bank is primary obligor of the acceptance instrument; however, the bank's customer, either the importer or the exporter, is in turn the bank's obligor under their prior credit arrangement (discussed later in this chapter).

According to negotiable instruments law (spelled out in Article 3 of the Uniform Commercial Code), the *primary obligor* of an acceptance is the party unconditionally obligated to pay at maturity. In the case of a BA, this party is the accepting bank. If the primary obligor fails to meet its payment obligation, the holder in due course has recourse through all previous endorsers back to the drawer of the draft who is the *secondary obligor*. The secondary obligor has the unconditional obligation to pay the acceptance if the primary obligor and subsequent endorsers dishonor it. In other words, the acceptance is *two-name paper*.

Most BAs are readily negotiable, because they represent the unconditional obligation of a "prime" commercial bank with good credit standing. No accepting bank has ever failed to honor its obligation. Consequently, no holder

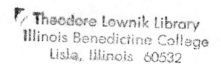

in due course has had to seek repayment from a secondary obligor or drawer of the draft.

An accepting bank may decide to *hold the BA in portfolio*. In this case the bank finances the transaction by purchasing the BA with its own funds. Its position is similar to the position it is in when it extends a loan directly to its customer. However, when the accepting bank sells the BA to another party it ties up none of its own funds, even though it has extended credit and assumed the obligation to pay the acceptance at maturity.

Eligibility Criteria

Eligibility criteria for BAs are spelled out in Section 13, paragraphs 7 and 12, of the Federal Reserve Act with subsequent interpretations of the Board of Governors and in the Federal Open Market Committee's (FOMC) Rules on Open Market Operations in Bankers Acceptances. These criteria determine two separate categories of eligibility, namely:

- Whether or not a specific transaction may be financed by the BA.
- Whether or not the proceeds from the sale of the BA are exempt from the reserve requirement mandated by the Federal Reserve (i.e., that a bank must hold in reserve a certain percentage of funds it gets from sources other than the sale of eligible BAs).

The type of transaction and tenor of the draft are the chief eligibility (and market-defining) criteria. In addition, there are other constraints defining BAs eligible for discount and hence exempt from reserve requirements. In general, these criteria stipulate:

- The BA must finance a self-liquidating trade transaction.
- BA funds cannot be used by the drawer for working capital purposes.
- Duplication of financing is not allowed.

Allowable Trade Transactions.   To be *eligible for discount* the Federal Reserve has stipulated that the BA must finance one of the following types of trade transactions. Except as noted below, the BA must be created to finance a "current" shipment (usually defined as being within 30 days of shipment), and the tenor must be no longer than <u>six</u> months (180 days):

- Import or export between the United States and a foreign country or between two foreign countries.

- United States domestic shipment of goods between companies in different cities.
- Domestic or foreign storage of readily marketable staples. Goods must be secured by a title document, usually a warehouse receipt. The Federal Reserve defines a readily marketable staple as "an article of commerce, agriculture, or industry, of such uses as to make it the subject of constant dealings in ready markets with such frequent quotations of price as to make (1) the price easily and definitely ascertainable and (2) the staple itself easy to realize upon by sale at any time." Furthermore, the goods in question must be nonperishable, that is, they must maintain their value as security at least for the life of the draft drawn against them. The Federal Reserve lists the following examples: cattle, coal, cotton, cottonseed, cotton yarns, flour, potatoes, sugar in bond, and wool.
- Dollar exchange, for example, to provide financing between harvests for one-crop countries; BA financing for this type of transaction is allowed only in approved countries and the tenor of the BA must be <u>three</u> months or less.

To be *eligible for purchase* as defined by the FOMC, the BA must finance one of the following types of trade transaction. It must be created within 30 days of shipment, and the tenor may be no longer than <u>nine</u> months (BAs with a tenor longer than six months, however, incur a reserve requirement):

- Import or export of goods between the United States and a foreign country or between two foreign countries (same as eligible for discount criterion).
- United States domestic shipment of goods between companies in different cities (same).
- Domestic storage of *any* goods in the United States under contract of sale or going into channels of trade within a reasonable period and secured by a title document at the time of acceptance.

Table 6.1 summarizes eligibility and reservability requirements.

Rules Governing the Bankers Acceptance Instrument Itself.   An eligible BA sold in the market must bear an eligibility stamp that notes the grounds on which the transaction is eligible, for example, the stamp might read, "The transaction that gives rise to this instrument is the *importation* of *steel* from *Japan* to *USA*."

Bankers acceptances cannot be drawn without recourse; that is, the BA must be two-name paper.

Table 6.1 Summary of Eligibility and Reserve Requirements

Type of Bankers Acceptance	Eligible For		Reserves Required[c]
	Purchase[a]	Discount[b]	
Export–import, including shipments between foreign countries			
Tenor—6 months or less	Yes	Yes	No
6 to 9 months	Yes	No	Yes
Domestic shipment, with or without documents conveying title attached at the time of acceptance[d]			
Tenor—6 months or less	Yes	Yes[e]	No
6 to 9 months	Yes	No	Yes
Shipment within foreign countries			
Tenor—any maturity	No	No	Yes
Foreign storage, readily marketable staples secured by warehouse receipt			
Tenor—6 months or less	No	Yes[e]	No
6 to 9 months	No	No	Yes
Domestic storage, readily marketable staples secured by warehouse receipt			
Tenor—6 months or less	Yes	Yes[e]	No
6 to 9 months	Yes	No	Yes
Domestic storage, any goods in the United States under contract of sale or going into channels of trade and secured throughout its life by warehouse receipt			
Tenor—6 months or less	Yes	No	Yes
6 to 9 months	Yes	No	Yes
Dollar exchange, required by usages of trade, only in approved countries			
Tenor—3 months or less	No	Yes	No
3 to 9 months	No	No	Yes
Finance or working capital, not related to any specific transaction			
Tenor—any maturity	No	No	Yes

[a]Authorizations announced by the Federal Open Market Committee on April 1, 1974.

[b]In accordance with Regulation A of the Federal Reserve Act.

[c]In accordance with Regulation D of the Federal Reserve Act.

[d]Before passage of the Bank Export Services Act of 1982, the Federal Reserve required that title documents be in possession of the accepting bank at the time the BA was created.

[e]Providing that the maturity of nonagricultural bills at the time of discount is not more than 90 days.

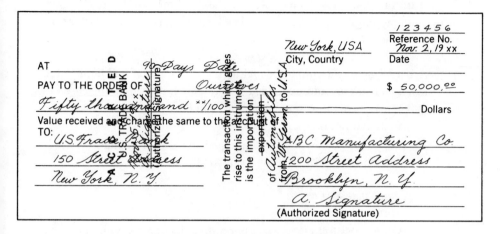

Figure 6.3 Typical bankers acceptance.

Alterations on the face of the BA must be guaranteed by the accepting bank.

Certain restrictive endorsements are prohibited, for example, "Payable to any Bank, Banker, or Trust Company," because the interpretation that foreign courts may place on such endorsements is unclear.

Bankers acceptances cannot cover trade transactions with countries with which the U.S. Treasury Department prohibits trade (e.g., Cuba).

Figure 6.3 illustrates typical acceptance and eligibility stamps found on a BA.

(*Note:* Tenor refers to the full length of time of the acceptance from date of inception to maturity.)

Source: Chart adapted from Ralph T. Helfrich, "Trading in Bankers' Acceptances: A View from the Acceptance Desk of the Federal Reserve Bank of New York," *Monthly Review* (Federal Reserve Bank of New York, February 1976), p. 54 (from an unpublished paper delivered by Arthur Bardenhagen, V.P., Irving Trust Company, at the Seventh Annual C.I.B. Conference in New Orleans, LA, October 13, 1975).

Legal Limitations.   The Federal Reserve has set limits on the total amount of outstanding eligible BAs each member bank may hold, and on the total amount for individual customers.

- A bank's aggregate limit is equal to 150% of paid-up and unimpaired stock and surplus and undivided profit. This limit can be increased to 200% with Federal Reserve approval, and only if there is intent to use the additional limit.
- An individual borrower's limit is equal to 10% of capital, which is separate from the 10% limit on loans to the same customer.

The Acceptance Market

In Figure 6.2 and the following transaction flow diagrams we lump dealers and investors together under the title "Acceptance Market." In this section we will separate these parties to show how they and the accepting bank interact.

Accepting Banks.   Who are these banks that create BAs? Any member bank of the Federal Reserve system and U.S. branches or agencies of foreign banks that are subject to reserve requirements are allowed to accept a draft; however, the overwhelming majority of BAs are created by prime commercial banks that do a significant volume of international business—primarily those located in New York, with some in other major port cities (e.g., Los Angeles, San Francisco, Houston, Seattle, Boston, and Chicago). These banks have the specialized staff, foreign trade connections, and established name necessary to administer the complex BA instrument. Their acceptances trade at the most favorable rate in the money market because investors consider their credit sounder than that of other banks. There is also a healthy market in the BAs of the larger regional banks even though they trade at somewhat higher rates in the market.

Dealers.   Dealers intermediate between accepting banks and investors and are therefore the first tier of the acceptance market. They "make the market" for BAs by quoting rates at which they are willing to buy and sell them. These rates fluctuate throughout the day reflecting the rates of other short-term money market instruments and Fed funds, the size of the dealer's portfolio, and supply and demand in the market.

Accepting banks use rates quoted by dealers to help establish the discount rate they charge their BA customers. Currently there are 20–25 active dealers, most of whom are located in New York. They include money market dealers who trade in BAs as well as other short-term paper, dealers who specialize in BAs, and a few banks and firms. Currently no dealer trades BAs of all the accepting banks.

Investors. Investors, who make up the second and third tiers of the acceptance market, are eager to purchase eligible BAs because these acceptances are safe, liquid, short-term investments with a relatively high yield. The second tier of the market is comprised of other banking institutions:

- United States commercial banks who purchase their own BAs as well as those of other banks.
- United States savings banks.
- Bank trust departments.
- Foreign central and commercial banks.

The third tier includes:

- Finance-related businesses such as mutual funds and insurance companies.
- Corporations.
- Individuals.

Funding and Profitability

Funding decisions are normally made by the treasury department of the accepting bank. Banks usually create BAs with the intention of funding them by selling them the same day in the money market. However, based on several variables including the bank's BA position, the cost of funds that day, rates of alternative instruments, and so on, the treasury department may decide to hold the BAs in portfolio. The bank must fund BAs held in portfolio from its own cash position as it funds any other borrowing instrument. Other funding methods are usually more expensive than selling the BA in the market and

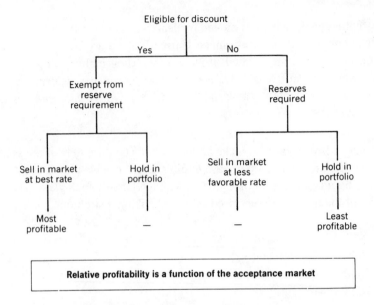

Figure 6.4   Funding and profitability relationships.

tend to reduce the bank's profitability. Figure 6.4 illustrates these funding and profitability relationships.

CLEAN BANKERS ACCEPTANCES

The participants in the financing and investment cycles of a clean BA (i.e., one that originates independently of a time letter of credit) are:

- *Drawer* (secondary obligor of the BA).
- *Drawee/accepting bank* (primary obligor).
- *Acceptance market.*

Figure 6.5 illustrates the relationship between the parties in a transaction financed by a clean BA. Typically, buyer and seller have concluded a sales agreement and

- The seller needs funds to purchase and repackage the goods for shipment, or for the period between shipment and receipt of payment from the buyer.
- Or the buyer needs funds to meet payment obligations under sight letter of credit, documentary collection, or open account terms.

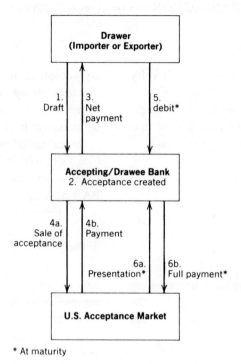

Figure 6.5 Clean acceptance financing.

TRANSACTION FLOW (Fig. 6.5)

Transaction Steps	Notes
1. The drawer presents the draft to the drawee/bank and asks the bank to accept. The drawer includes documentation necessary to establish that the transaction is eligible for acceptance financing.	Before the bank can accept, the account officer must verify that an acceptance agreement has been concluded with the drawer naming the conditions under which he may draw drafts (see section on Facility Setup below). The account officer must also determine whether the transaction is indeed eligible for BA financing (see section on Eligibility Criteria above).

TRANSACTION FLOW (Fig. 6.5) (Continued)

Transaction Steps	Notes
2. The bank creates the BA by stamping "Accepted" on the face of the draft. It also notes on an eligibility stamp the specifics of the trade transaction being financed.	By accepting, the bank substitutes its credit for the customer's and assumes the obligation to pay the BA at maturity. It charges an acceptance fee for taking this credit risk (see section on Pricing below). Notice that in this example of clean BA financing, the secondary obligor of the negotiable instrument is the same party as the credit obligor of the bank (i.e., the drawer).
3. The accepting bank immediately discounts the BA and credits the drawer's account for the net amount.	The buyer's discount rate (BDR) represents the bank's charge to the customer for replacing the funds advanced to him. (See section on Pricing below for how the BDR is determined.)
4. (a) The accepting bank funds the BA by selling it in the acceptance market, usually through a dealer. (b) The dealer pays the bank the face value minus dealer's discount.	
5. At maturity the bank debits the account of its obligor (the drawer) for the face amount of the BA.	
6. At or following maturity, (a) the investor presents the BA to the accepting bank, and (b) the bank pays the investor the full face amount of the BA.	The holder of the BA does not earn any additional interest beyond the due date.

DOCUMENTARY BANKERS ACCEPTANCES

The following diagrams illustrate the procedures involved in transacting financing via documentary BAs, that is, those that originate in connection with time (usance) letters of credit. Before charting documentary BAs, it will be helpful to highlight certain facts:

- The purpose of a documentary BA is *financing* a transaction, unlike the clean BA whose purpose is *funding*. Therefore a documentary BA is not necessarily discounted, as will be seen in the transaction flows that follow.
- The accepting bank may be any bank designated in the letter of credit as drawee (issuing, confirming, or paying agent bank but not negotiating bank).
- If the BA finances a U.S. import, the accepting bank is usually the U.S. bank that issued the letter of credit.
- If the BA finances a U.S. export, the accepting bank is usually the U.S. bank that advised or confirmed the Credit.

Figure 6.6 charts the transaction flow of a documentary BA that finances a U.S. import. When comparing Figure 6.6 with 6.7, notice that the U.S. bank normally creates the BA regardless of its role in the letter of credit transaction.

United States Import

Assume the acceptance is financing a U.S. import (i.e., the accepting bank is the U.S. bank that issued the letter of credit). The parties are:

- United States *importer* (issuing bank's obligor under the letter of credit).
- *Drawee/accepting bank* (primary obligor of the acceptance).
- Exporter's/*advising/negotiating bank*.
- *Exporter/drawer* (secondary obligor of the acceptance).
- United States *acceptance market*.

For the purpose of this flow, assume the draft will be drawn on the issuing bank.

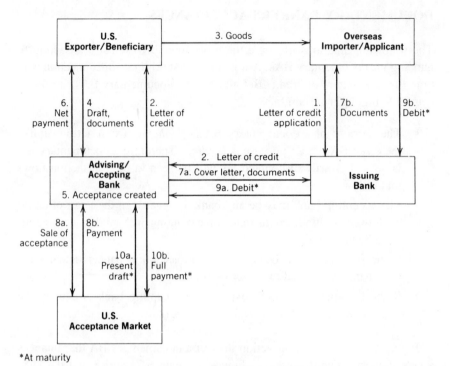

Figure 6.6 Documentary bankers acceptance financing a U.S. import.

TRANSACTION FLOW (Fig. 6.6)

Transaction Steps	Notes
1. The exporter and importer agree that their sales transaction will be carried out under a time letter of credit, and the importer applies for the Credit.	The importer's application for the letter of credit is the credit agreement that obligates the importer to repay the bank for acceptances it creates under the Credit.
2. (a) The importer's bank issues the letter of credit and sends it to a correspondent bank in the exporter's country (b) which advises the Credit to the exporter.	
3. The exporter prepares and ships the goods to the U.S. importer.	

TRANSACTION FLOW (Fig. 6.6) (Continued)

Transaction Steps	Notes
4. (a) After shipment, the exporter presents a time draft to the bank along with the other documents required under the letter of credit.	The exporter's dollar draft is drawn on the U.S. issuing bank as authorized in the letter of credit.
(b) The exporter's bank sends draft and documents to the U.S. issuing bank with the exporter's request to accept the draft and discount it.	Alternatively the exporter might ask the bank to accept the draft and hold it in safekeeping until maturity.
5. (a) The issuing bank reviews the documents and, if they conform to the terms of the Credit, accepts the draft, creating the BA by stamping "Accepted" on the face of the draft. It also notes the nature of the transaction on an eligibility stamp, for example, "The transaction that gives rise to this instrument is the importation of oil from Mexico to the U.S."	At acceptance, the contingent liability booked at issuance becomes an actual liability of a duration equal to the tenor of the draft. The accepting bank charges an acceptance fee that is normally for the account of the importer (see section on Pricing below).
(b) At the same time, the bank releases the documents to the importer.	The documents are usually released under a trust receipt unless the importer has previously signed a security agreement with the bank covering the goods.
6. At the exporter's request, the accepting bank discounts the BA and effects payment to the exporter through the negotiating bank.	The discount rate is determined in part by whether the BA is eligible for discount. The bank makes this determination based on the documents required under the time letter of credit. Who pays the discount charge is determined by the relative negotiating strengths of importer and exporter. The letter of credit will state explicitly if the importer

TRANSACTION FLOW (Fig. 6.6) (Continued)

Transaction Steps	Notes
	is to pay the discount charges. If the letter of credit is "silent," the exporter is to pay these charges. An exporter who wants to offer a more attractive sales package to boost sales, may agree to pay the discount charges. On the other hand, an importer who requires the financing, might agree to pay them.
7. The accepting bank funds the BA by selling it in the acceptance market. In payment the bank receives face value less dealer's discount rate.	
8. At maturity the accepting bank settles the BA by debiting the account of its obligor, the importer.	
9. At or following maturity, the investor presents the BA to the accepting bank, and the bank pays the investor the face value of the BA.	

United States Export

Now assume the BA is financing a U.S. export (i.e., the accepting bank is the U.S. bank that advises, pays as agent, or confirms the letter of credit). The parties are:

- *Importer* (issuing bank's obligor under the Credit).
- Importer's/*issuing bank* (advising/confirming bank's obligor under the Credit).
- United States exporter's/*accepting bank* (primary obligor of the acceptance).
- United States *exporter/drawer* (secondary obligor of the acceptance).
- United States *acceptance market*.

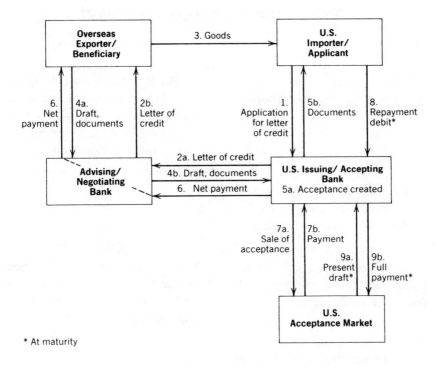

Figure 6.7 Documentary bankers acceptance financing a U.S. export.

TRANSACTION FLOW (Fig. 6.7)

Transaction Steps	Notes
1. The overseas importer applies for a letter of credit.	
2. The issuing bank sends the Credit to a correspondent in the United States, which advises the exporter.	
3. The U.S. exporter prepares and ships the goods.	
4. After shipping, the exporter presents documents and draft to the	The U.S. exporter could also ask the accepting bank to simply hold

TRANSACTION FLOW (Fig. 6.7) (Continued)

Transaction Steps	Notes
advising/confirming bank and asks it to accept and discount the draft.	the BA in safekeeping until maturity, or to return the BA to him, in which case the exporter himself could either hold it to maturity or seek a better discount rate at another bank.
5. The bank checks the documents and stamps "Accepted" on the face of the draft, thereby creating the BA.	
6. At the request of the drawer/exporter, the accepting bank discounts the acceptance.	The exporter receives the face amount *less* any charges named in the letter of credit for which he is responsible.
7. (a) The accepting bank notes on a cover letter that it has accepted the exporter's draft and sends letter and documents to the issuing bank in the importer's country (b) which releases the documents to the importer.	
8. The U.S. accepting bank funds the BA by selling it in the acceptance market.	
9. At maturity (a) the accepting bank debits the account of its obligor, the issuing bank, which in turn	The contractual obligation between the two banks rests in the issuing bank's request to confirm or its instructions to charge its account at maturity.
(b) debits the account of *its* obligor, the importer/applicant.	The applicant pays the face amount of the BA *plus* any charges for which he is responsible.

TRANSACTION FLOW (Fig. 6.7) (Continued)

Transaction Steps	Notes
10. At or following maturity (a) the investor presents the acceptance to the accepting bank for payment and (b) the bank pays the investor the full face value of the acceptance.	

IMPLEMENTATION

This discussion is concerned with the issues most common to persons engaged in financing, buying, or selling via bankers acceptances. We will first discuss pricing, then generic setup and booking procedures, including shipping details (documentation).

Pricing

By accepting the draft a bank obligates itself unconditionally to pay the face amount of the acceptance at maturity to whoever presents it at that time. The bank charges an *acceptance commission* on a *per annum* basis for assuming this credit risk on behalf of its customers. The commission is expressed as a percentage of the face value of the draft (usually about 1% per annum.).

In addition to the acceptance commission, the bank also charges a discount rate. The *buyer's discount rate* (BDR) is the bank's charge to the customer for replacing the funds advanced to him. This rate fluctuates throughout the day and is constantly revised by the bank's treasury department depending on:

- The *dealer's discount rate* (DDR), which is the rate at which the bank can sell BAs to a dealer.
- The bank's current BA position, which is whether the bank is within the aggregate limit on BAs set by the Federal Reserve. When the bank is approaching this limit it raises its rate, thereby pricing itself out of the market to discourage buyers.

The face amount of an acceptance can affect its negotiability and hence the rate at which it trades. Investors prefer drafts for $100,000 or $500,000. Larger denominations or odd amounts are not as attractive and may trade at slightly higher rates. For example, if total BA financing is for $2,055,000, the drawer might present four separate drafts for $500,000 each and one "odd lot" draft for $55,000.

In clean BAs the acceptance commission and discount rate are usually combined into one charge, called the *all-in rate,* which is deducted from the face amount of the draft when funds are advanced to the drawer:

Acceptance commission + discount rate = all-in rate

Normally the Treasury area of the accepting bank sets a minimum BDR, and the account officer for the borrower adds the acceptance commission and sets an all-in rate for each transaction based on:

- The customer's credit standing—the better the credit the lower the rate.
- The customer's current market environment.
- The rate being offered by competing banks.

In documentary BAs that arise within the terms of time letters of credit the acceptance fee is normally paid by the importer and the BDR charge is usually paid by the exporter/drawer unless the letter of credit specifically states otherwise. Who finally pays the charges is a function of the relative negotiating strengths of the trading parties.

Facility Setup

The procedures for setting up a bankers acceptance financing facility vary from bank to bank, but in general they follow those outlined below. Before a bank can accept drafts it must establish a line of credit for the customer up to which he or she may draw drafts. In addition, the bank usually concludes an acceptance agreement with the customer that stipulates the conditions under which he may draw drafts, including:

- The obligation of the drawer to repay BAs at maturity.
- The right of the bank to hold title documents and to take a security interest in the goods of the underlying trade transaction.

If the BA originated in the exporter's draft required under a time letter of credit, the credit application itself is the agreement obligating the importer to repay the bank. In clean, independent bankers acceptance transactions, however, a separate acceptance agreement is usually necessary.

It is also common practice for a bank to ask its bankers acceptance customers to presign a supply of blank drafts and return them to the bank. The purpose of using these presigned drafts is to avoid delays in selling the BA in the market on the same day it was created. If the bank does not have the customer's presigned draft or power of attorney, the customer must deliver the completed draft to the bank by a certain time. If the customer misses the delivery deadline, the bank cannot deliver the acceptance to the dealer to whom it has already been sold. Furthermore, the bank must hold the acceptance overnight, thereby increasing its funding costs. When the bank is finally able to sell the acceptance, the dealer's discount rate may be higher than it was when the account officer quoted the all-in rate to the customer. In this case, if the delay is the customer's fault, he or she is usually required to pay the difference.

Documentary Requirements

At the time the BA is created, the bank must have documentary evidence that the trade transaction is eligible for BA financing. For documentary BAs created under the terms of a time letter of credit, the letter of credit itself provides all necessary evidence. For clean BAs, requirements vary depending on the category of the transaction:

- *For pre-export*, the contract of sale is required.
- *For import or export and for shipment between foreign countries*, a statement of purpose is required that includes:
    Shipping date.
    Amount of financing.
    Countries of import and export.
    Nature of the goods.
    Period of financing required.
    A statement that no other financing exists for this transaction.
- *For U.S. domestic shipment*, a statement of purpose is required that is identical to the one described above, except that "countries of import and export" is replaced by "states of origin and destination."

- *For storage of readily marketable staples, U.S. domestic or foreign,* a limited statement of purpose and title document, usually the warehouse receipt, are required. Goods can be released to drawer/buyer under a trust receipt.
- *For dollar exchange acceptances,* request for financing with tenor is necessary.

SUMMARY

Bankers acceptances are attractive to banks, borrowers, and investors for a variety of reasons.

Advantages to the Bank

- The bank may use investors' money rather than its own to advance funds to borrowers, thus increasing the bank's lending supply.
- Proceeds from eligible acceptances are exempt from reserve requirements, thus increasing their profitability.
- Eligible BAs held in portfolio provide better liquidity than conventional loans, because they can be sold easily in the money market.

Advantages to Borrowers

- Acceptance financing can generally be obtained at a cost lower than that obtained on straight loans.(However, companies able to issue their own prime commercial paper will probably find BA rates relatively unattractive.)
- BA financing may represent expansion of a customer's borrowing capacity, because the legal limit on outstanding eligible BAs is separate from the limit on other loans.
- BAs may represent a source of funds in times of tight liquidity.

Attractiveness to Investors

Investors are eager to purchase bankers acceptances because they are short-term, low-risk, relatively high-yield investments with immediate liquidity:

- *Short term,* because acceptances eligible for discount are limited by the Federal Reserve to a tenor of six months.
- *Low-risk,* because they are the irrevocable obligation of a commercial bank.

  Note: "Prime" quality BAs are those created by prime commercial ("money center") banks. The large regional banks also create BAs. However, because investors perceive them to carry greater risk than prime acceptances they demand a higher rate of return, which reduces the bank's spread and makes these acceptances more expensive to obligors. In some cases the bank may absorb the additional cost in order to attract a larger share of the bankers acceptance market.

- Generally *higher yield* than Treasury Bills, especially when money is tight.
- Immediately *liquid,* because they can be converted to cash at any time by selling them to another investor.

Approximately 90% of all international trade is conducted in U.S. dollars, although there has been a marked increase in trade conducted in other currencies, notably Japanese yen. The predominant market for U.S. dollar BAs is in the United States. Therefore the overwhelming majority of U.S. dollar BAs are drawn on and accepted by U.S. banks. Dollar-denominated trade payments are, moreover, frequently routed through a U.S. bank in order to gain access to the U.S. acceptance market. Consequently, a solid understanding of the mechanics of the dollar acceptance market is a fundamental tool of trade finance.

7 Customer Service

In theory all areas of a bank work together to serve the customer, that is, to deliver customer satisfaction. Practically speaking, however, several different banking areas are involved in processing trade items, and interdepartmental cooperation is sometimes difficult. The difficulty has many causes, but one of them lies in the tendency of personnel employed in the various banking areas to have their own idiosyncratic view of the relative importance and technical requirements of the trade services.

THE ROLE OF CREDIT PERSONNEL

The customer's first point of contact with a bank is usually the account officer. Different banks classify this key person differently. Variously titled "loan officer," "credit officer," "calling officer," "line officer," or even "relationship manager," one major bank has simply named them "bankers." In any event, training in credit analysis* marks the beginning of their bank employment. The credit or lending perspective permeates the traditional banking environment; hence this training permanently distinguishes these officers from other bank personnel. Throughout their banking career, the question is asked: "Does this officer have credit training?" A positive answer gives credibility even when unjustified on other grounds, and a negative answer casts doubt despite all other evidence. To the extent that a narrowly defined "credit curriculum" inhibits many bankers' understanding of the technical logic and the processing requirements of the noncredit services and constrains the ability to respond imaginatively to the fundamental financial needs of their customers, the traditional credit perspective hampers the attempts of U.S. bankers to think innovatively about the business they are in and the services they provide.

Finally, the traditional credit bias leads many United States bankers to make what seems to non-U.S. bankers a spurious distinction between the credit function and the noncredit, or operating, services. Unfortunately for the banking customer dependent on the noncredit services, many U.S. account officers seem to perceive the operating services as being on a less than equal footing with the lending or credit function.

The Role of the Account Officer

United States bankers have historically viewed their role as one of accepting deposits and making loans, and they have traditionally focused on arranging

*Paul S. Nadler and Richard B. Miller, *The Banking Jungle: How to Survive and Prosper in a Business Turned Topsy Turvy*, Wiley, New York, 1985, pp. 99–102.

large short-term and working capital loans to the near exclusion of banking opportunities arising from their customers' trade flows (export sales and cross-border purchases of raw materials and supplies). This situation contrasts sharply to that prevailing outside the United States where a customer's banking needs arising from trade transactions may constitute the bulk of that customer's banking business. In banks outside the United States, training in credit analysis has traditionally been offered only at the conclusion of a lengthy (sometimes ten-year) clerical apprenticeship in which young bankers are systematically rotated through the various processing areas: Deposit Services, Collections, Letter of Credit (i.e., the "Bills Department"). To bankers trained in this tradition, credit is but one among many financial services offered by a bank, and the bank officer is as comfortable assisting the customer with transaction-based services as in performing a credit analysis.

Perhaps in response to this bias, when it became prudent in the 1970s to maximize fees to be derived from the noncredit or operating services, many U.S. bankers concluded that the proper role of the account officer was to be a generalist capable of identifying customer "need" and calling in the appropriate technical specialist to conduct and conclude the sale. To the extent that a bank's complete product line may include 60–70 financial services, the concept of the generalist banker able to orchestrate banking capability on behalf of the customer was a useful one. Perceptive account officers understood the marketing implications of the generalist role. They understood, often intuitively, that successful marketing no longer depended solely on "how much can I lend," but increasingly on "what service can I provide."

Those bankers who embraced the new point of view made a concerted effort to learn both the bank's traditional product line and the newly created financial services. It is standard practice in the banking industry to rotate account officers through a series of assignments covering a wide range of customers with differing needs. This practice enables enterprising bankers to learn in depth the various financial services required by a variety of bank customers. In addition, many banks also formed specialist or technical sales teams to support the marketing efforts of the account officer. Over time, account officers working with these technical specialists absorb a good deal of their expertise. Thus a "trickle-down" effect can be attributed to the activities of the specialist or technical sales teams.

Originally, the danger was that bankers would adopt a "product of the week" mentality, selling bank services indiscriminately to corporate customers. However, the less talented banker often used the generalist role as a screen to permit continued single-minded focus on the credit function. Banking customers are outspoken when they criticize the seeming inability of some bankers to consider customer banking needs in other than a narrow credit sense or, as one corporate treasurer put it, "Bankers have their own peculiar [credit-oriented] view of the business we're in."

Administrative Sales/Service Assistant

In those instances in which a bank's calling officer perceives his or her mission to be primarily concerned with the credit function, the servicing of noncredit transactions will generally fall to others. The customer service contact person in these situations will usually be an administrative sales or service assistant who is responsible for assisting customers with their noncredit banking transactions.

At a practical level, the account officer's administrative assistant is often the person both best situated and most qualified to coordinate banking personnel in a complex troubleshooting activity involving more than one processing area. Because an enterprising administrative assistant gains practical experience in resolving problems, this person may also become quite adept at helping customers initiate transactions, that is, at giving instructions to the bank in such a way that minimizes the likelihood of problems arising later.

ORGANIZATION OF BANKING OPERATIONS

Banks providing trade services perform two distinct functions: first, processing the item (i.e., initiating the appropriate debit and credit entries); and second, processing information pertaining to the item. From the perspective of banking operations, an item can be described in terms of three functional stages: receiving the customer's *instruction, processing* the item, and *advising* the customer of the bank's actions regarding the item. Thus item processing is sandwiched between two information processing steps—the instruction and the advice.

A trade service is initiated when a bank customer (either importer or exporter) *instructs* the bank to process a specific trade item (letter of credit, documentary collection, bankers acceptance). Instructions may be transmitted via various communication modes: The customer may pick up the telephone, write a letter or, in more sophisticated environments, communicate directly with banking operations via electronic hookup. Regardless of how the instructions are relayed to the bank, they constitute the customer's definitive orders for processing the item.

Once the bank receives the instruction, it *processes* it. Processing is performed by the operating department responsible for that category of item: International Paying and Receiving, Letter of Credit, Collections. The department processes the item according to the rules and regulations governing the particular class of item and in accordance with the customer's instructions. The last processing step is the appropriate computer entry to the customer's account, namely, the customer's account number, details of the transaction, and the appropriate debit or credit, which settles the item as far as the bank is concerned.*

Following the processing of the item, the bank *advises* the customer of actions it has taken on the customer's behalf and at the customer's request. Records stored for the Central Accounting Department are typically used to produce the customer's monthly statement of account ("statement"). Today many of the larger banks supplement their bank statement with other, more timely means of advising their customers, for example, via a proprietary cash management system.

The Technical Perspective

The banking operations area processes trade items according to instructions it receives from its customers and according to the rules governing them. Ultimately the goal is satisfactory settlement of the trade item. Responsibility for executing the transaction accurately and in a timely fashion normally rests with a specific processing department within banking operations.

The responsibility is a major one. At senior levels, technical specialists are charged with maintaining the integrity of the bank's service as it is perceived by others. Banks around the world are able to exchange services on a correspondent basis precisely because a common, reliable core of international banking practice has developed over time. Consistency or uniformity of practice is not 100%, and there are difficulties, but on the whole international commerce is possible because banks have confidence in the reliability and integrity of the services they exchange with each other.

Senior technical experts feel keenly the responsibility to maintain the reputation and integrity of the financial services their banks provide, and they tend to accept the responsibility as a personal one. These technical experts seem at times to be almost immune to "normal" bank concerns. Usually active members of professional technical societies, they tend to seek corroboration

---

*An item may have to clear through several banks before final settlement is achieved. See Chapter 2.

of the correctness of their actions from their technical counterparts in other banks rather than from senior (nontechnical) officials in their own bank. They seem to view customers and nontechnical officials skeptically, that is, with a general lack of confidence in their desire to uphold the technical integrity of a specific financial service. These experts often have great influence in their organization. With a letter of credit, for example, the bank's reputation and a portion of its bottom line may rest on the professional judgment of the bank's letter of credit technical experts.

At lower levels, clerical personnel process items according to established rules, which derive from government regulation, commercial law, banking regulations, and trade practice. Taken together these rules and regulations form the technical perspective or point of view which constitutes the "product or technical logic" governing a particular service such as funds transfer, letter of credit, or documentary collection. Bank managers assess individual job performance not only in terms of productivity but also in terms of the ability to master the rules and adhere to them in practice. Moreover, this ability is a major component in the job-related self-esteem that derives from peer recognition.

Customer Service Personnel

Most processing departments maintain a Customer Service area whose primary responsibility is handling customer inquiries. The quality of training that Customer Service personnel receive differs greatly, as does the quality of the inquiry systems they employ. Wide disparities may exist in the skill level of Customer Service personnel located in different banks, or even in different processing areas within the same bank. They may be trained to locate trouble items within their own department only (intradepartmental inquiry), or they may be trained to seek problem resolution in the broader banking channels (interbank inquiry).

Given the limitations of many Customer Service units attached to a bank's processing areas, often the person most qualified and best situated to conduct a complex troubleshooting activity is the administrative sales/service assistant in the credit area. Guidelines for effective troubleshooting are presented later in this chapter.

TRANSMITTAL SYSTEMS

Documents and payment instructions of various kinds (e.g., checks, collections, payment orders, foreign drafts, and drafts drawn under letters of credit) move between buyer and seller, between banks, and across national borders. The system for transmitting documents plus the network of correspondent banking relationships that enables banks to debit and credit each other's accounts on their books make up what are loosely referred to as *banking channels*.

Air mail, the least expensive mode of transmittal, may often be the least reliable as well. Delivery can take anywhere from two days to several weeks. The sender has no control, and no reliable way of tracking lost items. But bank and trading parties must rely on air mail when no alternative, such as a courier service, is available.

Courier Services

In recent years, private courier services have been established to reduce document transit time, and some banks have developed their own courier services as a way to enhance their customer service offering. Couriers offer more or less fixed schedules based on airline timetables, and most provide some measure of control—receipts and logs, for example. A good courier can guarantee delivery within one to two days of pickup depending on location and is responsive to customer concerns regarding lost or delayed items and changes in airline schedules. The courier service is often faster than airmail, usually more reliable, and always more expensive.

TROUBLESHOOTING

Troubleshooting may be described as coordinating the problem-solving activities required to locate and straighten a procedural kink in the processing of a single trade item. Recurring problems may present a significant opportunity to enable a customer to do a piece of business faster, cheaper, more easily, or with less risk. Normally improvements can be achieved by manipulating either:

- Technical elements to reduce or eliminate risks or processing delays.
- Or elements of the cash management and/or document transmittal system to speed up the processing and/or increase the level of detail provided about a trade item.

In today's cost-conscious world, the goal is to reduce costs and increase processing efficiency. Bankers and customers alike need to be able to pinpoint problems in order to seize an opportunity to streamline an existing system. Thus the first task of Customer Service is to solve the immediate problem as promptly as possible, but perhaps even more important in the long run is the need to identify the systemic source of the problem and arrange permanent improvement.

General Guidelines

As a practical matter, anything that *can* go wrong *may* go wrong with the processing of a trade item. However, when dealing with a bank's technical experts, bankers and customers would do well to remember two things: first, a bank obtains the authority to act from the customer's instruction to the bank, or from the rules and regulations governing processing of specific transactions and second, the perspective of a bank's technical personnel is permanently influenced by the rigorous training they receive in the technical rules and regulations governing the service. Moreover, most technical experts have completely internalized the rules giving legitimacy to the correctness of their actions. As technicians they know *what* can be done but are not accustomed to explaining *why* actions can or cannot be taken. Thus the expert who says impatiently, "You can't do that!" can be tactfully asked to explain the technical reasoning behind the judgment. Does it, for example, violate the customer's instruction to the bank, or a banking rule or regulation governing the transaction, or the bank's own standard operating procedure?

Once the technical logic governing the transaction is identified, it is possible to engage in a collaborative problem-solving activity with the technical expert in order to assess realistically the technical options available for resolving the problem. The effectiveness of this activity is usually enhanced by the ability to convey understanding and respect for the relevant technical issues. Therefore, when a troubleshooting activity requires problem solving with a technical expert, the following guidelines can prove useful in achieving the desired result.

First, *present your case as a problem* and ask the expert to suggest a viable solution. Technical experts are great problem solvers, but they are usually less than enthusiastic when "outsiders"—bankers and customers alike—offer their own solutions to a problem. The reason for their lack of enthusiasm is understandable: solutions posed by non-technicians rarely take into account all the relevant technicalities. As a result, their solutions are normally less than optimal or outright impossible. Stating your case as a problem has a second advantage: It ensures that underlying assumptions are made explicit, thus avoiding the common pitfall, "Oh, if I'd only known *that's* all you wanted."

Second, *identify the technical logic* governing the transaction. Does it derive from:

- the customer's instruction to the bank, or
- a rule or regulation governing the transaction, or
- the bank's own standard operating procedure?

Third, *confirm your understanding* of the technical reasoning involved in the point under discussion. One easy way to do this is to restate in your own words what the expert is telling you. At the same time it is possible to separate the immutable technicalities from those that may be altered.

This approach presents a concrete benefit to bankers: if resolution of the problem is unavoidably unattractive to the bank's customer, you are nonetheless prepared to explain the technical reasons why the bank cannot fulfill the customer's request. You can also be prepared to suggest an alternative structure to avoid a recurrence of the problem.

The materials that follow are designed to identify typical problems derived from the technical logic inherent in each of the classical trade services. They are divided into three major categories:

- *What Can Go Wrong?* describes the most common causes of procedural delay and suggests useful remedies.
- *Preventive Actions* describes actions a bank customer can take to *prevent* processing delays.
- *Initiating the Service* offers some practical suggestions for issuing instructions to a bank in a way that will reduce the likelihood of problems occurring later on.

What Can Go Wrong with A Money Transfer?

Because a transfer of funds may be executed entirely by electronic means and because both the amounts being transferred and the negative consequences of an error may be substantial (as in a large foreign exchange transaction), customers are understandably concerned that their payments be executed properly.

The procedures required for the settlement of claims from errors committed in connection with U.S. dollar transactions are laid down in the "Rules on Interbank Compensation," approved by the New York Clearing House and the Council on International Banking.

The most typical errors fall into three major categories:

- The payment is late.
- The payment was made to the correct bank, but credited to the account of the wrong beneficiary.
- The payment was made to the wrong bank.

Common procedural remedies for these three basic error types are described in Table 7.1. They are but a few of many possible.

The concept of value date is fundamental to understanding these remedies. The *value date* is the date on which the bank is to process the payment according to the customer's instructions, regardless of the date on which the payment is to be *settled* (i.e., when the funds are to become available as cash). Suppose, for example, that on June 1 a customer instructs the bank to execute a payment on June 3 and to settle the transaction using next-day funds. The value date is June 3, the date on which the bank is to execute the payment as instructed. The funds are available on June 4 (next day). To increase efficiency and accuracy, many banks are urging their customers to send instructions prior to the value date so the banks can process the payment (enter it into the computer) and have it ready to execute (release) early on the value date.

Table 7.1 Procedural Remedies for Three Common Money Transfer Claims

If (Error)	Then (Procedural Remedy)
Payment was late.	*Back valuation:* Payment will be corrected by posting an entry to the beneficiary's account as if it had taken place on the earlier (correct) value date.
Payment was made to correct bank but credited to account of wrong beneficiary.	*Amendment of beneficiary:* Payment will be corrected by adjustment on the books of the receiving bank (i.e., the bank will debit the demand deposit account of the wrong beneficiary and credit the demand deposit account of the correct beneficiary with back value or compensation).
Payment was made to wrong bank.	*Payment made in error:* Payment will be corrected by asking the incorrect receiving bank to return the funds, and compensation will be arranged.

The Money Transfer Instruction. The following information is likely to be required by any bank processing a payment instruction:

- Customer name
- Account number
- Value date
- Amount
- Funds paid to/in favor of
- Funds received from/by order of
- Test key

Preventive Actions. Errors do not occur in a vacuum. Sometimes banks make errors, sometimes customers make them. When errors occur, it is a basic concept of interbank compensation that whoever is responsible for the error pays for it. Customers cannot control their banks, but in general, anything they can do to improve the efficiency of their own operation is likely to result in improved service. For example, bank customers can improve the quality of money transfer service they receive from their banks by taking the following actions:

- Train clerical personnel to *conform to the format* suggested by the bank that processes most of their international payments. By accepting responsibility for formating their own payment instructions correctly, customers can gain control over quality by eliminating the necessity for the bank to reformat the data.
- *Perform a value date reconciliation* as soon as possible. Customers who do so are able to ensure that the beneficiary obtains the funds as quickly as possible, that compensation costs are kept to a minimum, and finally that a compensation claim can be made within time limits set by the rules.
- Ask a technical expert on compensation to *clarify the compensation procedures to be followed in the event of error*—whether *customer or bank*. Because of time limits set on bank liability in the event of errors incurred in the electronic transfer of funds, it is imperative that bank customers perform their role in a timely and accurate way.

What Can Go Wrong with a Documentary Collection?

Documentary collection problems generally fall into one of two categories: the transfer of title to the importer or the receipt of payment by the exporter.

In such cases customer and bank should work together to help resolve the difficulty. Remember, documentary collections are governed by the exporter's instructions as specified in the collection order, and by "The Uniform Rules For Collections," I.C.C. Publication 322.

Common remedies to typical problems are given in Tables 7.2 and 7.3.

Collection Instruction.   Exporters initiate collections. The U.S. exporter may send the collection through his U.S. bank for transmittal to the foreign collecting bank or, in order to speed transmittal, he may send it directly to the collecting bank with a copy to the collection department of his own bank.

In both cases, the required information is the same:

1. Drawer's (exporter's) name, address, and reference number.
2. Date of draft, tenor, and amount.
3. Drawee's (importer's) name and address.
4. Type and number of documents (Collection Department will count documents to verify their presence).
5. How documents are to be released—whether against payment or acceptance.
6. Advising mode (cable, air mail, etc.) in the event of importer's nonpayment or nonacceptance of the draft.
7. Protest instructions (do/do not protest) in the event the importer refuses to accept or pay the draft.
8. Document transmittal instructions (air mail, courier) and who is to pay charges (drawer/seller or drawee/buyer).
9. Who is to pay respective bank charges.
10. Whether charges refused by drawee (buyer) may be waived; if so, the drawer will pay them.
11. Whether the draft may be held for arrival of merchandise.
12. Identification of "case of need," the exporter's representative in the importer's country, and the extent of his authority—for example, to "act fully on exporter's behalf," or to "assist in obtaining acceptance or payment of the draft as drawn, but is not authorized to alter its terms in any way."
13. Finally, a clause may be included which holds the importer responsible for all exchange differences arising from the inability of the collecting bank to remit payment immediately in U.S. dollars. This

Table 7.2 United States Importer's View of Common Documentary Collection Problems

Transaction Type: Inward Collection, payable domestic
Major Concern: Receiving title to the goods
Bank Role: Presenting/collecting bank[a]

Importer's Problem	Account Officer Needs to Find Out	Suggested Action
"Are the documents here? The goods aren't due for another week, and I don't want to pay early."	*Did the exporter specify an arrival draft?*	An arrival draft allows the importer to wait until the goods arrive before requiring him to pay or accept the draft.
	No	Under I.C.C. Publication 322, the importer is responsible for paying promptly. However, legal action is required to *compel* him to do so.
	Yes	Exporter probably expects to wait to receive payment.
"Why haven't I received the title documents yet?"	*Are documents delayed in transit?*	Nothing can be done about this delay; suggest review of transit mode for subsequent transactions.
	Documents against payment transaction?	The bank can arrange for the release of the goods to the importer via steamship guarantee or airway release.
"I [importer] refuse to pay!"	*What is the importer refusing to pay?*	
	Fees, charges, and interest?	Fees, charges, and interest can usually be waived automatically by the collecting bank, unless the collection order specifically forbids waiver.
	Refusing to honor the draft?	If importer is refusing to honor the draft, operations will follow exporter's instructions regarding protest.

[a]The collecting bank has two customers: the foreign branch or correspondent bank from which it received the documents and the importer. Occasionally this dual set of customer relationships causes conflicts. At such times, the operating department typically feels most keenly its obligation to its customer, the remitting bank; and the account officer in the credit area typically identifies with the bank's obligation to its customer, the importer.

Table 7.3 United States Exporter's View of Common Documentary Collection Problems

Transaction Type:	Outward collection, payable overseas
Major Concern:	Receiving payment for goods shipped
Bank Role:	Remitting bank

Exporter's Problem	Account Officer Needs to Find Out	Suggested Action
"Why haven't I received payment yet?"	*How were documents sent?*	
	Mail	Mail service is slow. The exporter might consider using the bank's or an independent courier service next time.
	Courier	If bank's courier, check with appropriate operating area.
	How was payment to be remitted?	
	Cable	At exporter's expense, the collecting bank can be contacted to verify if/when payment was sent. *Note:* Payment is sent by cable only for large amounts because of the cost factor involved.
	Draft or check	Checks are less costly than cable but also slower. Bank's courier may be able to shorten transit time.
	Has the importer refused to pay the draft?	If so, the collecting bank will follow the exporter's protest instructions. Unless the exporter gave specific instructions to protest a dishonored draft or to pursue other legal processes, the collecting bank is under no obligation to do so. *Note:* This probably means the buyer has backed out but the seller has shipped the goods. The bank cannot help except to suggest letter of credit terms next time around.

"The bank overseas released the title documents, and I've lost control of the goods without receiving payment."

Discussion: Under I.C.C. Publication 322, the collecting bank is required to pay. However, it is unlikely to do so voluntarily, and the U.S. exporter may have to file a law suit in the importer's country against the collecting bank in order to obtain payment. The exporter may be understandably reluctant to initiate legal action in a foreign country; however, he may urge the operating area of the remitting bank to use moral persuasion to encourage the collecting bank to pay, but it cannot compel that bank to do so. In this situation, the remitting bank continues to act solely as the exporter's *agent* in the transaction.

clause theoretically mitigates the U.S. exporter's potential foreign exchange transfer risk.

Preventive Actions.   The importer or exporter can take the following actions to ensure that the transaction unwinds according to their preferences:

- Importer may request an arrival draft, which permits the buyer to wait until the goods arrive before being required to pay or accept the draft.
- Exporter must instruct the bank regarding protest in the event the importer dishonors the draft.
- If exporter does *not* wish to waive charges, the collection order must so state.

What Can Go Wrong with a Letter of Credit?

Letter of credit transactions, of course, do not always unwind smoothly. When they do not, it often takes bank and customer working together to resolve the problems. First, remember the rule governing letters of credit: *Banks deal in documents not goods.* Second, in order to diagnose the problem, the bank must know the information presented in the diagnostic checklist introduced in Table 7.4.

Table 7.4 Letter of Credit Diagnostic Guide

What currency is it in?	Indicates funds transfer options (see Chapter 2).
What side of the transaction is the bank on?	
Importer	*Import credit:* The bank is the issuing bank.
Exporter	*Export credit:* In the U.S. the bank is probably paying as agent.
Did the bank confirm?	*Yes:* The bank is obligated to pay against conforming documents.
	No: The bank is not obligated to pay, but will do so provided the exporter presents conforming documents and the issuing bank provides sufficient funds.
Are there documentary discrepancies?	*Yes:* Payment can be refused.
	No: Payment cannot be refused on grounds that documents do not conform.

Ultimately, most letter of credit problems reduce to:

- The exporter cannot get paid because of discrepancies.
- The importer cannot get the title documents because of delays.
- The importer refuses to waive discrepancies.
- The importer suspects fraud on the part of the exporter.

Tables 7.5 and 7.6 summarize typical letter of credit problems and suggested action steps.

Application for a Commercial Credit.   The buyer applies for a letter of credit, but successful completion of a letter of credit transaction requires the thoughtful actions of all parties to the transaction: buyer, seller, and their respective banks. As with the documentary collection, thorough understanding of the operational implications of the structural choices available on the Application for a Commercial Credit* can increase the likelihood of a company receiving quality letter of credit service from its bank.

The following items are required on the application:

1.   The L/C reference number, which is normally supplied by the issuing bank.
2.   The current date.
3.   How the Credit is to be advised to the beneficiary: *short cable* (L/C reference number and account party) followed by airmail transmittal of the complete text is acceptable in most instances; *airmail* is slowest and cheapest; *full cable* (full text of the Credit) is fastest and most expensive.
4.   Advising bank.
5.   Full name and address of the importer/applicant.
6.   Full name and address of the exporter/beneficiary.
7.   The amount and currency of the Credit in both words and figures.
8.   The expiry date of the Credit, which represents the last date by which the exporter can present documents.

---

*Actual forms relating to letter of credit transactions are not included in this book because these forms vary from one bank to another. The best source for real samples is a commercial bank in the reader's community. A booklet of generic forms relating to letter of credit transactions is currently being revised by the International Chamber of Commerce and will be available from them shortly (I.C.C. Publishing Corporation, 156 Fifth Ave., New York, NY, 10010).

Table 7.5 United States Importer's View of Common Letter of Credit Problems

Transaction Type: Import credit
Major Concern: Receiving title to the goods
Bank Role: Issuing/paying bank

Importer's Problem	Account Officer Needs to Find Out	Suggested Action
"I can't get the title documents from your letter of credit department!"	*Documents stuck in letter of credit operations?*	Account officer can call Letter of Credit Customer Service unit to expedite.
	Discrepant document?	Importer may choose to waive the discrepancy.
	Not received by operations?	
	Not sent by banking intermediary?	Bank can cable (at importer's expense) for status report.
	Delayed in transit and the importer needs the goods immediately?	Bank can issue steamship guarantee or airway release.
"Your letter of credit people conducted an improper review. I've found a discrepancy, and I won't pay."	*Is the discrepancy legitimate?*	Account officer can call letter of credit operations to verify.
	Why doesn't importer want to pay? (Has the price of the goods moved against him?)	The bank's role is to service the payment and financing needs of the transaction, not to get involved in underlying commercial disputes.
	Why can't he pay?	Account officer can discuss refinance options: straight loan, acceptance financing, etc.

"My foreign supplier is complaining to me that he's being paid late"; or "He's being charged extra days of transit interest."	*Where are delays occurring?* (Here, there, transit time?)	Account officer can call Letter of Credit Customer Service unit to research. Buyer might structure subsequent Credits to this exporter for cable reimbursement.
"I suspect the exporter is trying to cheat me."	*Have documents been paid?* No	Letter of credit operations can perform a meticulous documentary review when they arrive.
	Yes, and they comply.	Sorry, it's too late for the bank to do anything about it.

TABLE 7.6 United States Exporter's View of Common Letter of Credit Problems

Transaction Type: Export credit
Major Concern: Receiving payment for goods shipped
Bank Role: Advising/paying agent/confirming bank

Exporter's Problem	Account Officer Needs to Find Out	Suggested Action
"I can't get paid."	*When were documents presented?*	Under I.C.C. Publication 400, letter of credit operations are charged with performing a documentary review and paying "within a reasonable time." In the United States, this normally means within 72 hours. However, turnaround time varies from bank to bank.
	Is there a documentary discrepancy?	
	Yes	Letter of credit operations will notify the exporter that it is holding the documents pending further instructions. The exporter has four options:
		• Correct and resubmit the documents, if possible.
		• Ask operations to cable (at exporter's expense) issuing bank to ask importer for waiver.
		• Ask bank to pay against reserve or guarantee.
		• Ask bank to send documents and draft on collection basis.
	No	Go to next question below.

What is the bank's role in the transaction?

Paying as agent under an advised credit?

Issuing bank has probably failed to fund its account with exporter's bank (its agent/correspondent) in anticipaion of the debit.

Account officer for the issuing bank may be able to authorize an overdraft in order to effect payment.

Exporter might consider requesting confirmed credit on next transaction.

Customer Service may be able to expedite.

Confirming bank?

9. The tenor describing the payment terms (sight or time), and the party on whom drafts are to be drawn.

10. Required commercial, transport, official, and insurance documents.

11. A clear, concise description of the goods. Detailed description does not increase protection under the Credit and may cause delays in processing the documents.

12. Shipping terms outlining the respective responsibilities of importer and exporter in the transaction, including who is responsible for arranging and/or paying for insurance coverage. If the exporter will provide coverage it must be evidenced by a document. Otherwise the application must stipulate that insurance coverage will be provided by the importer/applicant.

13. Ports of origin and destination and the latest date for shipment of the goods, normally about two weeks prior to expiration date of the Credit.

14. Whether or not partial shipments are allowed, i.e., whether or not the Exporter may ship the order in more than one shipment.

15. Whether or not transshipment is allowed. (See I.C.C. Publication 400, Article 29a.)

16. Number of days following shipment (as evidenced by the on-board date of the bill of lading) for exporter to present documents to the bank. Note that the number of days specified here does not extend the expiry date of the Credit.

17. Special instructions including any additional payment information, or any additional information required to facilitate payment under the Credit.

18. Where the bank should send the documents: directly to buyer or to some other party.

19. The name and address of account party if different from the applicant for the Credit.

Preventive Actions.   Successful completion of a letter of credit transaction requires the cooperation of all parties to the transaction: buyer, seller, and their respective banks. Discrepancies are best avoided through actions taken in advance to prevent them. For example:

- When they conclude the sales contract, importer and exporter should identify precisely the terms and conditions to be included in the letter of credit.
- When the importer applies for the Credit, he or she must take care to complete the application accurately and completely.
- When the issuing bank opens the Credit, it must take care to issue it accurately and in a form that assures compliance.
- When the exporter/beneficiary is advised of issuance of the Credit, he or she must check the Credit to make sure that he can conform to its terms and conditions. If not, he is responsible for contacting the importer/applicant to request an amendment to the Credit so that compliance is possible.

All this care is taken to minimize the likelihood of discrepancies arising at the payment stage. It should be noted that fully 50% of documents presented under letters of credit contain major discrepancies. Discrepancies disrupt a letter of credit transaction. They slow payment. Additional costs are incurred to resolve them, thus adding to transaction costs and cutting into bank profitability. Moreover the delayed payment to the exporter/beneficiary may adversely affect his cash flow and potentially *his* profitability.

Exporter/Beneficiary's Review of Credit. As we noted above, the beneficiary is responsible for checking the letter of credit immediately upon receipt to ensure that (1) its terms and conditions are as agreed upon in the sales contract and (2) it is possible to deliver the goods specified within the time allowed for a price not to exceed the amount stipulated in the Credit, and to comply with the other terms and conditions of the Credit.

Within this framework the seller/beneficiary should check the following items:

- The names and addresses of importer and exporter are complete and correct.
- Details of the credit:
    The type is that stipulated in the sales contract (e.g., irrevocable, confirmed, etc.)
    The amount is in the currency agreed to and sufficient to cover all

costs permitted by the contract (cost of goods, freight, insurance, fees, etc.)

The expiry and shipping dates allow sufficient time to prepare shipment and present documents.

- The insurance amount, effective date, duration, and risks covered are as agreed to in the contract.

- Shipment:

  The ports are as agreed.

  Special requirements for shipping *this* cargo are authorized by the credit, e.g., on-deck, partial shipment, charter party bill of lading, combined transport B/L with transshipment, and so on.

Exporter/Beneficiary's Review of the Documents.   Many of the large international banks develop checklists to enable their exporting customers to prepare documents that will conform to the terms and conditions of the letter of credit. The bank's customers may then tailor these checklists to fit the requirements of their Credits. Following is a beneficiary's checklist developed by the Marine Midland Bank, N.A.

Checklist Concerning Document Preparation and Examination

DOCUMENTS

The beneficiary must remain alert to the fact that the documents they present to the paying bank must completely agree in all respects with the terms of the credit. Any deviation eliminates the protection of the credit and source of funds and places them at the discretion of the buyer. The expedience of guaranteeing discrepancies may enable their draft to be paid, but the beneficiary cannot consider the proceeds cleanly possessed until a release of the guarantee is forthcoming.

When documents are presented, particular attention must be paid to the following points as they emphasize valid reasons for preventing or delaying payment:

DRAFT
- Does it bear the credit number?
- Is the tenor correct?

- Is the amount the same as the invoice (or less if the credit stipulates)?
- Does the name of drawee agree with credit requirements?
- Is the name of the drawer exactly the same as the beneficiary?
- Does the city where drawer is located appear by the date?
- Is it endorsed by the one to whom it is payable?
- Are there any restrictions that would prevent clean negotiation?

INVOICE

- Is it issued by the beneficiary, and signed by him if required?
- Is it addressed to the account party?
- Is the merchandise description exactly as shown in the credit regardless of the foreign language (including any misspellings)?
- Do the prices shown conform with the price basis, i.e., FOB, CIF, etc., indicated in credit?
- Do marks and numbers shown tie the invoice directly to the bill of lading?
- Is the amount of packing units (boxes, cartons, bales, etc.) in agreement with the bill of lading, and do the weights coincide?

INSURANCE POLICY OR CERTIFICATE

- Are all required risks covered?
- Is insurance for at least the CIF value plus 10%? If CIF value cannot be determined from documents, insurance should be at least value of the drawing or value of the commercial invoice, whichever is greater.
- Is the packing shown in complete agreement with the bill of lading?
- Is it dated earlier or the same date as the bill of lading or if dated later refers specifically to the particular bill of lading?
- Is it endorsed and/or countersigned in order to validate and transfer title as required?
- Are any warranties indicated such as "steel strapped cases" or "new steel barrels" which are not substantiated by the invoice or bill of lading?
- Are all copies in the set being presented?
- Does coverage specifically include "on deck" shipment if bills of lading so indicate?

BILL OF LADING

- Is bill of lading drawn to order of consignee, not endorsed to his order unless credit permits?
- Does notify party name and address appear?
- Are ports of departure and arrival correct?
- Does the general description on the bill of lading cover all merchandise invoiced?
- Does the type of packing and weights agree with all other documents?
- Are there any clauses which might make the bills of lading unclean such as "rusty drums," "repacked and recoopered," etc.?
- Unless otherwise specified, bills of lading must show that the goods are loaded on board—if stamped on bill of lading, it must be dated and signed or initialed.
- The "freight prepaid" indication must be shown on the bill of lading, if the freight is invoiced whether or not the credit specifically requests it.
- All of the copies comprising a set must be presented unless the credit indicates a different disposition.

OTHER DOCUMENTS

- Are they definitely identifiable with each other and with the invoices and bills of lading?
- Are inspection, analysis and weight certificates signed by one who is acting in the capacity required by the credit, e.g., "public weigher," "independent inspector"?
- Is the document titled to comply with the credit requirement, e.g., "Certificate of Origin," "Weight Tally," "Certificate of Analysis"?*

Exporter/Beneficiary's Options in the Event of Discrepancies. If a bank discovers a discrepancy in an export credit, it notifies the exporter/beneficiary and holds the documents pending further instructions. The beneficiary has four options, ranked here in descending order of desirability for the beneficiary:

*The preceding checklist reprinted from "Introduction to International Banking Services," 1983 edition, pages 44–46, published by Marine Midland Bank. Reprinted with permission.

1. *Correct a discrepancy in documents that he prepared and resubmit the documents.* This is not always possible after shipment, because many of the documents relate directly to the shipment.

2. *Ask the intermediary bank to cable the issuing bank to ask the importer/applicant to waive the discrepancy.*

3. *Ask the intermediary bank to pay against reserve* (guarantee). In this case, if the importer/applicant refuses documents, the intermediary bank will be repaid by the exporter/beneficiary.

4. *Ask the intermediary bank to submit the documents and draft to the buyer/applicant via the issuing bank as a collection item.* The exporter/beneficiary loses the advantages and protection of the letter of credit. He must wait for payment until the issuing bank collects the funds from the importer/applicant, and the intermediary bank collects them from the issuing bank.

PART **2**

INTRODUCTION

From the perspective of a banking customer, a bank's role is subordinated to the primary trading relationship existing between buyer and seller, and a bank's principal function is to support that relationship. In the international trade arena banks provide a business-to-business service, and their success or failure is often measured in terms of their ability to be sensitive to the broader needs of all parties to a transaction. In fact, the excitement traditionally associated with trade lies in the challenge to banker and business manager of juggling the respective points of view of all parties to a transaction, a juggling act made necessary because payment and financing structures ideally serve equally the needs of *all* the trading parties.

This understanding of the practice of trade contradicts the antiquated notion that international trade is characterized by a "rug merchant" mentality—an idea in itself based on the fallacious assumption that most international sales are "one-shot" deals. In fact, quite the opposite is true: Probably the majority of today's sales are repetitive in nature, involving the sale or purchase of goods or services on a recurring basis (e.g., seasonal, bimonthly, monthly). The term *trade flows* is commonly applied to describe these repetitive buying and selling patterns—for example, the goods and payment flows of an automobile manufacturer purchasing components from country A for a vehicle manufactured in country B and exported to countries C and D.

By contrast from a banker's point of view, the primary sales relationship is the one existing between the bank and its customer acting as either importer or exporter. Bankers focus on their customers' *trade flows* and they ask: What is the full product line of goods or services a customer is currently offering, or intends to offer, for export? What supplies and/or raw materials is the customer currently importing? What plans are there to expand international sources of supply?

ENVIRONMENTAL DYNAMIC AND MARKETING RESPONSE

Like other commercial entities banks react more or less creatively to threats and opportunities arising in the marketplace. Banking practice is currently undergoing radical restructuring as a result of widespread technological and economic changes. Throughout the 1970s bank management looked to the fee-based (noncredit) services to boost profits in the face of eroding profit margins. Those eroding margins came about as the result of three dominant forces: The emergence of what have come to be known collectively as "cash management services," ever-rising processing costs, and the worldwide debt crisis.*

The tactical outlines of a bank's sales and service program reflect its strategic response to perceived environmental threats and opportunities. As we have already seen, when a bank undertakes to process a trade item, it not only processes the item but information about the item as well. In recent years, banks have instituted major changes to standardize and automate both these processing functions. Banking operations have largely been automated. Information processing, however, involves the communication of transaction data both between banks and between bank and customer. In Chapter 3 we described SWIFT as the major system developed to improve the exchange of interbank financial messages. However, banks have also developed their own automated systems to improve the way they communicate with their customers, and their customers with them.

Cash Management Systems

The customer statement prepared by the bank is the traditional communications link between bank and customer. In recent years, many of the larger banks have instituted major changes to standardize and automate this exchange of information. In fact, a cash management system might be described as an automated bank statement. A computer terminal located in the customer's office enables the customer to retrieve information about debit and credit activity in the customer's own business checking account (demand deposit account). From the customer's point of view, the primary advantage of having literally fingertip control over account information is the ability to increase the efficient use of funds. For example, knowing when an expected credit has in fact arrived can decrease the customer's short-term borrowing needs and enhance the profitability of a sale, because funds received in payment can be invested promptly.

Individual banks seek to distinguish their systems based on the timeliness of delivery of transaction information to the customer or on the level of detail provided on individual transaction items. In addition, most systems provide an on-line inquiry capability (making it possible, e.g., to determine the cur-

*A. F. Daiboch, "Trade Banking Steps into an Aggressive New Role," *American Import Export Management*, October 1983, p. 26.

rent status of trade items). Finally, the most sophisticated systems enable valued corporate customers to initiate certain kinds of trade items, specifically money transfers, documentary collections, and letters of credit. The timely availability of detailed account information has enabled the sophisticated corporate treasurer or cash manager to "run lean," that is, to keep minimal balances on deposit with his bank. Historically these balances were an important source of bank revenue; their loss has contributed to the erosion of bank profitability.

Initially banks reacted to the loss of excess balances by adopting several tactics. One of the first was to shift marketing focus to the noncredit or fee-based services. During 1980–1982 this business was attractive to bank management because incremental gains did not involve additional funding costs (hence bypassing the then-high cost of funds), and income derived from the noncredit or fee-based services went straight to the bottom line of a bank's income statement, thus bypassing the balance sheet by not increasing asset levels. This initial marketing strategy concentrated on offering the customer a superior processing service based on "our people deliver better service," and it probably rested on a traditional image banks held of themselves as quasi "public servants."* In line with this view, customers were permitted to initiate instructions to the bank in their own idiosyncratic way, confident that "the bank will make it right." However, increasing transaction volumes coupled with rising processing costs have made it virtually impossible for most banks to continue to provide quality personal service without customer cooperation, and gross operating inefficiencies have become intolerable in an increasingly cost-conscious operating environment.

As constraints in the marketplace persisted, only the large money center banks and the very largest regional banks committed to the international marketplace have been able to continue to offer international trade services profitably. Why? Because they are the only banks with adequate resources to make the capital expenditures required to automate the processing of trade items. At the same time, the largest banks have instituted a fee-for-service pricing mechanism designed to replace revenues formerly obtained through income derived from the excess balances corporate cash managers used to leave on deposit with their banks.

To contain costs and to strengthen their customer relationships, many of the major international banks are actively assisting their customers to improve

---

*Stephen E. McLane, "Strategic Planning in Retail Banking," in *Banker's Desk Reference*, Edwin B. Cox (ed.), Warren, Gorham & Lamont, New York, 1983, p. 106.

the processing efficiency of their trade items by helping them to structure their instructions to the bank in a way that conforms to the formating requirements of the bank's own automated system. Customers willing to conform are being rewarded with improved service at more realistic prices.

In retrospect it seems obvious that processing inefficiencies and excess balances would travel hand in hand. Cash management systems, then, have had this double impact: Originally the mechanism that enabled corporate cash managers to reduce their bank balances, they have also provided banks with the technical capability to rationalize processing charges. Consequently, the initial marketing thrust ("our *people* deliver better service") has been replaced by "our *system* delivers more of what you need when you need it."

Bank Marketing of Trade Services

In earlier times importers and exporters structured their own transactions and banks, acting as "order-takers," provided the desired financial service requested by the customer—whether letter of credit, documentary collection, or whatever. Companies often financed their imports on a working capital basis rather than using such transaction-based techniques as bankers acceptance financing. Working capital loans typically fall under the jurisdiction of a company's treasurer or vice-president of finance. On the export side, expertise in structuring international trade transactions has historically rested with a company's export credit manager who, typically, named the desired payment term and selected a bank to provide the service. Letter of credit and documentary collection business was often awarded to a bank (or, more likely, split between two or three banks) based either on tradition, personal relationships, or as a reward for good work done elsewhere—arranging a difficult credit, for example. The banking counterpart of a company's export credit manager has been the trade specialist, who is normally the letter of credit or documentary collection technical expert who has risen through the ranks and gained wide experience with the documentation and payment structures required to transmit goods and payment across national borders.

In the past few years, as bank management has aggressively pursued fees for the classical trade services and as cash management capabilities have become increasingly sophisticated, bank product management has sought ways to distinguish a bank's trade services from those of the competition. One effective tactic has been the formation of specialist or technical sales units. Central to their success has been their ability to analyze a company's trade flows and design payment/financing structures tailored to the unique characteristics of specific situations.

The Transaction Profile introduced in Chapter 8 is designed to assist bankers and companies who engage in international trade to assess the characteristics of cross-border purchases and sales. The Trade Finance Model introduced in Chapter 9 is designed to provide bankers and companies with a model for designing innovative structures or evaluating the technical adequacy of payment/financing arrangements tailored to specific situations. Bankers may employ these tools to develop customer proposals based on streamlining existing payment/financing structures, and corporate managers can use them to assess the value and soundness of such proposals.

8 Transaction Profile

Trade transactions are frequently structured and executed under acute time pressure. As a result, transaction details are more likely to be buried in a rush of details extraneous to the financial concerns than to be presented in a systematic and orderly fashion. Consequently, central to the task of either evaluating an existing payment/financing arrangement or designing a new one is the ability to pick out and prioritize key transaction information. The Transaction Profile presents in an orderly sequence information derived from the trade map introduced at the conclusion to the Introduction to Part I. The profile begins with objective analysis of the nature of the transaction itself and subsequently addresses the concerns of the various parties to it.

It serves a second useful function: By focusing attention on the chronology of the procedure it pinpoints potential problems. Thus it is useful in improving the efficiency of communication among all parties to the transaction— buyer, seller, and their respective banks.

Transaction Profile

1. Describe the transaction's salient characteristics.

    Comment: A transaction profile provides banker and businessperson with important financial background information. The banker needs the data in order to qualify the business, that is, determine its profit potential, and the trade partners need to weigh potential transaction costs against ultimate profitability.

    - Type of goods:

Raw materials (commodities)	Components
Supplies	Consumer goods
Spare parts	Other

    Comment: The type of goods being financed may be a factor in determining the kind of financing technique which can be employed.

    - Annual volumes.
    - Average transaction size.
    - Frequency (including peaks and troughs):

Annual	Quarterly
Seasonal	Monthly
One-off	Bimonthly, and so on

    Comment: Annual volumes, average transaction size, and frequency indicate profitability potential to the banker and flag transaction cost(s) to the trading parties.

2. Describe payment details.

Comment: Payment details constitute a portion of the basic transaction elements.

- Currency.

Comment: Dollar-denominated transactions predominate; therefore the majority settle through New York. This fact has structural implications, for example, a need to access the U.S. acceptance market may influence the financing mechanism selected.

- Tenor.

Comment: Tenor refers to the length of the financing period. United States Eximbank (following the Organization of Economic Cooperation and Development) defines short term as being 180 days or less, medium term as being two–five years, and long term as being greater than five years (and generally less than ten years).

- Payment term.

Comment: Existing business can be described according to how it is currently being done. New or proposed business requires evaluating the relative usefulness of each of these classical payment terms:

    Cash in advance (prepayment)
    Letter of credit (confirmed, unconfirmed)
    Collection (D/P, D/A)
    Open account (foreign draft, foreign remittance, etc.)

3. Record the primary participants in the transaction.

Comment: Draw four boxes to represent seller, buyer and their respective banks. Place the seller in the upper left box so the goods will always flow from left to right across the page. Finally, designate the boxes immediately below seller and buyer as their respective banks.

4. Record any additional participants (e.g., government agencies, private insurance carrier, investor).

Comment: Draw additional boxes. Place government agencies next to the banks along the outside border of the diagram and position the investment market below the banks.

5. Document the chronological flow of goods, documents, and funds, existing or proposed.

Comment: Draw lines with arrows and number the arrows sequentially.

6. Profile the trading partners.

Comment: Steps 6 and 7 provide the basic background information needed to determine an optimal transaction structure. Generally speaking, *constraints*—whether posed by the business or economic situation of buyer or seller, or by their countries—provide the impetus for the design of innovative transaction structures.

* Exporter:
  Relative bargaining power/financial strength.
  Credit policy considerations (buyer/country limits).
  Preferred payment mode.
  Access to and cost of funds.
  Balance sheet considerations: liquidity/leverage.
  Ability to perform under the sales contract.
  Ability to provide accurate and complete documentation.
* Importer:
  Relative bargaining power/financial strength (credit risk).
  Balance sheet considerations: liquidity/leverage.
  Preferred payment mode.
  Access to and cost of funds.

7. Profile the respective countries.

* Exporter's country:
  Political stability
    What changes are expected in the political or business climate?
    How might anticipated changes affect the seller's ability to deliver under the sales contract?
    What is the likelihood of governmental intervention or expropriation of the seller's business?
  Currency strength
  Interest rates
  Export subsidy, and other incentives or regulations
* Importer's country:
  Political stability

What changes are expected in the political or business climate?

What is the likelihood of civil disturbance or war?

How might anticipated events affect the country's ability to meet its foreign debt obligations?

Foreign exchange transfer risk

Interest rates

Government incentives/import regulations or restrictions

- International environment:
  Economic factors
  Industry trends
  Market practice

8. Analyze the risks in the transaction.

Comment: Isolate risk factors first identified in Steps 6 and 7. (For additional information on risk, see Chapter 1.)

- Performance.
- Transaction.
- Payment:
  Nonacceptance
  Political
  Foreign exchange transfer
  Foreign exchange rate

9. What is your interest in the transaction?

- Exporter: See Step 9a.
- Importer: See Step 9b.
- Banker: See Step 9c.

Comment: Mutual insight into the decision processes outlined in Steps 9a–c can increase efficiency and profitability.

9a. Exporter:

- What are your marketing goals in this transaction?
  Land the sale against competitive pressure.
  Maintain market share.
  Penetrate attractive market more deeply.
  Penetrate new market.

- How would you describe your related business concerns?
    Credit policy considerations: buyer limits, country limits
    Balance sheet considerations: liquidity, leverage, cost of funds
    Other

9b. Importer:

- What are your goals in this transaction?
    Expand current source(s) of supply to safeguard availability.
    Obtain raw materials/supplies at best cost.

- How are you financing cross-border purchases?
    Working capital basis
    Acceptance financing
    Other

- How would you describe your related business concerns?
    Balance sheet considerations: liquidity, leverage
    Other

9c. Banker:

- Who is your customer?
    Exporter
    Importer
    Both

- Summarize the customer's goals.

Comment: If your customer is the exporter, refer to Step 9a; if your customer is the importer, refer to Step 9b. These items may be used to guide a marketing conversation.

- What is the *profit potential** of this business?

Comment: Use information obtained during Steps 1 and 2 to determine the relative attractiveness of the business to the bank in profitability terms. This determination in turn may affect your strategy. If the business is marginally attractive, and the risk is unacceptably high, you may decide to decline the business. Conversely, attractive

---

*This section on assessing profit potential has been freely adapted from Alfred F. Daiboch's discussion of the commercial banker's decision-making process in "Introductory Presentation on Trade Financing" for the President's Task Force on International Private Enterprise (unpublished paper), December 1983, p. 25. Daiboch names Relationship, Risk, Rate of Interest, and Repayment Term as the "4Rs" making up the variables influencing trade finance decision making.

but very risky business may be worth the time required to develop a transaction structure that either reduces risk or transfers unacceptable risk to other entities, a possibility discussed in Chapter 9.

- What risk is your customer willing to take in the transaction?
- What risk is the bank willing to take?
- What, if any, risk remains (i.e., unacceptable risk)?

Comment: Use information obtained during Steps 6–8 to analyze the risk levels in the transaction in light of the transaction's profit potential (see above).

- Is the *tenor* (financing period) appropriate for the goods (or project) being financed? Is the bank willing to take the risks identified in item 8 above for the desired period of time?

Comment: This question is intended to identify a possible disguised working capital loan.

- How acceptable is the *rate* at which the bank can do the business?

Comment: Multiple issues are involved in this question. The bank's first concern is to ensure that it will realize a profit on the rate which it is prepared to offer. The trading partners are concerned with containing transaction costs—costs that the seller ultimately passes on to the buyer.

On a short-term basis, the issue of rate arises in connection with letter of credit payment commission and bankers acceptance rates.

10a. How *satisfactory* is the current payment/financing structure?

Comment: This question should be considered on two levels: the transaction level and the business level.

- How well does the payment term serve the requirements of the transaction [e.g., needs arising from the business realities (opportunities and constraints)] within which importer and exporter operate?
- Are there recurring problems? Recurring problems may arise as the result of technical misunderstanding or inefficiencies, or they may arise as the result of inefficiencies in the way a bank coordinates its *communications/information* (cash management) and *transmittal systems* to deliver a trade service.

10b. How might the processing flow be *streamlined?*

Comment: Chapter 7 introduces ways to improve processing efficiency based on reducing or eliminating technical inefficiency.

10c. How else might the transaction be *structured?*

Comment: Business transacted initially under a given payment term may in time outgrow the structure if the underlying business reality changes. For example, business conducted initially on a letter of credit basis might eventually be conducted more economically on a documentary collection basis or even on open account terms.

In other situations, shifting from one payment term to another does not bring about the desired result, and the financing arrangement must be altered in order to bring about significant improvement. Such alterations often require the collaborative efforts of experts from several different banking departments. A design team coordinated by the customer's account officer and composed of trade service and cash management experts, often working with the bank's legal department, may be required to design the most innovative structures.

The analytic process outlined in the Transaction Profile can also be applied successfully to more complex transactions. By making it possible to *record basic information the same way each time,* employment of the Transaction Profile makes it possible to routinize what is standard in a trade transaction. The Transaction Profile is thus related to a pilot's preflight checklist, and the purpose is identical, that is, to ensure uniform and consistent results.

9 Trade Finance Model

In preceding chapters we analyze letter of credit payment and bankers acceptance financing structures. We investigate the properties of the draft and the related rights of a holder in due course. We discuss the technical logic inherent in these classical trade services. Using elements derived from these classical structures, we have constructed a Trade Finance Model to delineate acceptable payment and financing practice. The model can be used both to design and evaluate payment and financing arrangements.

The Trade Finance Model is based on four principles:

1. The banking transaction is completely separate from the underlying commercial transaction.
2. Documents represent the banking transaction.
3. The bank's undertaking is conditional.
4. The obligation to repay a bank for the financing it provides is contained in a legally enforceable debt instrument.

THE FUNDAMENTAL PRINCIPLES

1.   *The banking transaction is completely separate from the underlying commercial transaction.*

In its most basic form, the issue embodied in this principle refers to a bank's reluctance to become involved in the following situations:

*   Nonacceptance of the goods by the importer.
*   Commercial disputes over the underlying sales contract.
*   Fraud.

As a practical matter, it is unfeasible in economic terms for a bank to attempt to police the commercial aspects of trade transactions, and banks have historically made every attempt to divorce the banking transaction from the risks involved in the underlying commercial transaction. Article 3 of I.C.C. Publication 400 governing letters of credit is explicit on this point: "Credits, by their nature, are separate transactions from the sales or other contract(s) on which they may be based and banks are in no way concerned with or bound by such contract(s). . . ."

We have seen that the issuing bank's payment to the exporter under a letter of credit is made *without recourse*, that is, the issuing bank cannot recover funds from the seller if the buyer cannot reimburse the bank for financial reasons, or will not reimburse it for any other reason. We have also observed that an intermediary bank will negotiate an exporter's draft drawn under a letter of credit *with recourse,* that is, if the issuing bank fails to reimburse the negotiating bank for any reason, the negotiating bank can recover the funds from the exporter. Any financing arrangement structured to provide a bank full recourse back to the exporter may be highly desirable to the bank but will normally be unacceptable to the exporter.

In structuring financing on other than letter of credit terms, a bank typically employs the recourse mechanism to divorce the banking transaction from the underlying commercial transaction. In such instances a bank may assume the financial risk of the importer while retaining *limited recourse* to the exporter for nonpayment due to the situations noted above, namely nonacceptance of the goods by the importer, commercial disputes over the underlying sales contract, and fraud.

Practically speaking, then, the recourse mechanism may be used to allocate risk in a financing arrangement. A bank, for example, may accept the political risk of the importer's country and the commercial credit risk of the importer but refuse to accept the risks outlined above.

2. *Documents represent the banking transaction.*

The I.C.C. Publication 400 (Article 4) governing letters of credit is explicit: "In documentary credit operations all parties concerned deal in documents and not in goods."

We have already discussed the two principal documents of control, that is, the bill of lading (which may control title to the goods) and the draft (which may supplement the commercial invoice as the means by which the seller charges the buyer for the goods). Moreover we have seen that a bank can control the timing of the exchange of documents (as in a documentary collection) or examine them to assure conformity (as in a letter of credit). In either case, the net effect is that banks act based on documentary representation rather than on the actual events or facts on which the documents are presumably based.*

3. *The bank's undertaking is conditional.*

Under a letter of credit a bank undertakes to pay the seller up to the stated

---

*Henry Harfield, *Bank Acceptances and Credits* (5th ed.) Wiley, New York, 1974, p. 69.

amount of the credit *provided* that the seller presents conforming documents before the Credit expires. In a documentary collection the remitting bank will pay the seller *provided* that it has received the necessary funds from the collecting bank. In a similar way, banks normally specify the conditions under which they undertake to make payment or to finance a transaction. In general bankers set conditions in order to delineate the risks they assume in the transaction.

4. *The importer's obligation to repay the bank for the financing is contained in a legally enforceable debt instrument.*

The legal debt instrument under a letter of credit is the agreement contained in the Application for a Commercial Credit; in a bankers acceptance the instrument is the acceptance agreement executed by the bank's customer prior to creation of a bankers acceptance; the debt instrument in a term loan is implicit in the standard loan documentation that accompanies the loan. Finally, in a documentary collection (documents against acceptance) situation, the draft is the legally enforceable debt instrument.

Zenoff and Zwick identify three advantages of financing with drafts: first, they provide written evidence of obligations in terse, comprehensible form; second, they enable both parties to reduce the costs of financing and to apportion remaining costs equitably; and third, they are negotiable and unconditional, that is, their authenticity is not subject to disputes which may arise between the trading parties.*

Banks have historically employed negotiable instruments—the draft or bill of exchange and the promissory note—as the instruments of debt when tailoring trade finance arrangements to satisfy the practical requirements of specific transactions. In use since the Middle Ages, bills of exchange are currently governed by negotiable instruments law; moreover the negotiable instruments laws of most trading nations derive from principles originally articulated in the International Convention for Commercial Bills established by the Geneva Conference of 1930. In general, then, negotiable instruments law is useful because it constitutes a common international legal framework that enables banks and other commercial lenders to use the draft or bill of exchange as a reliable basis for financing their customers' trade transactions. In the United States, negotiable instruments law is contained in Section 3 of the Uniform Commercial Code.

_____
* David B. Zenoff and Jack Zwick, *International Financial Management*, Prentice-Hall, Englewood Cliffs, NJ, 1969, p. 383.

Negotiable instruments law states that the rights of a bona fide holder in due course are specifically free of any commercial disputes that may exist between the trading partners.* This principle is essentially the same as Article 3 of I.C.C. Publication 400 (i.e., banks are in no way bound by the underlying sales or commercial contracts). It means, for example, that where a drawee (buyer) might legitimately refuse to pay the drawer (seller) based on a dispute over the underlying sales contract, *such a dispute does not free the drawee from the obligation to pay a holder in due course.* In this sense negotiable instruments law may be said to render the rights of the holder in due course (investor in the paper) more secure than those of the original drawer of the draft.

In structuring trade finance arrangements, a bank will normally exercise great care to protect its rights as a holder in due course. This care is necessary because negotiable instruments law is not always consistent from one country to another, and variations in local practice may jeopardize a bank's rights. Even with this limitation, negotiable instruments law nonetheless provides bankers with a valuable legal starting point for the structuring of international trade finance arrangements.

Building from these four principles, we have constructed the Trade Finance Model (Table 9.1) for assessing the technical adequacy of payment or financing structures.

Table 9.1 Trade Finance Model

1. *What mechanism is used to divorce the banking transaction from the underlying commercial transaction?*
   Limited recourse arrangement.
   Other arrangement.
2. *How does a bank use documents to insert control into a financing arrangement?*
   Time their release.
   Examine them.
   Other.
3. *What are the conditions of the bank's undertaking?*
   Conditions designed to reduce risk.
   Conditions deriving from external factors, for example, government regulations.
4. *What constitutes the legally enforceable debt instrument in the financing arrangement? Why was it chosen?*
   Draft or bill of exchange.
   Promissory note.

*Gerhard W. Schneider, *Export–Import Financing*, Wiley, New York, 1974, pp. 205–209.

Generally speaking financial arrangements may be structured to capitalize on the financial strength of either importer or exporter, or on opportunities or constraints (most generally in the form of incentives or regulations) deriving from their respective national governments. To obtain an optimal financing structure, the bank will normally try to extend financing to the party commanding a financial advantage of one kind or another.

EXPORT CREDIT SUPPORT

Sometimes, however, the bank is unable to do a particular transaction either because it is up against its own legal lending limit for a specific country and cannot accept the additional risk, or it is unwilling to do the transaction usually because, for whatever reason, it has judged the foreign risk to be unacceptable.

At such times banks and exporters look to government entities for support. Government support of international trade has historically occurred through two mechanisms: first, *insurance* and/or *guarantee* programs that protect the insured party (exporter or bank) against the risk of nonpayment by the importer due to commercial and political risks; and second, *funding* and/or *subsidized financing* programs that make funds available at attractive (often below market) rates.* Government-supported loans are typically structured as either *supplier credits* or *buyer credits*. Although these terms are confusing to those unacquainted with them, they accurately identify the bank's customer (i.e., the obligor of the loan): In a supplier credit the bank's customer is the exporter, whereas in a buyer credit it is the importer.

Under a *buyer credit* loan format a U.S. bank extends financing directly to a foreign obligor, whether importer or bank. The payment term is generally a confirmed letter of credit (enabling the U.S. exporter to be paid at shipment), and the U.S. bank is wholly responsible for the loan documentation. The

---

*For additional information, see *The Chase Guide to Government Export Credit Agencies* (available from The Chase Manhattan Bank, N.A., One World Trade Center, 78th floor, New York, NY 10048), which examines government-supported export programs in more than 30 countries around the world.

buyer credit loan format is usually associated with large projects; however, it may also be used for short-term and medium-term trade finance.*

By contrast, under a *supplier credit* loan format the bank extends financing directly to the U.S. exporter. In this case, the payment term is usually open account or documentary collection with trade drafts payable at a specified future date. Supplier credits are also employed in the medium-term financing of capital goods exports, in which case the foreign importer gives the U.S. exporter a promissory note payable to the exporter. The exporter subsequently sells the drafts or notes to his or her U.S. bank, which becomes a bona fide holder in due course. Under the supplier credit format, the U.S. exporter arranges the loan documentation directly with the overseas importer and is contingently liable for the validity and enforceability of all debt instruments sold to the bank. (See Chapter 10 for an example of a supplier credit format.)

---

*A. F. Daiboch "Trade Banking Steps into an Aggressive New Role," *American Import Export Management*, October 1983, p. 28.

10 Practical Applications of the Trade Finance Model: Financing Foreign Receivables

To demonstrate how the Trade Finance Model works, we are going to employ it to analyze the procedural mechanics associated with three traditional methods of finance available to an exporter requiring financing of his or her foreign receivables. In Chapter 6 we discussed the time letter of credit as a financing tool. In this chapter we investigate three methods of financing based on the draft (bill of exchange):

- Advances against collections.
- Discounting trade acceptances.
- Funding with bankers acceptances.

These three structures are complementary but not generally interchangeable. For our purposes we understand the elements making up these structures as constituting the building blocks of trade finance. Our goal in this chapter is to analyze these typical financial structures in terms of their constituent elements. Trade bankers typically arrange these elements to tailor payment/ financing structures to the practical requirements of specific transactions. The fundamental analytic and problem-solving approach suggested by the Trade Finance Model, however, is the same, and it normally indicates areas where customization or innovation is possible. We rely on published descriptions of these financing techniques, principally those presented by Gerhard Schneider in Chapter 10 of his text *Export–Import Financing*.*

In the Transaction Profile we identify "type of goods" as one determinant of an optimal financing structure. At the broadest level we can consider four major categories of trade shipments:

- Relatively low-value commercial shipments such as textiles, garments, and other retail goods or supplies.
- Relatively higher value shipments of raw materials and supplies, including components, such as are found in computers and other manufactured goods.
- Relatively high-value commodities shipments such as minerals and farm products (rice, cocoa, coffee, etc.).
- High-value capital purchases such as production machinery.

*Gerhard Schneider, *Export–Import Financing*, Wiley, New York, 1974, pp. 346–348.

Further segmentation is possible within each category, but this classification is useful in considering appropriate financing arrangements in which some financing techniques are more appropriate to each category than are others. We begin by examining advances against collections.

ADVANCES AGAINST COLLECTIONS: COLLATERAL POOL

A company engaging in domestic trade can obtain a working capital loan from its bank by using the company's accounts receivable as security. A similar financing arrangement is available to exporters who wish to finance their foreign receivables or outward collections. Advances against outward collections are sometimes considered a viable alternative to international factoring for the financing of relatively lower value commercial transactions. Under an advance against collection, the bank lends to the exporter under a collateral pool of export receivables. Although the cash to pay down the financing should come from the importer, the exporter retains the full obligation to pay the bank whether the importer pays or not.

From the bank's point of view, the exporter's receivables form a pool of collateral against which the bank is willing to lend up to a stated maximum percentage of the total amount of receivables in the pool at any one time. The exporter's bank weighs a number of factors in determining the percentage it is willing to advance.* The principal ones follow.

Exporter's Credit Strength, Reputation, and Performance History. The bank looks to the exporter for payment should the importer refuse to pay; therefore the exporter must be creditworthy and reputable. Thus, the bank also evaluates the commercial performance history of the exporter to determine the risk that the importer might refuse to accept and pay the draft due to some commercial failure on the part of the exporter.

Importer's Credit Strength and Reputation. The bank interprets these as indicators of the importer's likelihood to accept and pay the draft.

Collection Record of Importer's Country. Importers in some countries pay drafts drawn on them promptly, whereas importers in other countries are

---

*Gerhard W. Schneider, *Export–Import Financing,* Wiley, New York, 1974, p. 346.

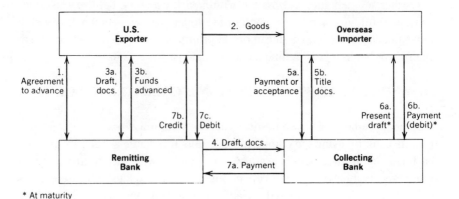

* At maturity

Figure 10.1   Advance against collections.

slower to pay.* A bank will advance a higher percentage against drafts drawn on importers in the prompt paying countries and may refuse to advance against receivables directed to the very slowest paying countries.

Nature of the Goods.   A lower percentage will be advanced for goods which are perishable, seasonal, or subject either to unpredictable changes in fashion or to stringent or difficult-to-meet quality standards.

TRANSACTION FLOW (Fig. 10.1)

Transaction Steps	Notes
1. The exporter's bank establishes a facility for advancing funds against the exporter's outward dollar collections.	In establishing the facility, the bank will weigh the following factors to establish a percentage of receivables up to which it is willing to lend: • Credit strength and business rep-

*These statistics are available through various banking publications, most notably through *The Chase World Guide for Exporters,* which publishes Chase's own collection experience; the credit terms being offered by U.S. exporting corporations in nine product categories; and the import and exchange regulations in more than 100 countries around the world.

TRANSACTION FLOW (Fig. 10.1) (Continued)

Transaction Steps	Notes
	utations of exporter and importer, respectively. • Collection experience in importer's country. • Nature of goods.
2. The exporter ships goods.	
3. The exporter (a) submits draft and documents to the bank, which (b) advances funds to the exporter up to the agreed-upon maximum percentage.	The bank will usually perfect its security interest in the goods by specifying that the bill of lading be consigned either to the order of the bank or to the order of the shipper and blank endorsed. The bank will also specify that the goods be covered by adequate insurance naming the bank loss payee.
4. The exporter's bank sends documents and draft to the collecting bank.	
5. The collecting bank notifies importer that documents have arrived and when the importer (a) either *pays* or *accepts* the draft, the bank (b) *releases* the title documents to him.	When a U.S. bank gives an advance on a U.S. exporter's foreign receivables, the legal jurisdiction for the transaction is the United States. Thus should a dispute arise between bank and exporter, the bank would be able to pursue the matter in the courts of the United States.
6. At maturity the collecting bank (a) presents the trade acceptance for payment and (b) debits the importer's account.	
7. When the Collection Department of the remitting (exporter's) bank (a) receives payment, it (b) credits	Under an advance against collections facility the bank retains recourse to the exporter should the

TRANSACTION FLOW (Fig. 10.1) (Continued)

Transaction Steps	Notes
the exporter's account and advises the Loan Department, which (c) debits the exporter's account, thus reducing the outstanding balance and freeing the line for additional advances.	importer fail to pay. Thus the exporter is obligated to repay advances made under the facility even in the event the proceeds of the collection fail to materialize.

Summary

In Chapter 2 we observed that the exporter does not normally obtain payment under collection terms until his bank receives the funds from the foreign buyer. An advance against collections facility provides one way for the exporter to finance these receivables using the underlying goods as security. An advance represents the bank's extension of a working capital loan to the exporter. One possible disadvantage to the exporter of financing deferred payment terms by obtaining advances is this: Both the receivables and the advances supporting them remain on the exporter's balance sheet and may affect his leverage and liquidity ratings. In a discount of the receivable (see next section), the receivable disappears and is replaced by cash which can be used to pay down the corresponding liabilities.

Advance Against Outward Collection: Single or Repetitive

Exporters of big-ticket trade shipments such as commodities sometimes wish to obtain financing for either a single collection or for repetitive shipments to a single foreign buyer. A bank may be willing to structure a financing arrangement based on advancing funds on a single receivable, or on a series of receivables to the same foreign obligor, with the underlying goods as security. However, it will weigh differently the factors it analyzes in establishing the maximum percentage of the draft(s) it is willing to advance. First, all parties to the transaction must have an undoubtedly sound reputation and credit standing. Second, the goods should be of a readily marketable nature, able to be sold easily and with little or no discount in the event the importer should refuse to pay or accept the draft. Finally, the importer should be located in a country known to pay its trade drafts promptly. The transaction flow is identical to that described previously for a collateral pool.

DISCOUNTING TRADE ACCEPTANCES

A *trade acceptance* is a draft or bill of exchange accepted by a buyer. As such, under negotiable instruments law it carries the full credit obligation of the importer to pay at maturity. An exporter may choose to hold a trade acceptance in portfolio and present it himself to the importer at maturity, although practically speaking trade acceptances are usually presented by a collecting bank in the importer's country acting on the instructions of the exporter's bank. However, an exporter who needs the funds prior to maturity may ask the bank to discount the acceptance with or without recourse to him.

In earlier times an exporter could shop around for the best rate. Today, however, international banks in general are reluctant to take the foreign risk represented by trade acceptances. Some banks, for example, only discount trade bills covered by export credit insurance, in which case the insurer must approve transactions prior to shipment. If the transaction is approved, the bank negotiates (i.e., purchases) the acceptance by discounting it. The discount mechanism is similar to the one employed in the discounting of a bankers acceptance: The bank advances to the exporter the face value of the acceptance less the discount charges until the maturity date. Because the bank is actually purchasing the instrument for value, it becomes a holder in due course and enjoys all the attendant rights under negotiable instruments law when demanding payment from the primary obligor, the buyer. Further, because the exporter actually sells the draft to the bank, the exporter is able to

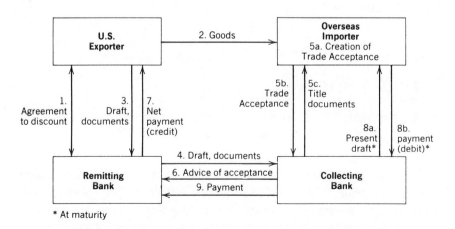

Figure 10.2 Discounting trade acceptances.

improve his balance sheet position by converting the receivable to cash without increasing his liabilities.

TRANSACTION FLOW (Fig. 10.2)

Transaction Steps	Notes
1. The exporter arranges for his bank to discount the trade acceptance(s).	Depending on the bank's policy, this may involve obtaining approval of the transaction from the bank's insurer.
2. The exporter ships the goods.	
3. The exporter submits documents to the remitting bank including a time draft drawn on the importer.	The draft is usually payable to the exporter and endorsed in blank.
4. The remitting bank sends documents, time draft, and collection order to the collecting/presenting bank in the importer's country.	
5. The importer's bank notifies the importer who (a) accepts the draft, thus creating a trade acceptance; (b) the importer returns the draft to the bank for safekeeping, whereupon (c) the bank releases the documents to him.	By accepting the draft, the importer accepts the unconditional obligation to pay the face amount at maturity to whoever presents the draft at that time. Upon receipt of the title documents, the importer can take possession of the goods.
6. The collecting/presenting bank normally advises the remitting bank of creation of the trade acceptance and holds it for presentation to the importer at maturity.	
7. The exporter asks the bank to discount the trade acceptance. The bank advances the face value of the draft minus discount charges until maturity.	The exporter's bank is now a bona fide holder in due course of the trade acceptance and has the right to receive payment at maturity.

TRANSACTION FLOW (Fig. 10.2) (Continued)

Transaction Steps	Notes
8. At maturity the collecting bank (a) presents the draft to the importer for payment and (b) debits the importer's account.	Settlement of the trade acceptance is final when the importer pays at maturity.
9. The collecting bank sends the payment to the exporter's bank (remitting bank).	

Summary

Discounting is relatively attractive to the exporter because it provides a means of obtaining off-balance-sheet financing. However, the practice of discounting trade acceptances is perhaps more common outside the United States. Certain prime quality U.S. importers have gained solid international reputations for immediately paying drafts drawn on them and for settling any commercial disputes directly with the seller. As a result, banks both inside and outside the United States have been willing to discount drafts drawn on these prime quality U.S. obligors. United States and/or overseas banks might be expected to be willing to discount the drafts drawn on foreign obligors with similar credit and business stature.

Under negotiable instruments law a trade acceptance is the technical equivalent of a bankers acceptance.* Thus theoretically trade acceptances could be routinely offered for rediscount to financial institutions willing to buy them as investments. The trade bills of the U.S. obligors described above might be especially attractive to financial institutions familiar with these prime quality obligors.

FUNDING WITH BANKERS ACCEPTANCES

A bank may choose to finance its customers' foreign receivables on an acceptance basis. Normally employed to finance goods sold on 180-day terms, acceptance financing is especially useful for raw materials, components, and general commodity financing. A deep secondary market for bankers accept-

---

*Henry Harfield, *Bank Credits and Acceptances* (5th ed.), Wiley, New York, 1974, p. 118.

ances combined with the lack of reserve requirements often makes it possible for the bank to obtain funding for eligible transactions at a cost significantly lower than alternative sources. This characteristic has perhaps contributed to the role bankers acceptances play in the structuring of supplier credits. The technical basis for the procedures governing acceptance financing combines negotiable instruments law and special Federal Reserve requirements (see Chapter 6).

The structure described here is one possible format for a supplier credit (see Chapter 9). In this arrangement the bankers acceptance serves as the underlying funding mechanism for the primary financing arrangement—discount of a trade acceptance under documents against acceptance payment terms. The analysis presented here is intended to raise issues and suggest possible solutions. Specific solutions are always found in the unique environmental factors surrounding a particular transaction. The elements of the transaction (e.g., acceptance, discount, and rediscount), including the associated rights of holder in due course have already been described in earlier chapters. Trade bankers employ these basic elements and others summarized in the Trade Finance Model to tailor payment and financing arrangements to the practical requirements of specific transactions.

TRANSACTION FLOW (Fig. 10.3)

Transaction Steps	Notes
1. The exporter and bank conclude an acceptance agreement.	
2. The exporter ships the goods.	
3. The exporter draws two drafts: • A time draft drawn on the foreign importer with a maturity date one–three days before the maturity date of the second draft described below. • A time draft drawn on the bank.	The difference in maturities allows the bank to collect the funds from the importer before it is obligated to make payment under the maturing BA. (See Steps 7 and 8 below.) Whether or not the exporter receives payment under the trade draft, he is still obligated to repay the bank under the BA.
4. The exporter's bank (a) accepts the draft drawn on itself and (b) dis-	By accepting the draft, the exporter's bank incurs a primary obliga-

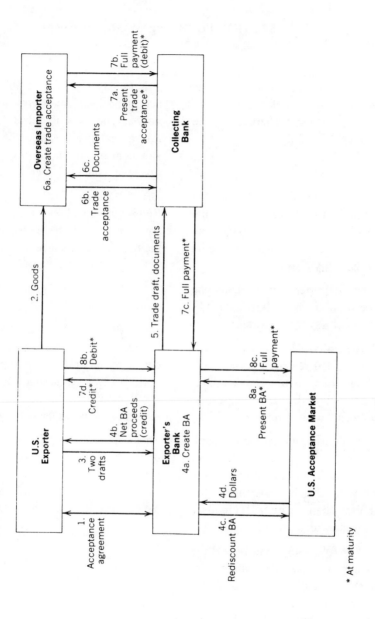

Figure 10.3 Funding with bankers acceptances.

TRANSACTION FLOW (Fig. 10.3) (Continued)

Transaction Steps	Notes
counts it, crediting the net proceeds (i.e., less an acceptance commission and discount charges) to the exporter's account.	tion to pay the face value of the acceptance at maturity to the holder. The bank is able to create this acceptance because the trade shipment is eligible for acceptance financing under Federal Reserve regulations.
In turn the bank (c) *rediscounts* the bankers acceptance and (d) uses the rediscounted proceeds to restore its own liquidity position.	Rediscounting allows the bank to shift funding of the transaction to the bankers acceptance market.
5. The exporter's bank sends the trade draft to the collecting bank, which notifies the importer.	
6. The importer (a) accepts the draft and (b) returns it to the collecting bank for safekeeping, whereupon (c) the bank releases the documents to the importer.	By accepting, the foreign buyer incurs a primary obligation to pay the trade acceptance at maturity, and legal jurisdiction for that obligation passes to the importer's country.
7. At maturity, the collecting bank (a) presents the trade acceptance to the importer and (b) receives the face value that it (c) remits to the exporter's bank, which (d) credits it to the exporter's account.	Should the importer fail to pay the draft, the exporter's bank has recourse to the exporter as drawer of the draft, unless bank and exporter have agreed otherwise.
8. At or following maturity, (a) the investor presents the bankers acceptance to the accepting bank for payment; the bank (b) debits the exporter's account for the face value of the bankers acceptance; and (c) pays the full face value of the bankers acceptance to the investor.	

Summary

In our hypothetical case the bank chose to create the bankers acceptance prior to the buyer's acceptance of the draft; therefore it accepts the risk that the buyer might refuse to accept or pay the draft, leaving the bank without funds to pay the holder of the bankers acceptance at maturity. From a strictly technical point of view, the bank would pay the holder of the bankers acceptance and could employ its right of recourse on the exporter as drawer of the draft to demand payment from him.

However, the bank will normally try to impose conditions to mitigate the perceived risk. The simplest solution, of course, is for the bank to agree to finance the transaction only from the time the foreign buyer accepts the trade draft to the maturity of the trade acceptance. However, the potential profit in a given trade flow may be such that a bank would wish to finance the entire period. In that case, there are several other structural alternatives. These structures are not prescriptive, but instead illustrate the procedural and technical elements which a bank manipulates to facilitate a given transaction. The bank might negotiate a limited recourse agreement with the exporter, reserving the right to look to the exporter in the event of nonpayment due to a commercial dispute or fraud. The exporter in turn might negotiate in the sales contract for the right to pursue the importer in the event of nonpayment. Finally, the financing arrangement might be structured under export credit insurance arranged either privately or through a government agency, in which case the bank would recover the funds under the appropriate insurance.

A bank will make an effort to structure payment/financing arrangements for a transaction or repetitive trade flow where it perceives the profit potential to justify the cost of arranging the structure. These costs are, of course, appropriately reflected in the rate quoted to the customer.

CONCLUSION

The Trade Finance Model can also be used to assess the technical adequacy of longer term payment and financing structures, such as note purchase, a forfait, or even countertrade arrangements. The basic issues are the same ones identified here. Often the complexity of a medium-term transaction requires the concerted efforts of an interdisciplinary marketing team, usually coordinated by the bank's account officer for that customer. In today's fast-paced and competitive world, optimal payment and financing arrangements are often only possible when customer and banker cooperate in an intelligent and informed manner to design structures tailored to particular commercial, economic, and political environments.

Appendix I Standby Credits

The basic principles underlying letters of credit are the same whether the credit is a documentary letter of credit or a standby letter of credit. However, the two instruments differ considerably from each other in purpose and procedure. As you recall, the *buyer* applies for a documentary credit in order to effect payment at shipment to the seller or supplier of goods. Under this letter of credit instrument the bank obligates itself to pay the beneficiary—the seller—upon presentation of documents that conform to the terms and conditions of the credit.

The roles are reversed under a standby credit in which the seller/supplier applies for the Credit to ensure his or her own performance. Under a standby credit, then, the bank obligates itself to pay the beneficiary/buyer up to a stated amount upon the beneficiary's presentation of a *claim*, or notice of default, that the seller/applicant has failed to discharge his responsibility as described in their underlying agreement.

Thus documentary and standby credits perform different and complementary functions in a trade transaction:

- Under a *documentary credit* the issuing bank undertakes to pay the seller/beneficiary up to a stated amount provided the seller presents conforming documents prior to expiration of the Credit.
- Under a *standby credit* the issuing bank undertakes to pay the buyer/beneficiary up to a stated amount provided the buyer presents a claim or notice of default prior to expiration of the Credit.

The parties are summarized in Table I.1.

Standby letters of credit demonstrate the remarkable flexibility of the letter of credit instrument whose range of applications is far broader than this discussion covers. Approximately 90% are issued to back up (i.e., to "stand by") the financial obligations of a third party; however, these standbys are not necessarily trade related and are outside the scope of this book.

Table I.1. Parties to Documentary and Trade-Related Standby Credits

	Documentary Credit	Trade-Related Standby Credit
Applicant	Importer	Exporter/supplier
Beneficiary	Exporter/supplier	Importer

The remaining 10% are used to back up performance in a trade-related transaction, most generally the project phases of a large-scale construction project. Typical uses are:

- *As a substitute for a bid bond.* The seller/applicant asks the bank to issue a standby credit for a percentage of the bid amount as a guarantee to the buyer/beneficiary that if the applicant wins the bid he or she will sign the contract to supply goods or services (thus ensuring that only serious bidders respond).
- *As a substitute for an advance payment bond.* The seller/applicant uses the standby credit to guarantee repayment of an advance if he or she defaults under the terms of the credit.
- *As a substitute for a performance bond.* The supplier/seller applies for a standby credit for a percentage of the contract price, guaranteeing the buyer/beneficiary that the supplier/applicant will perform as required under the terms of the standby credit.
- *As a substitute for a warranty bond.* The seller/supplier applies for a standby credit to ensure he or she will fulfill the warranty obligations. The buyer withholds a specified amount (usually 10%) until a certificate of satisfaction is issued at the conclusion of the warranty period.

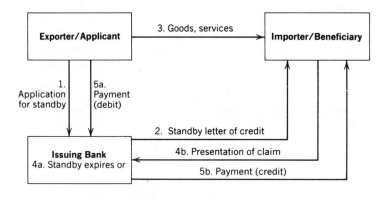

Figure I.1 Standby credit.

TRANSACTION FLOW (Fig. I.1)

Transaction Steps	Notes
1. The exporter/supplier applies for a standby letter of credit.	The issuing bank takes into account only the creditworthiness of its customer, principally the customer's ability to reimburse the bank if the beneficiary draws under the standby credit.
2. The issuing bank's letter of credit technical experts structure the standby credit, and the bank advises the importer/beneficiary.	
3. The exporter ships goods or delivers services in the contractually agreed upon manner.	
4. If necessary, the beneficiary presents a claim to the issuing bank in the form or manner stipulated in the Credit.	This claim is usually a simple statement that represents notice of default. (Capricious or unfair calling is a possibility described in the discussion which follows.)
	Because many suppliers perform as promised or stated in a contract, it is not unusual for the standby to expire unused. In this sense, a standby credit is similar to an insurance policy that one hopes to avoid having to use.
5(a) The issuing bank debits the applicant's account.	The bank is obligated to pay the importer/beneficiary upon presentation of a claim (notice of default) which conforms to the terms and conditions of the standby, and it will promptly debit the supplier/applicant's account.
(b) The issuing bank pays the beneficiary.	Remember that the cardinal principle of letter of credit is, "Banks

TRANSACTION FLOW (Fig. I.1) (Continued)

Transaction Steps	Notes
	deal in documents and not in goods, services, or other performances." Therefore the bank cannot be placed in the position of determining whether or not nonperformance has occurred.

DISCUSSION

Two principles govern standby credits. First, banks deal in documents not in goods, services, or other performances; and second, the issuing bank's obligation under a standby credit is to pay the importer/beneficiary up to a stated amount, provided that the claim is made prior to the expiration date of the standby credit. The integrity of the letter of credit instrument rests in the bank's unconditional undertaking to pay the beneficiary of the Credit against presentation of conforming documents, in this case, the notice of default. Although it appears simple on the surface, a review of the situation from the perspective of the exporter/applicant and the importer/beneficiary serves to highlight several important issues.

Typically an importer/beneficiary desires the simplest possible statement to trigger a drawing under a standby. However, the supplier/applicant might have reason to doubt the beneficiary's integrity and to fear the possibility of an *unfair* or *capricious calling*. In such cases an exporter/applicant might require that the documentation include, in addition to a simple statement, the attestation of a disinterested third party that nonperformance has in fact occurred.

Ultimately the utility of a standby credit rests on the integrity of the importer/beneficiary, and the exporter/applicant must understand his true vulnerability under a standby credit. It is natural for the applicant to wish to be able to claim unfair calling and ask "his" bank to intervene on his behalf. However, it is vitally important that the applicant understand fully that this action is not possible, because from a legal point of view the integrity of the letter of credit instrument itself is at stake. Article 4 of I.C.C. Publication 400 states that "Credits by their nature are separate transactions from the sales or other contract(s) on which they may be based and banks are in no way concerned with or bound by such contract(s). . . ." Thus if an importer/beneficiary presents a claim or notice of default which complies with the terms and conditions of the credit, *the bank is obligated to pay even if the applicant feels the claim is unfair.*

One reason why suppliers or contractors sometimes mistakenly believe that their bank would assume an active role in evaluating the validity of the claim derives from the traditional role of surety companies, which issued surety bonds. These bonds were ancillary to the underlying sales contract. In an instance of default, the surety company actively investigated the claims against the provisions of the underlying sales contract. At times the surety company undertook to cure the default itself and thus acted to complete the contract. If surety was awarded, the amount was decided through arbitration on the basis of actual damages.

The standby credit does not work like that. Standby credits are governed by I.C.C. Publication 400, and the basic principle is identical to that governing documentary credits: The issuing bank undertakes to pay the beneficiary up to a stated amount against the beneficiary's claim of default which conforms to the terms and conditions of the Credit.

Conversely the importer/beneficiary must understand the importance of presenting a claim which conforms *exactly* to the terms and conditions of a standby credit. Failure to do so will result in a discrepancy and constitute legitimate grounds for the issuing bank to refuse to pay. Definition of appropriate documentation renders the standby credit a complex instrument, and proper structuring of standby credits usually requires the technical assistance of the best letter of credit specialists.

Summary

Exposure.   At issuance the bank risks *financial exposure*. Because the bank undertakes to pay against a claim of default, it must pay against presentation of conforming documents, even if the applicant lacks the funds. The bank's exposure is usually unsecured because there is no merchandise to fall back upon for repayment as in a documentary letter of credit.

Liability.   The bank's liability at issuance is *contingent;* that is, it depends upon the beneficiary's presentation of a claim of default. The contingent liability becomes *actual* when the beneficiary presents, and the bank pays against, the claim. Provided that the applicant has sufficient funds in his or her account to cover the debit, the bank has no problem. In the event that the applicant lacks sufficient funds in the account, many banks will book a loan or some other financing arrangement. If this is necessary, the problem may be larger than it seems because the applicant may not be able to repay. Good credit analysis as well as a thorough understanding of the transaction will forestall a problem before it occurs.

As we have discussed previously, a standby credit does not protect the applicant from unfair or capricious calling on the part of the beneficiary.

Obligations, Rights, Responsibilities   The issuing bank:

- Has a responsibility to structure the standby credit to ensure that the terms are explicit, workable, and in compliance with I.C.C. Publication 400.
- Has a responsibility to review a claim of default submitted by the beneficiary to make sure it conforms to the terms and conditions of the standby credit.
- Is obligated to pay the beneficiary if the documents conform to all the terms and conditions of the Credit, and not to pay if the documents do not conform.
- Has a right to receive reimbursement from the applicant if claim is made and documents conform.

The applicant:

- Has a responsibility when applying for the Credit to require precise and accurate wording for the claim—wording that agrees with the provisions of the sales contract, if applicable.
- Is obligated to reimburse the issuing bank if it pays the beneficiary upon presentation of a claim which conforms to the terms and conditions of the Credit.
- Has a right to refuse to reimburse the bank if the claim does not conform to the terms and conditions of the Credit.

The beneficiary:

- Has a responsibility to examine the standby credit upon receipt to ensure that he can produce the claim in the required form.
- Has a responsibility to submit a claim which conforms to the terms and conditions of the Credit.
- Has a right to receive payment from the issuing bank against a claim which conforms to the terms and conditions of the Credit.

Risks.   The issuing bank has both issuance and documentary review risks, that is, if the bank issues a standby letter of credit incorrectly or pays the beneficiary against a claim which does not conform to the terms and conditions of the Credit, the applicant may legitimately refuse to reimburse the issuing bank.

The applicant risks being unable to perform as stipulated in the letter of credit and additionally risks that the beneficiary will call capriciously or unfairly under the Credit.

The function of a standby credit is to remove the beneficiary's risks in the transaction.

Sometimes as the expiry date draws near, a beneficiary will call under the standby credit to make sure he is covered. Such callings, though eventually resolved, can cause momentary uneasiness. Usually the beneficiary presents the claim and says to the issuing bank "extend or pay." Behind this request is the beneficiary's concern that he may lose the protection of the letter of credit due to expiration and what he really wants now is *not* payment but an extension of the expiry date. In such cases the issuing bank and the importer/applicant agree to amend the credit by extending the expiry date.

Appendix II Letter of Credit Variations

STRUCTURES USED IN MIDDLEMAN SITUATIONS

These variations allow the beneficiary to function as a middleman in arranging a sale between importer and supplier. Middlemen may be either independent entrepreneurs or they may be acting as agents of the importer. In either case, they tend to have certain characteristics in common:

- Their business is based on resale, and their profit usually depends on rapid turnover of goods.
- They are usually thinly capitalized and unable to get financing on their own.
- They need alternatives to financing in order to pay or guarantee payment to their primary suppliers.

The letter of credit variations that have developed for use in middlemen situations include:

- *Transferable Credit* whereby the middleman/beneficiary transfers all or a portion of his or her rights and obligations under the letter of credit to the supplier. If he wishes, the middleman may conceal the identity of the supplier from the importer by *substitution of invoices.*
- *Back-to-back (B–B) credit,* which allows the middleman/beneficiary to assign the proceeds of the primary letter of credit to the bank as security for a second, separate Credit in favor of the supplier. Back-to-back credits are rarely issued in the United States, but they are prevalent in the Far East, particularly in commodities markets.
- *Assignment of Proceeds,* whereby the supplier is paid with proceeds from the letter of credit after the middleman/beneficiary has submitted conforming documents.

These middleman variations are described in detail below.

Transferable Letter of Credit

Parties to the transaction are:

- *Importer/account party.*
- *Issuing bank.*
- *Exporter/*first beneficiary.

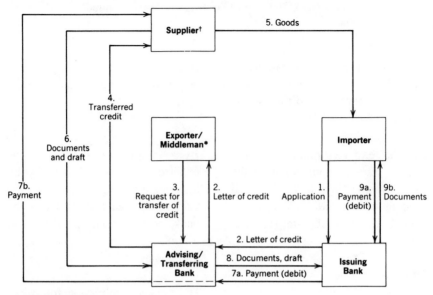

* First beneficiary
† Second beneficiary

Figure II.1   Transferable letter of credit.

- *Advising/transferring bank* (may be paying, accepting, or negotiating bank).
- *Supplier*/second beneficiary.

In the following example, assume the exporter has no need to conceal the identity of the supplier from the importer and that therefore no substitution of documents is required.

TRANSACTION FLOW (Fig. II.1)

Transaction Steps	Notes
1. The importer applies for a transferable letter of credit.	The importer's instructions to the bank must specifically state that the letter of credit is to be transferable.
2. The bank issues a Credit in favor of the exporter/middleman and	The exporter must examine the Credit to be sure that it is transfer-

TRANSACTION FLOW (Fig. II.1) (Continued)

Transaction Steps	Notes
sends it to a branch or correspondent in the exporter's country, which advises the Credit to the exporter.	able. If it is not, he can ask the importer to request an amendment.
3. The exporter/middleman submits a transfer application to the bank requesting that the full amount of the letter of credit be transferred to his supplier (the second beneficiary).	By submitting this application, the exporter transfers to the supplier all his obligations and rights under the Credit. Any amendments that the bank receives would go directly to the ultimate supplier, not to the middleman.
	The bank's commission for transferring the Credit is normally paid by the seller/first beneficiary unless the letter of credit specifically states otherwise.
	The exporter is now out of the transaction. The exporter usually receives a commission for arranging the sale, but this payment is outside the terms of the letter of credit.
4. The advising bank effects the transfer by sending the letter of credit to the supplier. This is the original letter of credit with a notation that the full amount has been transferred to the supplier (second beneficiary).	

TRANSACTION FLOW (Fig. II.1) (Continued)

Transaction Steps	Notes
5. The supplier ships the goods directly to the importer.	Normally the goods will be consigned to the order of the issuing bank on the bill of lading, thus allowing the bank to keep control of the goods until the importer pays.
6. After shipment, the supplier submits required documents and a draft to the advising/transferring bank for payment.	
7. The bank examines the documents and, if they comply with the terms and conditions of the Credit, (a) debits the issuing bank's account and (b) pays the supplier.	The advising/transferring bank has now become the paying bank (or negotiating bank depending upon what type of letter of credit was issued).
8. The advising/paying bank then forwards the documents and draft to the issuing bank.	
9. The issuing bank reviews the documents and, if they conform to the terms and conditions of the Credit, it (a) debits the importer's account and (b) releases the documents to him.	

Transferable Letter of credit: *Substitution of invoice.* In the following example of a Transferable Credit, assume that the exporter wishes to conceal the identity of the importer from the supplier. Also assume that the buyer is paying $200,000 for the goods; the supplier will receive $175,000 and the middleman's share for arranging the sale is $25,000.

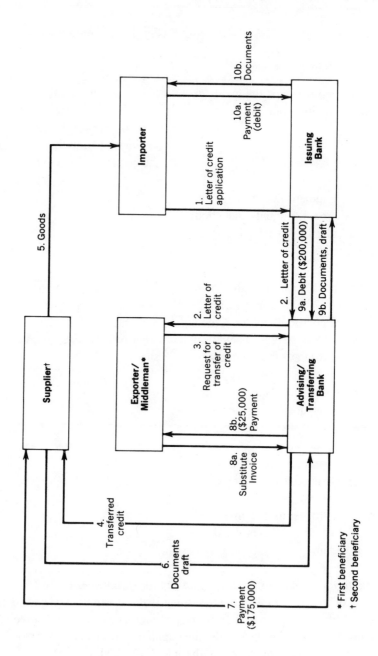

Figure II.2 Transferable letter of credit with substitution of invoice.

200

TRANSACTION FLOW (Fig. II.2)

Transaction Steps	Notes
1. The importer applies for a transferable letter of credit in the amount of $200,000.	
2. The importer's bank issues the letter of credit in favor of the exporter/middleman and sends it to a branch or correspondent in the exporter's country, which advises the Credit to the exporter.	
3. The exporter submits a transfer request to the advising bank asking that a portion of the Credit (say, $175,000) be transferred to his supplier.	The terms and conditions of the transferred Credit must be identical to those of the original letter of credit with the following possible exceptions: • The name and address of the exporter/beneficiary are substituted for those of the importer. • The unit price and total amount are reduced. • The latest shipment and expiry dates are earlier, as is the latest date for presentation of documents. • Insurance cover may be adjusted to comply with original letter of credit provisions.
4. The advising bank effects the transfer.	Usually the bank retypes the letter of credit on its own form. Any amendment would be advised to the primary beneficiary (middleman) who instructs the transferring bank whether or not to advise it to the second beneficiary (supplier).
5. After examining the Credit, the supplier ships the goods directly to the original importer.	The supplier's name would not usually appear on the bill of lading, and the goods would be consigned

TRANSACTION FLOW (Fig. II.2) (Continued)

Transaction Steps	Notes
	to the order of the issuing bank, thus concealing the identity of the importer. In addition, the supplier's identity can be concealed from the importer by having the bill of lading name the shipper as the original beneficiary of the credit.
6. After shipment, the supplier gathers the required documents and presents them to the transferring bank along with an invoice and a draft for $175,000.	If consular documents are required, they must usually be completed by the supplier, not the exporter. In this case the identity of the supplier cannot be kept from the importer.
7. The bank examines the documents to make sure they conform to the terms and conditions of the Credit and if so it pays the supplier $175,000.	
8. (a) The exporter must present a substitute invoice to the bank with a draft for the full amount of the Credit, that is, $200,000. (b) The bank pays the exporter the difference between the two invoices, that is, $25,000.	If the exporter does not deliver these items to the bank by the time specified, UCP Article 54 allows the bank to forward the *supplier's* draft and invoice to the issuing bank for payment and to collect the lower amount only.
9. The transferring bank (a) debits the issuing bank's account for $200,000 and (b) forwards the documents and exporter's invoice to it.	
10. The issuing bank examines the documents and, if they conform	

TRANSACTION FLOW (Fig. II.2) (Continued)

Transaction Steps	Notes

to the terms of the Credit, it (a) debits the importer's account for $200,000 and (b) releases the documents to him.

Back-to-Back Letter of Credit.   The parties involved in a back-to-back credit are the following.

Primary credit.

- *Importer/account party.*
- *Importer's bank* (issues the Credit).
- *Middleman's bank* (advises and usually pays the Credit).
- *Middleman/primary beneficiary.*

Secondary back-to-back credit.

- *Middleman/account party.*
- *Middleman's bank* (issues the back-to-back credit).
- *Supplier/beneficiary* of back-to-back credit.

Generally the exporter's bank would agree to issue a back-to-back credit only if:

- It is the paying bank of the original Credit.
- It is willing to accept the credit risk of both the exporter and the original issuing bank, and the political risk of the importing country.

In the following example, assume that the exporter/middleman's advising bank is also the paying bank for the original letter of credit, that is, it pays the Credit as the agent of its foreign branch or correspondent. Also assume that the importer is paying $100,000 for the goods, the supplier will receive $80,000 and the middleman's share is $20,000.

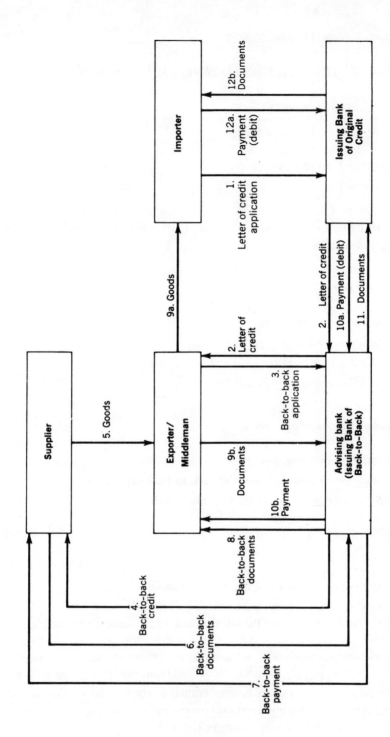

*If middleman's bank delays payment until it receives proceeds of the primary letter of credit, Step 7 becomes part of Step 10.

Figure II.3 Back–to–back credit.

TRANSACTION FLOW (Fig. II.3)

Transaction Steps	Notes
1. The importer applies for a letter of credit in the amount of $100,000.	
2. The importer's bank issues the letter of credit in favor of the exporter, and sends it to a branch or correspondent, which advises the Credit to the exporter.	
3. The exporter applies for a back–to–back credit for $80,000 in order to pay his supplier.	The exporter's application for the back-to-back credit is usually made at the request of the supplier.
4. The exporter's bank issues the back–to–back credit for $80,000 in favor of the supplier.	Before it issues a back-to-back credit the bank will usually require that the exporter assign the proceeds of the original letter of credit to it as security, thereby reducing the credit risk somewhat.
	However, by issuing the back-to-back credit the bank unconditionally obligates itself to pay this Credit against conforming documents whether or not the original letter of credit is completed. The documentary requirements of the second Credit should be identical to those of the primary letter of credit with the following exceptions: • The account party is now the exporter/middleman. • The beneficiary is the supplier. • The amount is reduced to reflect the exporter's costs and profit. • The expiry date is earlier to allow time for the exporter to gather and submit documents to the bank be-

TRANSACTION FLOW (Fig. II.3) (Continued)

Transaction Steps	Notes
	fore the original letter of credit expires.
	The bank collects two fees in back-to-back transactions: one for advising the primary letter of credit and one for issuing the second Credit.
5. The supplier prepares and ships the goods to the middleman.	
6. After shipment, the supplier presents the required back-to-back documents to the bank along with an invoice and draft for $80,000.	
7. The bank examines the documents and, if they comply with the terms and conditions of the back-to-back credit, it pays the supplier $80,000.	In reality, the bank may try to delay payment to the supplier until it receives the proceeds from the primary letter of credit (Step 9 below). If this cannot be done, a temporary loan is set up to provide the funds to pay the supplier. This loan will be paid from the proceeds of the primary letter of credit.
8. The bank releases the back-to-back documents to the middleman/account party.	
9. The middleman (a) ships to the importer and (b) submits to the same bank the documents required under the primary letter of credit along with an invoice for $100,000.	There is a timing risk at this point: If there is a delay in the back-to-back documents, the primary letter of credit may not be completed before the expiry date, and the bank may lose the payment. (Unlike the Transferable Credit, the importer is not obligated to accept the sup-

TRANSACTION FLOW (Fig. II.3) (Continued)

Transaction Steps	Notes
	plier's documents if the middleman's are not available.)

10. The bank examines the middleman's documents and if they conform to the terms and conditions of the primary letter of credit, it (a) debits the account of the correspondent or branch that issued the primary letter of credit for $100,000, as authorized in that Credit; and (b) pays the middleman $20,000 (the difference between the two letters of credit).

If the bank has delayed payment under the back-to-back credit until it receives the proceeds of the primary letter of credit, it now also pays the supplier $80,000, or uses the funds to pay off the loan.

11. The middleman's bank sends the documents to the importer's bank.

12. The importer's bank examines the documents and, if they conform, it (a) debits the importer's account for $100,000 and (b) releases the documents to the importer.

Assignment of Proceeds.   Assignment of Proceeds is an alternative to transferable and back-to-back credits as a means for the middleman/beneficiary to pay the supplier.

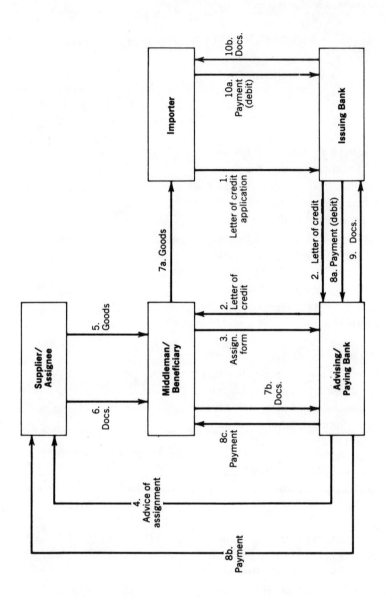

Figure II.4 Assignment of Proceeds.

TRANSACTION FLOW (Fig. II.4)

Transaction Steps	Notes
1. The importer applies for the letter of credit.	
2. The importer's bank issues the Credit and sends it to the advising bank, which notifies the middleman/beneficiary.	
3. The middleman/beneficiary completes an Assignment of Proceeds form instructing the advising/paying bank to pay the supplier/assignee a specific percentage of the value of the shipment against conforming documents prepared and submitted by the middleman/beneficiary.	
4. The bank advises the supplier of the assignment.	
5. The supplier/assignee prepares and ships the goods to the middleman.	
6. The supplier/assignee presents the shipping documents (usually domestic) to the middleman.	In other words, the supplier relinquishes control over the goods and must depend on the middleman to submit conforming documents.
7. The middleman ships to the importer and submits all documents required under the Credit to the advising/paying bank, along with an invoice for the full value of the shipment.	
8. The bank examines the documents and, if they comply with the terms and conditions of the letter of credit, it (a) debits the account of	

TRANSACTION FLOW (Fig. II.4) (Continued)

Transaction Steps	Notes
the issuing bank; (b) pays the supplier a percentage of the invoice as instructed on the assignment form; and (c) pays the balance of the invoice to the middleman.	
9. The advising/paying bank sends the documents to the issuing bank.	
10. The issuing bank examines the documents and, if they conform, the bank (a) debits the importer's account and (b) releases the documents to the importer.	

Table II.1 on page 212 summarizes the allocation of risk, responsibility and obligations among the various parties in middleman situations.

STRUCTURES USED TO CONTROL REPETITIVE SHIPMENTS

Various letter of credit structures have developed to control repetitive shipments from a regular exporter/beneficiary over a specific period of time. In addition to simply issuing a new Credit for each installment, some of the more common structures are described briefly below.

(*Note:* The "variation" is in the statement of terms and conditions; once the documents are presented, these repetitive Credits tend to unwind the same way standard letters of credit do. Consequently, detailed descriptions of the transaction flows are omitted.)

- *Revolving credit.* A revolving credit specifies that the exporter is authorized to draw up to a certain amount each month for a certain number of months to cover shipment of the goods described. The Credit could be reinstated *automatically* in relation to either time or value, or it could revolve *by amendment.* For example, a credit *revolving by time* might be for $50,000 a month for six months to cover repetitive shipments. Any unused balance from one period would either be cancelled automatically or added automatically to amounts available in subsequent months, depending upon whether the amounts were noncumulative or cumulative. The same Credit *revolving by value* would stipulate that total drawings not exceed $3 million within the 6-month period but provide for reinstatement either automatically or by amendment.

The issuing bank of a revolving credit is obligated to make payments over a period of time, for as long as the Credit is in effect whether or not the importer/applicant can repay. The bank can reduce its credit risk somewhat by structuring the Credit to *revolve by amendment* rather than automatically. The amendment procedure allows the issuing bank to re-examine its customer's credit before obligating itself to pay the exporter's draft covering the next installment.

- *Installment Credit.* This structure is more precise than a revolving credit. It makes continuation of the Credit contingent upon strict compliance with the terms and conditions of the Credit, and provides for automatic invalidation of the Credit should the exporter fail to comply. For example, it might stipulate that the exporter is to ship 30,000 units a month for six consecutive months beginning January 1984. If the exporter fails to comply one month, the letter of credit automatically ceases to exist. (See Article 45 of I.C.C. Publication 400.)

STRUCTURES USED TO INFLUENCE PAYMENT TERMS

Still other structures have developed to alter the payment date. In one case— *Deferred Payment Credit*—payment is delayed for a specified time period *following* shipment. In this case the exporter agrees to delay presentation of a sight draft until a specified number of days. Notice that, in contrast to the mechanism of acceptance under a usance (time) credit, the exporter is out the funds for the duration of the "deferred sight." In this way the exporter is able to finance the importer, who gets the financing needed without incurring the interest charges of a direct loan.

In another case—the *Red Clause Credit,* so called because the clause was originally stamped on the letter of credit in red ink—the issuing bank authorizes the negotiating bank to advance funds to the exporter *prior to* shipment of goods and presentation of documents. In effect, the negotiating bank extends a loan to the exporter under the importer's line of credit guaranteed by the issuing bank's letter of credit.

Table II.1 Summary of Risks, Rights, Responsibilities, and Obligations, Under the Middleman Variations

Credit	Supplier	Exporter	Importer	Exporter's Bank	Importer's Bank
Transfer without substitution of draft and invoice.	Right to full payment as beneficiary under letter of credit. Responsible for submitting conforming documents.	Gets paid via commission *outside* letter of credit structure.	May know identity of supplier. Same risks as those under any other Credit. Must request Transferable Credit in Application.	Risks, and so on, same as paying agent or negotiating bank.	Risks and obligations normally associated with a standard letter of credit.
Transfer with substitution of draft and invoice	Same as above.	Gets paid *inside* letter of credit structure. Timing risk: Submit substitute draft and invoice before expiry date or lose payment protection of letter of credit.	Must request Transferable Credit in Application. Must accept ultimate supplier's draft and documents if submitted.	Substitutes exporter's invoice and draft for that of ultimate supplier and sends to issuing bank.	Same as above.

Back-to-back (B–B)	Right to full payment under (B–B) upon presentation of conforming documents. Responsible for submitting conforming documents.	Account party of second (B–B) credit. Timing risk: Responsible to repay bank for payment under second (B–B) credit whether or not payment is received under first letter of credit.	May be ignorant of back-to-back arrangement.	Assumes credit risk of exporter/middleman Timing/documentary risk: Obligated to pay under second (B–B) credit whether or not payment received under first letter of credit.	Same as above.
Assignment of proceeds	Very risky because supplier must rely on exporter/middleman to present conforming documents before he receives payment.	Responsible for presenting conforming documents.	Probably unaware of assignment arrangement and not interested in it.	Risks and obligations normally associated with a standard letter of credit.	Same as above.

The effect of the red clause credit is similar to that of the middleman credits: It enables the exporter/beneficiary to pay his suppliers using another party's funds. The difference is that under a red clause the exporter remains the sole beneficiary, as opposed to the transferable credit in which the supplier becomes a secondary beneficiary, or the back-to-back credit in which the exporter opens a second Credit in favor of the ultimate supplier.

Deferred payment credits and red clause credits are described in detail below.

Deferred Payment Credit

The parties are:

- *Importer/account party.*
- *Issuing bank.*
- *Advising/paying bank.*
- *Exporter/beneficiary.*

It is used when the time of deferral exceeds six months; at times the deferral may extend for several years.

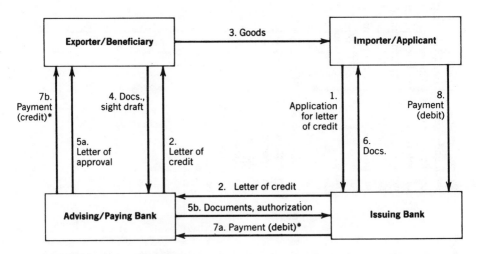

* At specified date of "deferred sight."

Figure II.5   Deferred Payment Credit.

TRANSACTION FLOW (Fig. II.5)

Transaction Steps	Notes
1. The importer applies for a deferred payment letter of credit in favor of the exporter.	The terms and conditions will stipulate that the exporter's sight draft must be presented X number of days following the bill of lading date. In contrast, a time credit would stipulate presentation of the exporter's time draft with a specific tenor. (See Chapter 6, *Bankers Acceptance*.) In either case, the expiry date of the Credit must be late enough to allow for the period until presentation of the draft.
2. The importer's bank issues the Credit and sends it to a branch or correspondent in the exporter's country, which advises the Credit to the exporter.	
3. The exporter ships the goods to the importer.	
4. Immediately following shipment, the exporter submits the required documents and a sight draft to the advising bank along with his authorization to release the documents to the importer.	Normally the exporter would ask the bank to hold the documents and draft in safekeeping until the presentation date.
5. The bank examines the documents and, if they comply with the terms and conditions of the Credit, it (a) sends an approval letter to the exporter; and (b) sends the original documents and authorization to the issuing bank.	The exporter is out of funds until he presents the sight draft and receives payment. To cover his financing needs for the period he could ask the bank to grant a loan using the deferred payment letter of credit as collateral.

TRANSACTION FLOW (Fig. II.5) (Continued)

Transaction Steps	Notes

6. The issuing bank examines the documents and, if they comply, it releases them to the importer.

7. On the deferred payment due date, the advising/paying bank retrieves the draft from safekeeping. It then (a) debits the issuing bank's account and (b) pays the exporter.

8. The issuing bank debits the importer's account.

Red Clause Credit

The parties are:

- *Importer/account party.*
- *Issuing bank.*
- *Advising/negotiating bank.*
- *Exporter/beneficiary.*

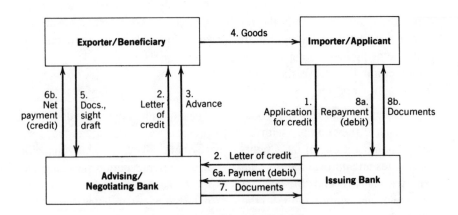

Figure II.6   Red Clause Credit.

A red clause credit may be used when the exporter needs pre-export financing to purchase goods for shipment, and either a high degree of trust exists between importer and exporter or their business relationship is legally linked as, for example, is the case when the exporter is an agent of the importer.

TRANSACTION FLOW (Fig. II.6)

Transaction Steps	Notes
1. The importer applies for a red clause credit in favor of the exporter.	The importer will be obligated to repay any advances made under this Credit to the exporter plus interest and bank charges whether or not the exporter ships and presents documents as required. For this reason an importer is unlikely to request a red clause credit unless he trusts the exporter to perform as stipulated in the Credit.
2. The bank issues the Credit and sends it to a branch or correspondent in the exporter's country, which advises the Credit to the exporter.	By issuing the Credit, the bank essentially authorizes the advising/ negotiating bank to make an unsecured loan to the exporter, under the importer's line of credit. Usually it will issue a red clause only if it is sure of the creditworthiness of the importer.
3. The advising bank advances the amount stipulated in the Credit to the exporter.	The advance may be either in the exporter's local currency or in a foreign currency if allowed by foreign exchange regulations in the importer's country. Usually the exporter gives the bank a receipt for the funds along with a statement to the effect that the advance will be used to buy and ship the goods described in the Credit.
4. The exporter purchases the goods and ships them to the importer.	

TRANSACTION FLOW (Fig. II.6) (Continued)

Transaction Steps	Notes
5. After shipment, the exporter submits documents and a sight draft to the advising/negotiating bank.	
6. The bank examines the documents and, if they conform to the terms and conditions of the Credit, it (a) debits the issuing bank's account; then (b) deducts the advance and interest and pays the exporter the net difference.	If the exporter fails to ship the goods or present conforming documents, the bank has the right to recover its advance plus interest from the issuing bank, which has recourse to the importer.
7. The advising/negotiating bank sends the documents to the issuing bank.	
8. The issuing bank examines them and, if they conform, it (a) debits the account of the importer and (b) releases the documents to him.	An alternative to the regular red clause is the *anticipatory red clause* under which the importer allows his account to be debited at the time the advance is made.

SUMMARY

Deferred payment credits may be either advised or confirmed. In the case of an advised credit, the exporter assumes the commercial credit risk of the issuing bank and the political risk of the importer's country, as he does with any other advised credit. In the case of a confirmed deferred payment credit, the exporter's bank adds its undertaking to that of the issuing bank and assumes the commercial and political risks described above.

Under a red clause credit the importer assumes almost all the risk since he is obligated to repay any advances made under the Credit plus interest and charges—whether or not the exporter ships.

The issuing bank has the credit risk of the importer. The advising/negotiating bank has only the credit risk of the issuing bank and the political risk of the importing country.

Appendix III Revised American Foreign Trade Definitions— 1941

Adopted July 30, 1941, by a Joint Committee representing the Chamber of Commerce of the United States of America, the National Council of American Importers, Inc., and the National Foreign Trade Council, Inc.

The following *Revised American Foreign Trade Definitions—1941* are recommended for general use by both exporters and importers. These revised definitions have no status at law unless there is specific legislation providing for them, or unless they are confirmed by court decisions. Hence, it is suggested that sellers and buyers agree to their acceptance as part of the contract of sale. These definitions will then become legally binding upon all parties.

Adoption by exporters and importers of these revised terms will impress on all parties concerned their respective responsibilities and rights.

GENERAL NOTES OF CAUTION

1. As foreign trade definitions have been issued by organizations in various parts of the world, and as the courts of countries have interpreted these definitions in different ways, it is important that sellers and buyers agree that their contracts are subject to the *Revised American Foreign Trade Definitions—1941* and that the various points listed are accepted by both parties.

2. In addition to the foreign trade terms listed herein, there are terms that are at times used, such as Free Harbor, C.I.F. & C. (Cost, Insurance, Freight, and Commission), C.I.F.C. & I. (Cost, Insurance, Freight, Commission, and Interest), C.I.F. Landed (Cost, Insurance, Freight, Landed), and others. None of these should be used unless there has first been a definite understanding as to the exact meaning thereof. It is unwise to attempt to interpret other terms in the light of the terms given herein. Hence, whenever possible, one of the terms defined herein should be used.

3. It is unwise to use abbreviations in quotations or in contracts which might be subject to misunderstanding.

4. When making quotations, the familiar terms "hundredweight" or "ton" should be avoided. A hundredweight can be 100 pounds of the short ton, or 112 pounds of the long ton. A ton can be a short ton of 2,000 pounds or a metric ton of 2,204.6 pounds, or a long ton of 2,240 pounds. Hence, the type of hundredweight or ton should be clearly stated in quotations and in sales confirmations. Also, all terms referring to quantity, weight, volume, length, or surface should be clearly defined and agreed upon.

5. If inspection, or certificate of inspection, is required, it should be agreed, in advance, whether the cost thereof is for account of seller or buyer.

6. Unless otherwise agreed upon, all expenses are for the account of seller up to the point at which the buyer must handle the subsequent movement of goods.

7. There are a number of elements in a contract that do not fall within the scope of these foreign trade definitions. Hence, no mention of these is made herein. Seller and buyer should agree to these separately when negotiating contracts. This particularly applies to so-called "customary" practices.

DEFINITIONS OF QUOTATIONS

(I) EX (point of origin).
"Ex Factory," "Ex Mill," "Ex Mine," "Ex Plantation," "Ex Warehouse," etc. (named point of origin). Under this term, the price quoted applies only at the point of origin, and the seller agrees to place the goods at the disposal of the buyer at the agreed place on the date or within the period fixed.

Under this quotation:

Seller must

1. bear all costs and risks of the goods until such time as the buyer is obliged to take delivery thereof;

2. render the buyer, at the buyer's request and expense, assistance in obtaining the documents issued in the country of origin, or of shipment, or of both, which the buyer may require either for purposes of exportation, or of importation at destination.

Buyer must

1. take delivery of the goods as soon as they have been placed at this disposal at the agreed place on the date or within the period fixed;

2. pay export taxes, or other fees or charges, if any, levied because of exportation;

3. bear all costs and risks of the goods from the time when he is obligated to take delivery thereof;

4. pay all costs and charges incurred in obtaining the documents issued in the country of origin, or of shipment, or of both, which may be

required either for purposes of exportation, or of importation at destination.

(II) F.O.B. (free on board).

Note: Seller and buyer should consider not only the definitions but also the "Comments on All F.O.B. Terms" given at end of this section in order to understand fully their respective responsibilities and rights under the several classes of "F.O.B." terms.

(II-A) "F.O.B. (named inland carrier at named inland point of departure)."

Under this term, the price quoted applies only at inland shipping point, and the seller arranges for loading of the goods on, or in, railway cars, trucks, lighters, barges, aircraft, or other conveyance furnished for transportation.

Under this quotation:

Seller must

1. place goods on, or in, conveyance, or deliver to inland carrier for loading;
2. provide clean bill of lading or other transportation receipt, freight collect;
3. be responsible for any loss or damage, or both, until goods have been placed in, or on, conveyance at loading point, and clean bill of lading or other transportation receipt has been furnished by the carrier;
4. render the buyer, at the buyer's request and expense, assistance in obtaining the documents issued in the country of origin, or of shipment, or of both, which the buyer may require either for purposes of exportation, or of importation at destination.

Buyer must

1. be responsible for all movement of the goods from inland point of loading, and pay all transportation costs;
2. pay export taxes, or other fees or charges, if any, levied because of exportation;
3. be responsible for any loss or damage, or both, incurred after loading at named inland point of departure;
4. pay all costs and charges incurred in obtaining the documents issued in the country of origin, or of shipment, or of both, which may be

required either for purposes of exportation, or of importation at destination.

(II-B) "F.O.B. (named inland carrier at named inland point of departure) Freight Prepaid to (named point of exportation)."

Under this term, the seller quotes a price including transportation charges to the named point of exportation and prepays freight to named point of exportation, without assuming responsibility for the goods after obtaining a clean bill of lading or other transportation receipt at named inland point of departure.

Under this quotation:
Seller must

1. assume the seller's obligations as under II-A, except that under (2) he must provide clean bill of lading or other transportation receipt, freight prepaid to named point of exportation.

Buyer must

1. assume the same buyer's obligations as under II-A, except that he does not pay freight from loading point to named point of exportation.

(II-C) "F.O.B. (named inland carrier at named inland point of departure) freight allowed to (named point)."

Under this term, the seller quotes a price including the transportation charges to the named point, shipping freight collect and deducting the cost of transportation, without assuming responsibility for the goods after obtaining a clean bill of lading or other transportation receipt at named inland point of departure.

Under this quotation:
Seller must

1. assume the same seller's obligations as under II-A, but deduct from his invoice the transportation cost to named point.

Buyer must

1. assume the same buyer's obligations as under II-A, including pay-

ment of freight from inland loading point to named point, for which seller has made deduction.

(II-D) "F.O.B. (named inland carrier at named point of exportation)."

Under this term, the seller quotes a price including the costs of transportation of the goods to named point of exportation, bearing any loss or damage, or both, incurred up to that point.

Under this quotation:

Seller must

1. place goods on, or in, conveyance, or deliver to inland carrier for loading;
2. provide clean bill of lading or other transportation receipt, paying all transportation costs from loading point to named point of exportation;
3. be responsible for any loss or damage, or both, until goods have arrived in, or on, inland conveyance at the named point of exportation;
4. render the buyer, at the buyer's request and expense, assistance in obtaining the documents issued in the country of origin, or of shipment, or of both, which the buyer may require either for purposes of exportation, or of importation at destination.

Buyer must

1. be responsible for all movement of the goods from inland conveyance at named point of exportation;
2. pay export taxes, or other fees or charges, if any, levied because of exportation;
3. be responsible for any loss or damage, or both, incurred after goods have arrived in, or on, inland conveyance at the named point of exportation;
4. pay all costs and charges incurred in obtaining the documents issued in the country of origin, or of shipment, or of both, which may be required either for purposes of exportation, or of importation at destination.

(II-E) "F.O.B. Vessel (named port of shipment)."

Under this term, the seller quotes a price covering all expenses up to, and including, delivery of the goods upon the overseas vessel provided by, or for, the buyer at the named port of shipment.

Under this quotation:

Seller must

1. pay all charges incurred in placing goods, actually on board the vessel designated and provided by, or for, the buyer on the date or within the period fixed;
2. provide clean ship's receipt or on-board bill of lading;
3. be responsible for any loss or damage, or both, until goods have been placed on board the vessel on the date or within the period fixed;
4. render the buyer, at the buyer's request and expense, assistance in obtaining the documents issued in the country of origin, or of shipment, or of both, which the buyer may require either for purposes of exportation, or of importation at destination.

Buyer must

1. give seller adequate notice of name, sailing date, loading berth of, and delivery time to, the vessel;
2. bear the additional costs incurred and all risks of the goods from the time when the seller has placed them at his disposal if the vessel named by him fails to arrive or to load within the designated time;
3. handle all subsequent movement of the goods to destination;
   (a) provide and pay for insurance;
   (b) provide and pay for ocean and other transportation;
4. pay export taxes, or other fees or charges, if any, levied because of exportation;
5. be responsible for any loss or damage, or both, after goods have been loaded on board the vessel;
6. pay all costs and charges incurred in obtaining the documents, other than clean ship's receipt or bill of lading, issued in the country of origin, or of shipment, or of both, which may be required either for purposes of exportation, or of importation at destination.

(II-F) "F.O.B. (named inland point in country of importation)."

Under this term, the seller quotes a price including the cost of the merchandise and all costs of transportation to the named inland point in the country of importation.

Under this quotation:
Seller must

1. provide and pay for all transportation to the named inland point in the country of importation;
2. pay export taxes, or other fees or charges, if any, levied because of exportation;
3. provide and pay for marine insurance;
4. provide and pay for war risk insurance, unless otherwise agreed upon between the seller and buyer;
5. be responsible for any loss or damage, or both, until arrival of goods on conveyance at the named inland point in the country of importation;
6. pay the costs of certificates of origin, consular invoices, or any other documents issued in the country of origin, or of shipment, or of both, which the buyer may require for the importation of goods into the country of destination and, where necessary, for their passage in transit through another country;
7. pay all costs of landing, including wharfage, landing charges, and taxes, if any;
8. pay all costs of customs entry in the country of importation;
9. pay customs duties and all taxes applicable to imports, if any, in the country of importation.

Note: The seller under this quotation must realize that he is accepting important responsibilities, costs, and risks, and should therefore be certain to obtain adequate insurance. On the other hand, the importer or buyer may desire such quotations to relieve him of the risks of the voyage and to assure him of his landed costs at inland point in country of importation. When competition is keen, or the buyer is accustomed to such quotations from other sellers, seller may quote such terms, being careful to protect himself in an appropriate manner.
Buyer must

1. take prompt delivery of goods from conveyance upon arrival at destination;
2. bear any costs and be responsible for all loss or damage, or both, after arrival at destination.

COMMENTS ON ALL F.O.B. TERMS

In connection with F.O.B. terms, the following points of caution are recommended:

1. The method of inland transportation, such as trucks, railroad cars, lighters, barges, or aircraft should be specified.
2. If any switching charges are involved during the inland transportation, it should be agreed, in advance, whether these charges are for account of the seller or the buyer.
3. The term "F.O.B. (named port)," without designating the exact point at which the liability of the seller terminates and the liability of the buyer begins, should be avoided. The use of this term gives rise to disputes as to the liability of the seller or the buyer in the event of loss or damage arising while the goods are in port, and before delivery to or on board the ocean carrier. Misunderstandings may be avoided by naming the specific point of delivery.
4. If lighterage or trucking is required in the transfer of goods from the inland conveyance to ship's side, and there is a cost therefore, it should be understood, in advance, whether this cost is for account of the seller or the buyer.
5. The seller should be certain to notify the buyer of the minimum quantity required to obtain a carload, a truckload, or a barge-load freight rate.
6. Under F.O.B. terms, excepting "F.O.B. (named inland point in country of importation)," the obligation to obtain ocean freight space, and marine and war risk insurance, rests with the buyer. Despite this obligation on the part of the buyer, in many trades the seller obtains the ocean freight space, and marine and war risk insurance, and provides for shipment on behalf of the buyer. Hence, seller and buyer must

have an understanding as to whether the buyer will obtain the ocean freight space, and marine and war risk insurance, as is his obligation, or whether the seller agrees to do this for the buyer.

7. For the seller's protection, he should provide in his contract of sale that marine insurance obtained by the buyer include standard warehouse to warehouse coverage.

(III) F.A.S. (free along side).
Note: Seller and buyer should consider not only the definitions but also the "Comments" given at the end of this section, in order to understand fully their respective responsibilities and rights under "F.A.S." terms.

"F.A.S. Vessel (named port of shipment)."
Under this term, the seller quotes a price including delivery of the goods along side overseas vessel and within reach of its loading tackle.

Under this quotation:
Seller must

1. place goods along side vessel or on dock designated and provided by, or for, buyer on the date or within the period fixed; pay any heavy lift charges, where necessary, up to this point;
2. provide clean dock or ship's receipt;
3. be responsible for any loss or damage, or both, until goods have been delivered along side the vessel or on the dock;
4. render the buyer, at the buyer's request and expense, assistance in obtaining the documents issued in the country of origin, or of shipment, or of both, which the buyer may require either for purposes of exportation, or of importation at destination.

Buyer must

1. give seller adequate notice of name, sailing date, loading berth of, and delivery time to, the vessel;
2. handle all subsequent movement of the goods from along side the vessel;
   (a) arrange and pay for demurrage or storage charges, or both, in warehouse or on wharf, where necessary;

    (b)   provide and pay for insurance;

    (c)   provide and pay for ocean and other transportation;

3.   pay export taxes, or other fees or charges, if any, levied because of exportation;

4.   be responsible for any loss or damage, or both, while the goods are on a lighter or other conveyance along side vessel within reach of its loading tackle, or on the dock awaiting loading, or until actually loading on board the vessel, and subsequent thereto;

5.   pay all costs and charges incurred in obtaining the documents, other than clean dock or ship's receipt, issued in the country of origin, or of shipment, or of both, which may be required either for purposes of exportation, or of importation at destination.

F.A.S. COMMENTS

1.   Under F.A.S. terms, the obligation to obtain ocean freight space, and marine and war risk insurance, rests with the buyer. Despite this obligation on the part of the buyer, in many trades the seller obtains ocean freight space, and marine and war risk insurance, and provides for shipment on behalf of the buyer. In others, the buyer notifies the seller to make delivery along side a vessel designated by the buyer and the buyer provides his own marine and war risk insurance. Hence, seller and buyer must have an understanding as to whether the buyer will obtain the ocean freight space, and marine and war risk insurance, as is his obligation, or whether the seller agrees to do this for the buyer.

2.   For the seller's protection, he should provide in his contract of sale that marine insurance obtained by the buyer include standard warehouse to warehouse coverage.

(IV) C.&F. (cost and freight).
Note: Seller and buyer should consider not only the definitions but also the "C.&F. Comments" and the "C.&F. and C.I.F. Comments", in order to understand fully their respective responsibilities and rights under "C.&F." terms.

"C.&F. (named point of destination)."

Under this term, the seller quotes a price including the cost of transportation to named point of destination.

Under this quotation:

Seller must

1. provide and pay for transportation to named point of destination;
2. pay export taxes, or other fees or charges, if any, levied because of exportation;
3. obtain and dispatch promptly to buyer, or his agent, clean bill of lading to named point of destination;
4. where received-for-shipment ocean bill of lading may be tendered, be responsible for any loss or damage, or both, until the goods have been delivered into the custody of the ocean carrier;
5. where on-board ocean bill of lading is required, be responsible for any loss or damage, or both, until the goods have been delivered on board the vessel;
6. provide, at the buyer's request and expense, certificates of origin, consular invoices, or any other documents issued in the country of origin, or of shipment, or of both, which the buyer may require for importation of goods into country of destination and, where necessary, for their passage in transit through another country.

Buyer must

1. accept the documents when presented;
2. receive goods upon arrival, handle and pay for all subsequent movement of the goods, including taking delivery from vessel in accordance with bill of lading clauses and terms; pay all costs of handling, including any duties, taxes, and other expenses at named point of destination;
3. provide and pay for insurance;
4. be responsible for loss of or damage to goods, or both, from time and place at which seller's obligations under (4) and (5) above have ceased;
5. pay the costs of certificates of origin, consular invoices, or any other documents issued in the country of origin, or of shipment, or of both,

which may be required for the importation of goods into the country of destination and, where necessary, for their passage in transit through another country.

C. & F. COMMENTS

1.   For the seller's protection, he should provide in his contract of sale that marine insurance obtained by the buyer include standard warehouse to warehouse coverage.

2.   The comments listed under the following C.I.F. terms in many cases apply to C. & F. terms as well, and should be read and understood by the C. & F. seller and buyer.

(V) C.I.F. (cost, insurance, freight).
Note: Seller and buyer should consider not only the definitions but also the "Comments" at the end of this section, in order to understand fully their respective responsibilities and rights under "C.I.F." terms.

"C.I.F. (named point of destination)."
Under this term, the seller quotes a price including the cost of the goods, the marine insurance, and all transportation charges to the named point of destination.

Under this quotation:
Seller must

1.   provide and pay for transportation to named point of destination;
2.   pay export taxes, or other fees or charges, if any, levied because of exportation;
3.   provide and pay for marine insurance;
4.   provide war risk insurance as obtainable in seller's market at time of shipment at buyer's expense, unless seller has agreed that buyer provide for war risk coverage (See Comment 10 (c));
5.   obtain and dispatch promptly to buyer, or his agent, clean bill of lading to named point of destination, and also insurance policy or negotiable insurance certificate;

6. where received-for-shipment ocean bill of lading may be tendered, be responsible for any loss or damage, or both, until the goods have been delivered into the custody of the ocean carrier;

7. where on-board ocean bill of lading is required, be responsible for any loss or damage, or both, until the goods have been delivered on board the vessel;

8. provide, at the buyer's request and expense, certificates of origin, consular invoices, or any other documents issued in the country of origin, or of shipment, or both, which the buyer may require for importation of goods into country of destination and, where necessary, for their passage in transit through another country.

Buyer must

1. accept the documents when presented;

2. receive the goods upon arrival, handle and pay for all subsequent movement of the goods, including taking delivery from vessel in accordance with bill of lading clauses and terms; pay all costs of landing, including any duties, taxes, and other expenses at named point of destination;

3. pay for war risk insurance provided by seller;

4. be responsible for loss of or damage to goods, or both, from time and place at which seller's obligations under (6) or (7) above have ceased;

5. pay the cost of certificates of origin, consular invoices, or any other documents issued in the country of origin, or of shipment, or both, which may be required for importation of the goods into the country of destination and, where necessary, for their passage in transit through another country.

C. & F. AND C.I.F. COMMENTS

Under C. & F. and C.I.F. contracts there are the following points on which the seller and the buyer should be in complete agreement at the time that the contract is concluded:

1. It should be agreed upon, in advance, who is to pay for miscellaneous expenses, such as weighing or inspection charges.

2. The quantity to be shipped on any one vessel should be agreed upon, in advance, with a view to the buyer's capacity to take delivery upon arrival and discharge of the vessel, within the free time allowed at the port of importation.

3. Although the terms C. & F. and C.I.F. are generally interpreted to provide that charges for consular invoices and certificates of origin are for the account of the buyer, and are charged separately, in many trades these charges are included by the seller in his price. Hence, seller and buyer should agree, in advance, whether these charges are part of the selling price, or will be invoiced separately.

4. The point of final destination should be definitely known in the event the vessel discharges at a port other than the actual destination of the goods.

5. When ocean freight space is difficult to obtain, or forward freight contracts cannot be made at firm rates, it is advisable that sales contracts, as an exception to regular C. & F. or C.I.F. terms, should provide that shipment within the contract period be subject to ocean freight space being available to the seller, and should also provide that changes in the cost of ocean transportation between the time of sale and the time of shipment be for account of the buyer.

6. Normally, the seller is obligated to prepay the ocean freight. In some instances, shipments are made freight collect and the amount of the freight is deducted from the invoice rendered by the seller. It is necessary to be in agreement on this, in advance, in order to avoid misunderstanding which arises from foreign exchange fluctuations which might affect the actual cost of transportation, and from interest charges which might accrue under the letter of credit financing. Hence, the seller should always prepay the ocean freight unless he has a specific agreement with the buyer, in advance, that goods can be shipped freight collect.

7. The buyer should recognize that he does not have the right to insist on inspection of goods prior to accepting the documents. The buyer should not refuse to take delivery of goods on account of delay in the receipt of documents, provided the seller has used due diligence in their dispatch through the regular channels.

8. Sellers and buyers are advised against including in a C.I.F. contract any indefinite clause at variance with the obligations of a C.I.F. contract as specified in these Definitions. There have been numerous

court decisions in the United States and other countries invalidating C.I.F. contracts because of the inclusion of indefinite clauses.

9. Interest charges should be included in cost computations and should not be charged as a separate item in C.I.F. contracts, unless otherwise agreed upon, in advance, between the seller and buyer; in which case, however, the term C.I.F. and I. (Cost, Insurance, Freight, and Interest) should be used.

10. In connection with insurance under C.I.F. sales, it is necessary that seller and buyer be definitely in accord upon the following points:
   (a) The character of the marine insurance should be agreed upon in so far as being W.A. (With Average) of F.P.A. (Free of Particular Average), as well as any other special risks that are covered in specific trades, or against which the buyer may wish individual protection. Among the special risks that should be considered and agreed upon between seller and buyer are theft, pilferage, leakage, breakage, sweat, contact with other cargoes, and others peculiar to any particular trade. It is important that contingent or collect freight and customs duty should be insured to cover Particular Average losses, as well as total loss after arrival and entry but before delivery.
   (b) The seller is obligated to exercise ordinary care and diligence in selecting an underwriter that is in good financial standing. However, the risk of obtaining settlement of insurance claims rests with the buyer.
   (c) War risk insurance under this term is to be obtained by the seller at the expense and risk of the buyer. It is important that the seller be in definite accord with the buyer on this point, particularly as to the cost. It is desirable that the goods be insured against both marine and war risk with the same underwriter, so that there can be no difficulty arising from the determination of the cause of the loss.
   (d) Seller should make certain that in his marine or war risk insurance, there be included the standard protection against strikes, riots and civil commotions.
   (e) Seller and buyer should be in accord as to the insured valuation, bearing in mind that merchandise contributes in General Average on certain bases of valuation which differ in various trades. It is desirable that a competent insurance broker be consulted, in order that full value be covered and trouble avoided.

(VI) "Ex Dock (named port of importation)"

Note: Seller and buyer should consider not only the definitions but also the "Ex Dock Comments" at the end of this section, in order to understand fully their respective responsibilities and rights under "Ex Dock" terms.

Under this term, seller quotes a price including the cost of the goods and all additional costs necessary to place the goods on the dock at the named port of importation, duty paid, if any.

Under this quotation:

Seller must

1. provide and pay for transportation to named port of importation;
2. pay export taxes, or other fees or charges, if any, levied because of exportation;
3. provide and pay for marine insurance;
4. provide and pay for war risk insurance, unless otherwise agreed upon between the buyer and seller;
5. be responsible for any loss or damage, or both, until the expiration of the free time allowed on the dock at the named port of importation;
6. pay the costs of certificates of origin, consular invoices, legalization of bill of lading, or any other documents issued in the country of origin, or of shipment, or of both, which the buyer may require for the importation of goods into the country of destination and, where necessary, for their passage in transit through another country;
7. pay all costs of landing, including wharfage, landing charges, and taxes, if any;
8. pay all costs of customs entry in the country of importation;
9. pay customs duties and all taxes applicable to imports, if any, in the country of importation, unless otherwise agreed upon.

Buyer must

1. take delivery of the goods on the dock at the named port of importation within the free time allowed;
2. bear the cost and risk of the goods if delivery is not taken within the free time allowed.

EX DOCK COMMENTS

This term is used principally in United States import trade. It has various modifications, such as "Ex Quay," "Ex Pier," etc., but it is seldom, if ever, used in American export practice. Its use in quotations for export is not recommended.

Appendix IV SUMMARY OF INCOTERMS

Shipping terms	ICC int'l abbreviations	The seller must:	The buyer must:
Ex-works	EXW	Deliver goods at his premises	Make all arrangements at his own cost and risk to take goods to their destination
Free carrier . . . at a named point	FRC	Provide export licence and pay any export taxes; provide evidence of delivery of goods to the carrier	Contract for the carriage, pay the freight and nominate the carrier; pay insurance premium
Free on rail, or free on truck	FOR	Deliver goods to railway; provide buyer with an invoice and transport document	Pay freight; notify seller of destination of the goods; obtain export licence and pay any export taxes
FOB airport	FOA	Deliver goods to airport of departure; contract for carriage or notify the buyer if he wants him to do so	Pay freight; notify seller if he does not wish him to contract for carriage; pay insurance premium
Free alongside ship	FAS	Deliver goods alongside ship; provide an 'alongside' receipt	Nominate the carrier; contract for carriage, pay freight, obtain export licence and pay any export taxes; pay insurance premium
Free on board	FOB	Deliver goods on board and provide a clean on board receipt; provide export licence, pay export taxes and loading costs if not included in the freight charge	Nominate the carrier; contract for carriage and pay the freight; pay discharge costs and loading costs if included in the freight charges; pay insurance premium
Cost and freight	CFR (often seen as C & F)	Contract for carriage, pay freight to named destination; deliver goods on board and provide buyer with an invoice and clean on board bill of lading;	Accept delivery of goods on shipment after documents are tendered to him; pay unloading costs if not included in the freight charges; pay insurance premium

Shipping terms	ICC int'l abbrevi- ations	The seller must:	The buyer must:
		obtain export licence and pay export taxes, loading costs and unloading costs if included in the freight charges	
Cost, insurance and freight	CIF	As with 'cost and freight' above, *plus* contract for the insurance of goods, pay the premium and provide the buyer with the policy or certificate	Accept delivery of goods on shipment after documents are tendered to him; pay unloading costs if not included in the freight charges
Freight/carriage paid to . . .	DCP	Contract for carriage, pay freight to named destination; deliver goods to first carrier; obtain export licence and pay any export taxes; provide buyer with invoice and transport document	After tender of documents, accept delivery of goods when they are delivered to first carrier; arrange and pay insurance premium
Freight/carriage and insurance paid to . . .	CIP	As with 'freight/carriage paid to' above, *plus* contract for insurance of goods and pay the premium, providing the buyer with a policy or certificate	Accept delivery of goods after documents are tendered to him
Ex-ship	EXS	Deliver goods on board at destination; provide buyer with documents to enable delivery to be taken from the ship	Pay discharge costs, import duties, taxes and fees, if any; obtain import licence
Ex-quay	EXQ	Deliver goods on to quay at destination. Provide buyer with documents to enable him to take delivery; obtain import licence	Take delivery of goods from the quay at destination

Shipping terms	ICC int'l abbrevi- ations	The seller must:	The buyer must:
		and pay import duties, taxes, fees, unloading costs and insurance	
Delivered at frontier	DAF	Deliver goods cleared for export at a place named on the frontier; provide the buyer with documents to take delivery	Pay for on-carriage; obtain import licence and pay import duties, taxes and fees if any
Delivered duty paid	DDP	Obtain import licence and pay import duties, taxes and fees if any; arrange and pay insurance; provide documents to enable the buyer to take delivery	Take delivery of the goods at the named place of destination

Source: From Alasdair Watson, *Finance of International Trade* (3rd ed.), The Institute of Bankers, London, 1985, pp. 34–35. Reprinted with permission.

Appendix V Uniform Rules for Collections*

GENERAL PROVISIONS AND DEFINITIONS

A

These provisions and definitions and the following articles apply to all collections as defined in (B) below and are binding upon all parties thereto unless otherwise expressly agreed or unless contrary to the provisions of a national, state or local law and/or regulation which cannot be departed from.

B

For the purpose of such provisions, definitions and articles:

1. **i** "Collection" means the handling by banks, on instructions received, of documents as defined in (ii) below, in order to
   a) obtain acceptance and/or, as the case may be, payment, or
   b) deliver commercial documents against acceptance and/or, as the case may be, against payment, or
   c) deliver documents on other terms and conditions.
   ii "Documents" means financial documents and/or commercial documents:
   a) "financial documents" means bills of exchange, promissory notes, checks, payment receipts or other similar instruments used for obtaining the payment of money;
   b) "commercial documents" means invoices, shipping documents, documents of title or other similar documents, or any other documents whatsoever, not being financial documents.
   iii "Clean collection" means collection of financial documents not accompanied by commercial documents.
   iv "Documentary collection" means collection of
   a) financial documents accompanied by commercial documents;
   b) commercial documents not accompanied by financial documents.
2. The "parties thereto" are:
   i the "principal" who is the customer entrusting the operation of collection to his bank;
   ii the "remitting bank" which is the bank to which the principal has entrusted the operation of collection;
   iii the "collecting bank" which is any bank, other than the remitting bank, involved in processing the collection order;
   iv the "presenting bank" which is the collecting bank making presentation to the drawee.
3. The "drawee" is the one to whom presentation is to be made according to the collection order.

C.

All documents sent for collection must be accompanied by a collection order giving complete and precise instructions. Banks are only permitted to act upon the instructions given in such collection order, and in accordance with these Rules.

If any bank cannot, for any reason, comply with the instructions given in the collection order received by it, it must immediately advise the party from whom it received the collection order.

LIABILITIES AND RESPONSIBILITIES

Article 1
Banks will act in good faith and exercise reasonable care.

Article 2
Banks must verify that the documents received appear to be as listed in the collection order and must immediately advise the party from whom the collection order was received of any documents missing.

Banks have no further obligation to examine the documents.

Article 3
For the purpose of giving effect to the instructions of the principal, the remitting bank will utilize as the collecting bank:
i the collecting bank nominated by the principal, or, in the absence of such nomination,
ii any bank, of its own or another bank's choice, in the country of payment or acceptance, as the case may be.

The documents and the collection order may be sent to the collecting bank directly or through another bank as intermediary.

Banks utilizing the services of other banks for the purpose of giving effect to the instructions of the principal do so for the account of and at the risk of the latter.

The principal shall be bound by and liable to indemnify the banks against all obligations and responsibilities imposed by foreign laws or usages.

Article 4
Banks concerned with a collection assume no liability or responsibility for the consequences arising out of delay and/or loss in transit of any messages, letters or documents, or for delay, mutilation or other errors arising in the

transmission of cables, telegrams, telex, or communication by electronic systems, or for errors in translation or interpretation of technical terms.

Article 5

Banks concerned with a collection assume no liability or responsibility for consequences arising out of the interruption of their business by Acts of God, riots, civil commotions, insurrections, wars, or any other causes beyond their control or by strikes or lockouts.

Article 6

Goods should not be dispatched direct to the address of a bank or consigned to a bank without prior agreement on the part of that bank.

In the event of goods being dispatched direct to the address of a bank or consigned to a bank for delivery to a drawee against payment or acceptance or upon other terms without prior agreement on the part of that bank, the bank has no obligation to take delivery of the goods, which remain at the risk and responsibility of the party dispatching the goods.

Article 7

Documents are to be presented to the drawee in the form in which they are received, except that remitting and collecting banks are authorized to affix any necessary stamps, at the expense of the principal unless otherwise instructed, and to make any necessary endorsements or place any rubber stamps or identifying marks or symbols customary to or required for the collection operation.

Article 8

Collection orders should bear the complete address of the drawee or of the domicile at which presentation is to be made. If the address is incomplete or incorrect, the collecting bank may, without obligation and responsibility on its part, endeavour to ascertain the proper address.

Article 9

In the case of documents payable at sight the presenting bank must make presentation for payment without delay.

In the case of documents payable at a tenor other than sight the presenting bank must, where acceptance is called for, make presentation for acceptance without delay, and where payment is called for, make presentation for payment not later than the appropriate maturity date.

Article 10

In respect of a documentary collection including a bill of exchange payable at a future date, the collection order should state whether the commercial documents are to be released to the drawee against acceptance (D/A) or against payment (D/P).

In the absence of such statement, the commercial documents will be released only against payment.

Payment

Article 11

In the case of documents payable in the currency of the country of payment (local currency), the presenting bank must, unless otherwise instructed in the collection order, only release the documents to the drawee against payment in local currency which is immediately available for disposal in the manner specified in the collection order.

Article 12

In the case of documents payable in a currency other than that of the country of payment (foreign currency), the presenting bank must, unless otherwise instructed in the collection order, only release the documents to the drawee against payment in the relative foreign currency which can immediately be remitted in accordance with the instructions given in the collection order.

Article 13

In respect of clean collections partial payments may be accepted if and to the extent to which and on the conditions on which partial payments are authorized by the law in force in the place of payment. The documents will only be released to the drawee when full payment thereof has been received.

In respect of documentary collections partial payments will only be accepted if specifically authorized in the collection order. However, unless otherwise instructed, the presenting bank will only release the documents to the drawee after full payment has been received.

In all cases partial payments will only be accepted subject to compliance with the provisions of either Article 11 or Article 12 as appropriate.

Partial payment, if accepted, will be dealt with in accordance with the provisions of Article 14.

Article 14

Amounts collected (less charges and/or disbursements and/or expenses where applicable) must be made available without delay to the bank from which the collection order was received in accordance with the instructions contained in the collection order.

ACCEPTANCE

Article 15

The presenting bank is responsible for seeing that the form of the acceptance of a bill of exchange appears to be complete and correct, but is not responsible for the genuineness of any signature or for the authority of any signatory to sign the acceptance.

PROMISSORY NOTES, RECEIPTS AND OTHER SIMILAR INSTRUMENTS

Article 16

The presenting bank is not responsible for the genuineness of any signature or for the authority of any signatory to sign a promissory note, receipt, or other similar instrument.

PROTEST

Article 17

The collection order should give specific instructions regarding protest (or other legal process in lieu thereof), in the event of non-acceptance or non-payment.

In the absence of such specific instructions the banks concerned with the collection have no obligation to have the documents protested (or subjected to other legal process in lieu thereof) for non-payment or non-acceptance.

Any charges and/or expenses incurred by banks in connection with such protest or other legal process will be for the account of the principal.

CASE-OF-NEED (PRINCIPAL'S REPRESENTATIVE) AND PROTECTION OF GOODS

Article 18

If the principal nominates a representative to act as case-of-need in the event of non-acceptance and/or non-payment the collection order should clearly and fully indicate the powers of such case-of-need.

In the absence of such indication banks will not accept any instructions from the case-of-need.

Article 19

Banks have no obligation to take any action in respect of the goods to which a documentary collection relates.

Nevertheless in the case that banks take action for the protection of the goods, whether instructed or not, they assume no liability or responsibility with regard to the fate and/or condition of the goods and/or for any acts and/or omissions on the part of any third parties entrusted with the custody and/or protection of the goods. However, the collecting bank must immediately advise the bank from which the collection order was received of any such action taken.

Any charges and/or expenses incurred by banks in connection with any action for the protection of the goods will be for the account of the principal.

ADVICE OF FATE, ETC.

Article 20

Collecting banks are to advise fate in accordance with the following rules:

i *Form of advice.* All advices or information from the collecting bank to the bank from which the collection order was received, must bear appropriate detail including, in all cases, the latter bank's reference number of the collection order.

ii *Method of advice.* In the absence of specific instructions, the collecting bank must send all advices to the bank from which the collection order was received by quickest mail but, if the collecting bank considers the matter to be urgent, quicker methods such as cable, telegram, telex, or communication by electronic systems, etc. may be used at the expense of the principal.

iii   **a.** *Advice of payment.* The collecting bank must send without delay
advice of payment to the bank from which the collection order was
received, detailing the amount or amounts collected, charges and/or
disbursements and/or expenses deducted, where appropriate, and
method of disposal of the funds.

   b. *Advice of acceptance.* The collecting bank must send without delay
advice of acceptance to the bank from which the collection order
was received.

   c. *Advice of non-payment or non-acceptance.* The collecting bank
must send without delay advice of non-payment or advice of non-
acceptance to the bank from which the collection order was received.

   The presenting bank should endeavour to ascertain the reasons for
such non-payment or non-acceptance and advise accordingly the
bank from which the collection order was received.

   On receipt of such advice the remitting bank must, within a reasonable time, give appropriate instructions as to the further handling of
the documents. If such instructions are not received by the presenting bank within 90 days from its advice of non-payment or non-
acceptance, the documents may be returned to the bank from which
the collection order was received.

INTEREST, CHARGES, AND EXPENSES

Article 21
If the collection order includes an instruction to collect interest which is not
embodied in the accompanying financial document(s), if any, and the drawee
refuses to pay such interest, the presenting bank may deliver the document(s)
against payment or acceptance as the case may be without collecting such
interest, unless the collection order expressly states that such interest may
not be waived. Where such interest is to be collected the collection order
must bear an indication of the rate of interest and the period covered. When
payment of interest has been refused the presenting bank must inform the
bank from which the collection order was received accordingly.

If the documents include a financial document containing an unconditional
and definitive interest clause the interest amount is deemed to form part of
the amount of the documents to be collected. Accordingly, the interest

amount is payable in addition to the principal amount shown in the financial document and may not be waived unless the collection order so authorizes.

Article 22

If the collection order includes an instruction that collection charges and/or expenses are to be for account of the drawee and the drawee refuses to pay them, the presenting bank may deliver the document(s) against payment or acceptance as the case may be without collecting charges and/or expenses unless the collection order expressly states that such charges and/or expenses may not be waived. When payment of collection charges and/or expenses has been refused the presenting bank must inform the bank from which the collection order was received accordingly. Whenever collection charges and/or expenses are so waived they will be for the account of the principal, and may be deducted from the proceeds.

Should a collection order specifically prohibit the waiving of collection charges and/or expenses then neither the remitting nor collecting nor presenting bank shall be responsible for any costs or delays resulting from this prohibition.

Article 23

In all cases where in the express terms of a collection order, or under these Rules, disbursements and/or expenses and/or collection charges are to be borne by the principal, the collecting bank(s) shall be entitled promptly to recover outlays in respect of disbursements and expenses and charges from the bank from which the collection order was received and the remitting bank shall have the right promptly to recover from the principal any amount so paid out by it, together with its own disbursements, expenses and charges, regardless of the fate of the collection.

Appendix VI Uniform Customs and Practice for Documentary Credits*

A. GENERAL PROVISIONS AND DEFINITIONS

Article 1

These articles apply to all documentary credits, including, to the extent to which they may be applicable, standby letters of credit, and are binding on all parties thereto unless otherwise expressly agreed. They shall be incorporated into each documentary credit by wording in the credit indicating that such credit is issued subject to Uniform Customs and Practice for Documentary Credits, 1983 revision, ICC Publication number 400.

Article 2

For the purposes of these articles, the expressions "documentary credit(s)" and "standby letter(s) of credit" used herein (hereinafter referred to as "credit(s)"), mean any arrangement, however named or described, whereby a bank (the issuing bank), acting at the request and on the instructions of a customer (the applicant for the credit),

i is to make a payment to or to the order of a third party (the beneficiary), or is to pay or accept bills of exchange (drafts) drawn by the beneficiary, or

ii authorizes another bank to effect such payment, or to pay, accept or negotiate such bills of exchange (drafts),

against stipulated documents, provided that the terms and conditions of the credit are complied with.

Article 3

Credits, by their nature, are separate transactions from the sales or other contract(s) on which they may be based and banks are in no way concerned with or bound by such contract(s), even if any reference whatsoever to such contract(s) is included in the credit.

Article 4

In credit operations all parties concerned deal in documents, and not in goods, services and/or other performances to which the documents may relate.

Article 5

Instructions for the issuance of credits, the credits themselves, instructions for any amendments thereto and the amendments themselves must be complete and precise.

In order to guard against confusion and misunderstanding, banks should discourage any attempt to include excessive detail in the credit or in any amendment thereto.

Article 6
A beneficiary can in no case avail himself of the contractual relationships existing between the banks or between the applicant for the credit and the issuing bank.

B. FORM AND NOTIFICATION OF CREDITS

Article 7
a. Credits may be either
  i revocable, or
  ii irrevocable.
b. All credits, therefore, should clearly indicate whether they are revocable or irrevocable.
c. In the absence of such indication the credit shall be deemed to be revocable.

Article 8
A credit may be advised to a beneficiary through another bank (the advising bank) without engagement on the part of the advising bank, but that bank shall take reasonable care to check the apparent authenticity of the credit which it advises.

Article 9
a. A revocable credit may be amended or cancelled by the issuing bank at any moment and without prior notice to the beneficiary.
b. However, the issuing bank is bound to:
  i reimburse a branch or bank with which a revocable credit has been made available for sight payment, acceptance or negotiation, for any payment, acceptance or negotiation made by such branch or bank prior to receipt by it of notice of amendment or cancellation, against documents which appear on their face to be in accordance with the terms and conditions of the credit.
  ii reimburse a branch or bank with which a revocable credit has been made available for deferred payment, if such branch or bank has,

prior to receipt by it of notice of amendment or cancellation, taken up documents which appear on their face to be in accordance with the terms and conditions of the credit.

Article 10

a. An irrevocable credit constitutes a definite undertaking of the issuing bank, provided that the stipulated documents are presented and that the terms and conditions of the credit are complied with:

i if the credit provides for sight payment—to pay, or that payment will be made;

ii if the credit provides for deferred payment—to pay, or that payment will be made, on the date(s) determinable in accordance with the stipulations of the credit;

iii if the credit provides for acceptance—to accept drafts drawn by the beneficiary if the credit stipulates that they are to be drawn on the issuing bank, or to be responsible for their acceptance and payment at maturity if the credit stipulates that they are to be drawn on the applicant for the credit or any other drawee stipulated in the credit;

iv if the credit provides for negotiation—to pay without recourse to drawers and/or bona fide holders, draft(s) drawn by the beneficiary, at sight or at a tenor, on the applicant for the credit or on any other drawee stipulated in the credit other than the issuing bank itself, or to provide for negotiation by another bank and to pay, as above, if such negotiation is not effected.

b. When an issuing bank authorizes or requests another bank to confirm its irrevocable credit and the latter has added its confirmation, such confirmation constitutes a definite undertaking of such bank (the confirming bank), in addition to that of the issuing bank, provided that the stipulated documents are presented and that the terms and conditions of the credit are complied with:

i if the credit provides for sight payment—to pay, or that payment will be made;

ii if the credit provides for deferred payment—to pay, or that payment will be made, on the date(s) determinable in accordance with the stipulations of the credit;

iii if the credit provides for acceptance—to accept drafts drawn by the beneficiary if the credit stipulates that they are to be drawn on the confirming bank, or to be responsible for their acceptance and payment at maturity if the credit stipulates that they are to be drawn on the applicant for the credit or any other drawee stipulated in the credit;

iv if the credit provides for negotiation—to negotiate without recourse to drawers and/or bona fide holders, draft(s) drawn by the beneficiary, at sight or at a tenor, on the issuing bank or on the applicant for the credit or on any other drawee stipulated in the credit other than the confirming bank itself.

c. If a bank is authorized or requested by the issuing bank to add its confirmation to a credit but is not prepared to do so, it must so inform the issuing bank without delay. Unless the issuing bank specifies otherwise in its confirmation authorization or request, the advising bank will advise the credit to the beneficiary without adding its confirmation.

d. Such undertakings can neither be amended nor canceled without the agreement of the issuing bank, the confirming bank (if any), and the beneficiary. Partial acceptance of amendments contained in one and the same advice of amendment is not effective without the agreement of all the above named parties.

ARTICLE 11

a. All credits must clearly indicate whether they are available by sight payment, by deferred payment, by acceptance or by negotiation.

b. All credits must nominate the bank (nominated bank) which is authorized to pay (paying bank), or to accept drafts (accepting bank), or to negotiate (negotiating bank), unless the credit allows negotiation by any bank (negotiating bank).

c. Unless the nominated bank is the issuing bank or the confirming bank, its nomination by the issuing bank does not constitute any undertaking by the nominated bank to pay, to accept, or to negotiate.

d. By nominating a bank other than itself, or by allowing for negotiation by any bank, or by authorizing or requesting a bank to add its confirmation, the issuing bank authorizes such bank to pay, accept or negotiate, as the case may be, against documents which appear on their face to be in accordance with the terms and conditions of the credit, and undertakes to reimburse such bank in accordance with the provisions of these articles.

Article 12

a. When an issuing bank instructs a bank (advising bank) by any teletransmission to advise a credit or an amendment to a credit, and intends the mail confirmation to be the operative credit instrument, or the operative amendment, the teletransmission must state "full details to follow" (or words of similar effect), or that the mail confirmation will be the operative credit instrument or the operative amendment. The issuing bank must forward the operative credit instrument or the operative amendment to such advising bank without delay.

b. The teletransmission will be deemed to be the operative credit instrument or the operative amendment, and no mail confirmation should be sent, unless the teletransmission states "full details to follow" (or words of similar effect), or states that the mail confirmation is to be the operative credit instrument or the operative amendment.

c. A teletransmission intended by the issuing bank to be the operative credit instrument should clearly indicate that the credit is issued subject to Uniform Customs and Practice for Documentary Credits, 1983 revision, ICC Publication number 400.

d. If a bank uses the services of another bank or banks (the advising bank) to have the credit advised to the beneficiary, it must also use the services of the same bank(s) for advising any amendments.

e. Banks shall be responsible for any consequences arising from their failure to follow the procedures set out in the preceding paragraphs.

Article 13

When a bank is instructed to issue, confirm or advise a credit similar in terms to one previously issued, confirmed or advised (similar credit) and the previous credit has been the subject of amendment(s), it shall be understood that the similar credit will not include any such amendment(s) unless the instructions specify clearly the amendment(s) which is/are to apply to the similar credit. Banks should discourage instructions to issue, confirm or advise a credit in this manner.

Article 14

If incomplete or unclear instructions are received to issue, confirm, advise or amend a credit, the bank requested to act on such instructions may give preliminary notification to the beneficiary for information only and without responsibility. The credit will be issued, confirmed, advised or amended only when the necessary information has been received and if the bank is then prepared to act on the instructions. Banks should provide the necessary information without delay.

C. LIABILITIES AND RESPONSIBILITIES

Article 15
Banks must examine all documents with reasonable care to ascertain that they appear on their face to be in accordance with the terms and conditions of the credit. Documents which appear on their face to be inconsistent with one another will be considered as not appearing on their face to be in accordance with the terms and conditions of the credit.

Article 16
a. If a bank so authorized effects payment, or incurs a deferred payment undertaking, or accepts, or negotiates against documents which appear on their face to be in accordance with the terms and conditions of a credit, the party giving such authority shall be bound to reimburse the bank which has effected payment, or incurred a deferred payment undertaking, or has accepted, or negotiated, and to take up the documents.

b. If, upon receipt of the documents, the issuing bank considers that they appear on their face not to be in accordance with the terms and conditions of the credit, it must determine, on the basis of the documents alone, whether to take up such documents, or to refuse them and claim that they appear on their face not to be in accordance with the terms and conditions of the credit.

c. The issuing bank shall have a reasonable time in which to examine the documents and to determine as above whether to take up or to refuse the documents.

d. If the issuing bank decides to refuse the documents, it must give notice to that effect without delay by telecommunication or, if that is not possible, by other expeditious means, to the bank from which it received the documents (the remitting bank), or to the beneficiary, if it received the documents directly from him. Such notice must state the discrepancies in respect of which the issuing bank refuses the documents and must also state whether it is holding the documents at the disposal of, or is returning them to, the presentor (remitting bank or the beneficiary, as the case may be). The issuing bank shall then be entitled to claim from the remitting bank refund of any reimbursement which may have been made to that bank.

e. If the issuing bank fails to act in accordance with the provisions of paragraphs (c) and (d) of this article and/or fails to hold the documents at the disposal of, or to return them to, the presentor, the issuing bank shall be precluded from claiming that the documents are not in accordance with the terms and conditions of the credit.

f. If the remitting bank draws the attention of the issuing bank to any discrepancies in the documents or advises the issuing bank that it has paid, incurred a deferred payment undertaking, accepted or negotiated under reserve or against an indemnity in respect of such discrepancies, the issuing bank shall not be thereby relieved from any of its obligations under any provision of this article. Such reserve or indemnity concerns only the relations between the remitting bank and the party towards whom the reserve was made, or from whom, or on whose behalf, the indemnity was obtained.

Article 17

Banks assume no liability or responsibility for the form, sufficiency, accuracy, genuineness, falsification or legal effect of any documents, or for the general and/or particular conditions stipulated in the documents or superimposed thereon; nor do they assume any liability or responsibility for the description, quantity, weight, quality, condition, packing, delivery, value or existence of the goods represented by any documents, or for the good faith or acts and/or omissions, solvency, performance or standing of the consignor, the carriers, or the insurers of the goods, or any other person whomsoever.

Article 18

Banks assume no liability or responsibility for the consequences arising out of delay and/or loss in transit of any messages, letters or documents, or for delay, mutilation or other errors arising in the transmission of any telecommunication. Banks assume no liability or responsibility for errors in translation or interpretation of technical terms, and reserve the right to transmit credit terms without translating them.

Article 19

Banks assume no liability or responsibility for consequences arising out of the interruption of their business by Acts of God, riots, civil commotions, insurrections, wars or any other causes beyond their control, or by any strikes or lockouts. Unless specifically authorized, banks will not, upon resumption of their business, incur a deferred payment undertaking, or effect payment, acceptance or negotiation under credits which expired during such interruption of their business.

Article 20

a. Banks utilizing the services of another bank or other banks for the purpose of giving effect to the instructions of the applicant for the credit do so for the account and at the risk of such applicant.

b. Banks assume no liability or responsibility should the instructions they transmit not be carried out, even if they have themselves taken the initiative in the choice of such other bank(s).

c. The applicant for the credit shall be bound by and liable to indemnify the banks against all obligations and responsibilities imposed by foreign laws and usages.

Article 21

a. If an issuing bank intends that the reimbursement to which a paying, accepting or negotiating bank is entitled shall be obtained by such bank claiming on another branch or office of the issuing bank or on a third bank (all hereinafter referred to as the reimbursing bank) it shall provide such reimbursing bank in good time with the proper instructions or authorization to honour such reimbursement claims and without making it a condition that the bank entitled to claim reimbursement must certify compliance with the terms and conditions of the credit to the reimbursing bank.

b. An issuing bank will not be relieved from any of its obligations to provide reimbursement itself it and when reimbursement is not effected by the reimbursing bank.

c. The issuing bank will be responsible to the paying, accepting or negotiating bank for any loss of interest if reimbursement is not provided on first demand made to the reimbursing bank, or as otherwise specified in the credit, or mutually agreed, as the case may be.

D. DOCUMENTS

Article 22

a. All instructions for the issuance of credits and the credits themselves and, where applicable, all instructions for amendments thereto and the amendments themselves, must state precisely the document(s) against which payment, acceptance or negotiation is to be made.

b. Terms such as "first class", "well known", "qualified", "independent", "official", and the like shall not be used to describe the issuers of any documents to be presented under a credit. If such terms are incorporated in the credit terms, banks will accept the relative documents as presented, provided that they appear on their face to be in accordance with the other terms and conditions of the credit.

c. Unless otherwise stipulated in the credit, banks will accept as originals documents produced or appearing to have been produced:

i by reprographic systems;

ii by, or as the result of, automated or computerized systems;

iii as carbon copies,

if marked as originals, always provided that, where necessary, such documents appear to have been authenticated.

Article 23

When documents other than transport documents, insurance documents and commercial invoices are called for, the credit should stipulate by whom such documents are to be issued and their wording or data content. If the credit does not so stipulate, banks will accept such documents as presented, provided that their data content makes it possible to relate the goods and/or services referred to therein to those referred to in the commercial invoice(s) presented, or to those referred to in the credit if the credit does not stipulate presentation of a commercial invoice.

Article 24

Unless otherwise stipulated in the credit, banks will accept a document bearing a date of issuance prior to that of the credit, subject to such document being presented within the time limits set out in the credit and in these articles.

D.1. TRANSPORT DOCUMENTS (DOCUMENTS INDICATING LOADING ON BOARD OR DISPATCH OR TAKING IN CHARGE)

Article 25

Unless a credit calling for a transport document stipulates as such document a marine bill of lading (ocean bill of lading or a bill of lading covering carriage by sea), or a post receipt or certificate of posting:

a. banks will, unless otherwise stipulated in the credit, accept a transport document which:

  i appears on its face to have been issued by a named carrier, or his agent, and

  ii indicates dispatch or taking in charge of the goods, or loading on board, as the case may be, and

  iii consists of the full set of originals issued to the consignor if issued in more than one original, and

  iv meets all other stipulations of the credit.

b. Subject to the above, and unless otherwise stipulated in the credit, banks will not reject a transport document which:

  i bears a title such as "Combined transport bill of lading", "Combined transport document", "Combined transport bill of lading or port-to-port bill of lading", or a title or a combination of titles of similar intent and effect, and/or

  ii indicates some or all of the conditions of carriage by reference to a source or document other than the transport document itself (short form/blank back transport document), and/or

  iii indicates a place of taking in charge different from the port of loading and/or a place of final destination different from the port of discharge, and/or

  iv relates to cargoes such as those in containers or on pallets, and the like, and/or

  v contains the indication "intended", or similar qualification, in relation to the vessel or other means of transport, and/or the port of loading and/or the port of discharge.

c. Unless otherwise stipulated in the credit in the case of carriage by sea or by more than one mode of transport but including carriage by sea, banks will reject a transport document which:

  i indicates that it is subject to a charter party, and/or

  ii indicates that the carrying vessel is propelled by sail only.

d. Unless otherwise stipulated in the credit, banks will reject a transport document issued by a freight forwarder unless it is the FIATA Combined Transport Bill of Lading approved by the International Chamber of Commerce or otherwise indicates that it is issued by a freight forwarder acting as a carrier or agent of a named carrier.

Article 26

If a credit calling for a transport document stipulates as such document a marine bill of lading:

a. banks will, unless otherwise stipulated in the credit, accept a document which:

    i appears on its face to have been issued by a named carrier, or his agent, and

    ii indicates that the goods have been loaded on board or shipped on a named vessel, and

    iii consists of the full set of originals issued to the consignor if issued in more than one original, and

    iv meets all other stipulations of the credit.

b. Subject to the above, and unless otherwise stipulated in the credit, banks will not reject a document which:

    i bears a title such as "Combined transport bill of lading", "Combined transport document", "Combined transport bill of lading or port-to-port bill of lading", or a title or a combination of titles of similar intent and effect, and/or

    ii indicates some or all of the conditions of carriage by reference to a source or document other than the transport document itself (short form/blank back transport document), and/or

    iii indicates a place of taking in charge different from the port of loading, and/or a place of final destination different from the port of discharge, and/or

    iv relates to cargoes such as those in containers or on pallets, and the like.

c. Unless otherwise stipulated in the credit, banks will reject a document which:

    i indicates that it is subject to a charter party, and/or

    ii indicates that the carrying vessel is propelled by sail only, and/or

    iii contains the indication "intended", or similar qualification in relation to

        • the vessel and/or the port of loading—unless such document bears an on board notation in accordance with article 27 (b) and also indicates the actual port of loading, and/or

        • the port of discharge—unless the place of final destination indicated on the document is other than the port of discharge, and/or

iv is issued by a freight forwarder unless it indicates that it is issued by such freight forwarder acting as a carrier, or as the agent of a named carrier.

Article 27

a. Unless a credit specifically calls for an on board transport document, or unless inconsistent with other stipulation(s) in the credit, or with article 26, banks will accept a transport document which indicates that the goods have been taken in charge or received for shipment.

b. Loading on board or shipment on a vessel may be evidenced either by a transport document bearing wording indicating loading on board a named vessel or shipment on a named vessel, or, in the case of a transport document stating "received for shipment", by means of a notation of loading on board on the transport document signed or initialled and dated by the carrier or his agent, and the date of this notation shall be regarded as the date of loading on board the named vessel or shipment on the named vessel.

Article 28

a. In the case of carriage by sea or by more than one mode of transport but including carriage by sea, banks will refuse a transport document stating that the goods are or will be loaded on deck, unless specifically authorized in the credit.

b. Banks will not refuse a transport document which contains a provision that the goods may be carried on deck, provided it does not specifically state that they are or will be loaded on deck.

Article 29

a. For the purpose of this article transhipment means a transfer and reloading during the course of carriage from the port of loading or place of dispatch or taking in charge to the port of discharge or place of destination either from one conveyance or vessel to another conveyance or vessel within the same mode of transport or from one mode of transport to another mode of transport.

b. Unless transhipment is prohibited by the terms of the credit, banks will accept transport documents which indicate that the goods will be transhipped, provided the entire carriage is covered by one and the same transport document.

c. Even if transhipment is prohibited by the terms of the credit, banks will accept transport documents which:

   i incorporate printed clauses stating that the carrier has the right to tranship, or

   ii state or indicate that transhipment will or may take place, when the credit stipulates a combined transport document, or indicates carriage from a place of taking in charge to a place of final destination by different modes of transport including a carriage by sea, provided that the entire carriage is covered by one and the same transport document, or

   iii state or indicate that the goods are in a container(s), trailer(s), "LASH" barge(s), and the like and will be carried from the place of taking in charge to the place of final destination in the same container(s), trailer(s), "LASH" barge(s), and the like under one and the same transport document.

   iv state or indicate the place of receipt and/or of final destination as "C.F.S." (container freight station) or "C.Y." (container yard) at, or associated with, the port of loading and/or the port of destination.

Article 30

If the credit stipulates dispatch of goods by post and calls for a post receipt or certificate of posting if it appears to have been stamped or otherwise authenticated and dated in the place from which the credit stipulates the goods are to be dispatched.

Article 31

a. Unless otherwise stipulated in the credit, or inconsistent with any of the documents presented under the credit, banks will accept transport documents stating that freight or transportation charges (hereinafter referred to as "freight") have still to be paid.

b. If a credit stipulates that the transport document has to indicate that freight has been paid or prepaid, banks will accept a transport document on which words clearly indicating payment or prepayment of freight appear by stamp or otherwise, or on which payment of freight is indicated by other means.

c. The words "freight prepayable" or "freight to be prepaid" or words of similar effect, if appearing on transport documents, will not be accepted as constituting evidence of the payment of freight.

d. Banks will accept transport documents bearing reference by stamp or otherwise to costs additional to the freight charges, such as costs of, or disbursements incurred in connection with, loading, unloading or similar operations, unless the conditions of the credit specifically prohibit such reference.

Article 32
Unless otherwise stipulated in the credit, banks will accept transport documents which bear a clause on the face thereof such as "shippers load and count" or "said by shipper to contain" or words of similar effect.

Article 33
Unless otherwise stipulated in the credit, banks will accept transport documents indicating as the consignor of the goods a party other than the beneficiary of the credit.

Article 34
a. A clean transport document is one which bears no superimposed clause or notation which expressly declares a defective condition of the goods and/or the packaging.
b. Banks will refuse transport documents bearing such clauses or notations unless the credit expressly stipulates the clauses or notations which may be accepted.
c. Banks will regard a requirement in a credit for a transport document to bear the clause "clean on board" as complied with if such transport document meets the requirements of this article and of article 27(b).

D2. INSURANCE DOCUMENTS

Article 35

a. Insurance documents must be as stipulated in the credit, and must be issued and/or signed by insurance companies or underwriters, or their agents.
b. Cover notes issued by brokers will not be accepted, unless specifically authorized by the credit.

Article 36

Unless otherwise stipulated in the credit, or unless it appears from the insurance document(s) that the cover is effective at the latest from the date of loading on board or dispatch or taking in charge of the goods, banks will refuse insurance documents presented which bear a date later than the date of loading on board or dispatch or taking in charge of the goods as indicated by the transport document(s).

Article 37

a. Unless otherwise stipulated in the credit, the insurance document must be expressed in the same currency as the credit.
b. Unless otherwise stipulated in the credit, the minimum amount for which the insurance document must indicate the insurance cover to have been effected is the CIF (cost, insurance and freight . . . "named port of destination") or CIP (freight/carriage and insurance paid to "named point of destination") value of the goods, as the case may be, plus 10%. However, if banks cannot determine the CIF or CIP value, as the case may be, from the documents on their face, they will accept as such minimum amount the amount for which payment, acceptance or negotiation is requested under the credit, or the amount of the commercial invoice, whichever is the greater.

Article 38

a. Credits should stipulate the type of insurance required and, if any, the additional risks which are to be covered. Imprecise terms such as "usual risks" or "customary risks" should not be used; if they are used, banks will accept insurance documents as presented, without responsibility for any risks not being covered.
b. Failing specific stipulations in the credit, banks will accept insurance documents as presented, without responsibility for any risks not being covered.

Article 39

Where a credit stipulates "insurance against all risks", banks will accept an insurance document which contains any "all risks" notation or clause, whether or not bearing the heading "all risks", even if indicating that certain risks are excluded, without responsibility for any risk(s) not being covered.

Article 40
Banks will accept an insurance document which indicates that the cover is subject to a franchise or an excess (deductible), unless it is specifically stipulated in the credit that the insurance must be issued irrespective of percentage.

D3. COMMERCIAL INVOICE

Article 41
a. Unless otherwise stipulated in the credit, commercial invoices must be made out in the name of the applicant for the credit.
b. Unless otherwise stipulated in the credit, banks may refuse commercial invoices issued for amounts in excess of the amount permitted by the credit. Nevertheless, if a bank authorized to pay, incur a deferred payment undertaking, accept, or negotiate under a credit accepts such invoices, its decision will be binding upon all parties, provided such bank has not paid, incurred a deferred payment undertaking, accepted or effected negotiation for an amount in excess of that permitted by the credit.
c. The description of the goods in the commercial invoice must correspond with the description in the credit. In all other documents, the goods may be described in general terms not inconsistent with the description of the goods in the credit.

D4. OTHER DOCUMENTS

Article 42
If a credit calls for an attestation or certification of weight in the case of transport other than by sea, banks will accept a weight stamp or declaration of weight which appears to have been superimposed on the transport document by the carrier or his agent unless the credit specifically stipulates that the attestation or certification of weight must be by means of a separate document.

E. MISCELLANEOUS PROVISIONS

QUANTITY AND AMOUNT

Article 43

a. The words "about", "circa" or similar expressions used in connection with the amount of the credit or the quantity or the unit price stated in the credit are to be construed as allowing a difference not to exceed 10% more or 10% less than the amount or the quantity or the unit price to which they refer.

b. Unless a credit stipulates that the quantity of the goods specified must not be exceeded or reduced, a tolerance of 5% more or 5% less will be permissible, even if partial shipments are not permitted, always provided that the amount of the drawings does not exceed the amount of the credit. This tolerance does not apply when the credit stipulates the quantity in terms of a stated number of packing units or individual terms.

PARTIAL DRAWINGS AND/OR SHIPMENTS

Article 44

a. Partial drawing and/or shipments are allowed, unless the credit stipulates otherwise.

b. Shipments by sea, or by more than one mode of transport but including carriage by sea, made on the same vessel and for the same voyage, will not be regarded as partial shipments, even if the transport documents indicating loading on board bear different dates of issuance and/or indicate different ports of loading on board.

c. Shipments made by post will not be regarded as partial shipments if the post receipts or certificates of posting appear to have been stamped or otherwise authenticated in the place from which the credit stipulates the goods are to be dispatched, and on the same date.

d. Shipments made by modes of transport other than those referred to in paragraphs (b) and (c) of this article will not be regarded as partial shipments, provided the transport documents are issued by one and the same carrier or his agent and indicate the same date of issuance, the same place of dispatch or taking in charge of the goods, and the same destination.

DRAWINGS AND/OR SHIPMENTS BY INSTALMENTS

Article 45
If drawings and/or shipments by instalments within given periods are stipulated in the credit and any instalment is not drawn and/or shipped within the period allowed for that instalment, the credit ceases to be available for that and any subsequent instalments, unless otherwise stipulated in the credit.

EXPIRY DATE AND PRESENTATION

Article 46
a. All credits must stipulate an expiry date for presentation of documents for payment, acceptance or negotiation.
b. Except as provided in Article 48 (a), documents must be presented on or before such expiry date.
c. If an issuing bank states that the credit is to be available "for one month", "for six months" or the like, but does not specify the date from which the time is to run, the date of issuance of the credit by the issuing bank will be deemed to be the first day from which such time is to run. Banks should discourage indication of the expiry date of the credit in this manner.

Article 47
a. In addition to stipulating an expiry date for presentation of documents, every credit which calls for a transport document(s) should also stipulate a specified period of time after the date of issuance of the transport document(s) during which presentation of documents for payment, acceptance or negotiation must be made. If no such period of time is stipulated, banks will refuse documents presented to them later than 21 days after the date of issuance of the transport document(s). In every case, however, documents must be presented not later than the expiry date of the credit.

b. For the purpose of these articles, the date of issuance of a transport document(s) will be deemed to be:

  i in the case of a transport document evidencing dispatch, or taking in charge, or receipt of goods for shipment by a mode of transport other than by air—the date of issuance indicated on the transport document or the date of the reception stamp thereon whichever is the later.

  ii in the case of a transport document evidencing carriage by air—the date of issuance indicated on the transport document or, if the credit stipulates that the transport document shall indicate an actual flight date, the actual flight date as indicated on the transport document.

  iii in the case of a transport document evidencing loading on board a named vessel—the date of issuance of the transport document or, in the case of an on board notation in accordance with Article 27(b), the date of such notation.

  iv in cases to which Article 44(b) applies, the date determined as above of the latest transport document issued.

Article 48

a. If the expiry date of the credit and/or the last day of the period of time after the date of issuance of the transport document(s) for presentation of documents stipulated by the credit or applicable by virtue of Article 47 falls on a day on which the bank to which presentation has to be made is closed for reasons other than those referred to in article 19, the stipulated expiry date and/or the last day of the period of time after the date of issuance of the transport document(s) for presentation of documents, as the case may be, shall be extended to the first following business day on which such bank is open.

b. The latest date for loading on board, or dispatch, or taking in charge shall not be extended by reason of the extension of the expiry date and/or the period of time after the date of issuance of the transport document(s) for presentation of document(s) in accordance with this article. If no such latest date for shipment is stipulated in the credit or amendments thereto, banks will reject transport documents indicating a date of issuance later than the expiry date stipulated in the credit or amendments thereto.

c. The bank to which presentation is made on such first following business day must add to the documents its certificate that the documents were presented within the time limits extended in accordance with Article 48

(a) of the Uniform Customs and Practice for Documentary Credits, 1983 revision, ICC Publication Number 400.

Article 49

Banks are under no obligation to accept presentation of documents outside their banking hours.

LOADING ON BOARD, DISPATCH AND TAKING IN CHARGE (SHIPMENT)

Article 50

a. Unless otherwise stipulated in the credit, the expression "shipment" used in stipulating an earliest and/or a latest shipment date will be understood to include the expressions "loading on board", "dispatch" and "taking in charge".

b. The date of issuance of the transport document determined in accordance with Article 47(b) will be taken to be the date of shipment.

c. Expression such as "prompt", "immediately", "as soon as possible", and the like should not be used. If they are used, banks will interpret them as a stipulation that shipment is to be made within thirty days from the date of issuance of the credit by the issuing bank.

d. If the expression "on or about" and similar expressions are used, banks will interpret them as a stipulation that shipment is to be made during the period from five days before to five days after the specified date, both end days included.

DATE TERMS

Article 51

The words "to", "until", "till", "from", and words of similar import applying to any date term in the credit will be understood to include the date mentioned. The word "after" will be understood to exclude the date mentioned.

Article 52

The terms "first half", "second half" of a month shall be construed respectively as from the 1st to the 15th, and the 16th to the last day of each month, inclusive.

Article 53
The terms "beginning", "middle", or "end" of a month shall be construed respectively as from the 1st to the 10th, the 11th to the 20th, and the 21st to the last day of each month, inclusive.

F. TRANSFER

Article 54
a. A transferable credit is a credit under which the beneficiary has the right to request the bank called upon to effect payment or acceptance or any bank entitled to effect negotiation to make the credit available in whole or in part to one or more other parties (second beneficiaries).

b. A credit can be transferred only if it is expressly designated as "transferable" by the issuing bank. Terms such as "divisible", "fractionable", "assignable", and "transmissible" add nothing to the meaning of the term "transferable" and shall not be used.

c. The bank requested to effect the transfer (transferring bank), whether it has confirmed the credit or not, shall be under no obligation to effect such transfer except to the extent and in the manner expressly consented to by such bank.

d. Bank charges in respect of transfers are payable by the first beneficiary unless otherwise specified. The transferring bank shall be under no obligation to effect the transfer until such charges are paid.

e. A transferable credit can be transferred once only. Fractions of a transferable credit (not exceeding in the aggregate the amount of the credit) can be transferred separately, provided partial shipments are not prohibited, and the aggregate of such transfers will be considered as constituting only one transfer of the credit. The credit can be transferred only on the terms and conditions specified in the original credit, with the exception of the amount of the credit, of any unit prices stated therein, of the period of validity, of the last date for presentation of documents in accordance with Article 47 and the period for shipment, any or all of which may be reduced or curtailed, or the percentage for which insurance cover must be effected, which may be increased in such a way as to provide the amount of cover stipulated in the original credit, or these articles. Additionally, the name of the first beneficiary can be substituted for that of the applicant for the credit, but if the name of the applicant for the credit is specifically required by the original credit to appear in any document other than the invoice, such requirement must be fulfilled.

f. The first beneficiary has the right to substitute his own invoices (and drafts if the credit stipulates that drafts are to be drawn on the applicant for the credit) in exchange for those of the second beneficiary, for amounts not in excess of the original amount stipulated in the credit and for the original unit prices if stipulated in the credit, and upon such substitution of invoices (and drafts) the first beneficiary can draw under the credit for the difference, if any, between his invoices and the second beneficiary's invoices. When a credit has been transferred and the first beneficiary is to supply his own invoices (and drafts) in exchange for the second beneficiary's invoices (and drafts) but fails to do so on first demand, the paying, accepting or negotiating bank has the right to deliver to the issuing bank the documents received under the credit, including the second beneficiary's invoices (and drafts) without further responsibility to the first beneficiary.

g. Unless otherwise stipulated in the credit, the first beneficiary of a transferable credit may request that the credit be transferred to a second beneficiary in the same country, or in another country. Further, unless otherwise stipulated in the credit, the first beneficiary shall have the right to request that payment or negotiation be effected to the second beneficiary at the place to which the credit has been transferred, up to and including the expiry date of the original credit, and without prejudice to the first beneficiary's right subsequently to substitute his own invoices and drafts (if any) for those of the second beneficiary and to claim any difference due to him.

BIBLIOGRAPHY

Beehler, Paul J., *Contemporary Cash Management: Principles, Practices and Perspectives* (2nd ed.), Wiley, New York, 1983.

The Chase Manhattan Bank, N.A., One World Trade Center, 78th Floor, New York, N.Y.:
>   *The Chase World Guide for Exporters;*
>   *The Chase Guide to Government Export Credit Agencies.*
>   *Dynamics of Trade Finance,* 1984.

Daiboch, A.F., "Trade Banking Steps into an Aggressive New Role," *American Import Export Management,* October, 1983.
>   "Introductory Presentation on Trade Financing," for the President's Task Force on International Private Enterprise (unpublished paper), December 1983.

Davis, Stephen I., *The Management Function in International Banking,* Wiley, New York, 1979.

Duffield, Jeremy G., and B. J. Summers, "Bankers' Acceptances," in *Instruments of the Money Market* (5th ed.), Federal Reserve Bank of Richmond, 1981.

Fuchs, Victor R., "The Growing Importance of the Service Industry," National Bureau of Economics Research, 1965.

Goldsmith, Howard R., *How to Make a Fortune in Import/Export,* Reston Publishing Company, Reston, VA, 1980.

Harfield, Henry, *Bank Credits and Acceptances,* Wiley, New York, 1974.

Helfrich, Ralph T., "Trading in Bankers' Acceptances: A View from the Acceptance Desk of the Federal Reserve Bank of New York," *Monthly Review,* Federal Reserve Bank of New York, February, 1976.

International Chamber of Commerce, Publication No. 400, *Uniform Customs and Practice for Documentary Credits,* 1983 revision.
>   Publication 322, *Uniform Rules for Collections.*
>   Publication 350, *Incoterms.*
>   Publication 354, *Guide to Incoterms.*
>   Publication 325, *Uniform Rules for Contract Guarantees.*
>   Publication 365, *Introduction to I.C.C. Rules on International Contracts.*
>   Publication 417, *Key Words in International Trade.*

Johnson, E.M., "The Selling of Services," in V.P. Buell and C. Heyel (eds.), *Handbook of Modern Marketing,* McGraw-Hill, New York, 1970.

Kettell, Brian, *The Finance of International Business*, Quorum Books, Westport, CT, 1981.

Levitt, Theodore, *The Marketing Imagination*, Free Press, New York, 1984.

Marine Midland Bank, N.A., *International Banking Services* (1983).

McLane, Stephen E., "Strategic Planning in Retail Banking," in *Banker's Desk Reference*, Edwin B. Cox (ed.), Warren, Gorham & Lamont, New York, 1983.

The Morgan Guaranty Trust Company, *Export and Import Procedures*, International Banking Division, 23 Wall Street, New York, NY 10008.

Moriarty, R.T., R.C. Kimball, and J.H. Gay, "The Management of Corporate Banking Relationships," *Sloan Management Review*, Spring, 1983.

Nadler, Paul S., and Richard B. Miller, *The Banking Jungle: How to Survive and Prosper in a Business Turned Topsy Turvy*, Wiley, New York, 1985.

Perry, F. E., *The Elements of Banking*, Methuen & Co. Ltd., London, 1981.

Richardson, Linda, *Bankers in the Selling Role*, Wiley, New York, 1981.

Schneider, Gerhard W., *Export-Import Financing: A Practical Guide*, Wiley, New York, 1974.

Shaw, John C., *The Quality-Productivity Connection in Service-Sector Management*, Van Nostrand Reinhold Company, New York, 1978.

Uniform Commercial Code, 9th ed., 1978.

Walter, Ingo, and Tracy Murray (eds.), *Handbook of International Business*, Wiley, New York, 1982.

Wilson, Aubrey, *The Marketing of Professional Services*, McGraw-Hill, London, 1972.

Zenoff, D. B., and J. Zwick, *International Financial Management*, Prentice-Hall, Englewood Cliffs, NJ, 1969.

INDEX